AFRICAN NGENUITY

An Investor's Guide to a Vital Tech Ecosystem

MARSHA WULFF, EMBA

A maverick investor whose
strategies succeed in Africa

African Ngenuity:
An Investor's Guide to a Vital Tech Ecosystem

Copyright © Marsha Wulff (2025)

ISBN Paperback: 979-8-89576-166-3

Published by:

Dedicated to:

Investors who seek the next big thing,
Development funders who want better outcomes, and
Afropreneurs who need informed funders.

Table of Contents

Front Matter

Foreword
By Jon Gosier

Photo: Jon Gosier, May 2012
Source: https://appfrica.wordpress.com/2012/05/

Africa in the early aughts was something to behold. A wave of tech-driven optimism, entrepreneurship, and self-reliance seemed to be taking hold everywhere from Mombasa to Dakar, Cairo to Cape Town. The most inspiring part was that it wasn't a reaction to old wrongs and injustices; it was a collective understanding that all the tools that were needed to transform the continent were right there—in the hands and minds of people coming of age at the time. Much of this wasn't even limited to Africa. From 2006 to around 2014, the wave of techno-optimism spread globally.

Linux was celebrated for freeing personal computers from corporate control, Google emerged boldly claiming it would organize all the world's information, Twitter (now X.com) was founded as a real-time torrent of information, almost acting as a pair of binoculars seemingly allowing users to tune in to events and conversations taking place anywhere around the world as they were happening. All of this tech would liberate the oppressed, limit corruption, and build wealth that previous generations could only dream of.

When I moved to Uganda in 2008, I arrived to find this infectious spirit of technologists and entrepreneurs was very much growing already. Even though it was infinitely more difficult to build a tech business from the continent compared to most places in the world (with its rolling brownouts, expensive connectivity, and global skeptics), what I was reminded of every day was what was still possible anyway.

I paid no attention to the people who were quick to remind me of what wasn't possible in Africa; I fixated on the people who dared to try anyway. Entrepreneurs, who took all those challenges and turned them into part of their business models. The people who looked at a landscape that may appear arid and underdeveloped, but who still saw a better future in the distance. It was the entrepreneurs who were chasing that ambitious horizon that I found myself employing and investing in.

The major difference between this optimism for tech in Africa versus most other parts of the world was that in Africa, there was very little incumbent tech to replace. In the developed world, economies developed from feudal, to agrarian, to industrial, to post-industrial, to the information age over the course of several hundred years. Africa, on the other hand, had the opportunity to leapfrog a lot of that, heading directly into the mobile and internet-powered future there now.

It wasn't just a vision. It was happening. It happened.

I had the pleasure of working with a number of genius software developers and entrepreneurs dead set on using tech and business to change the course of the continent's development outside the traditional authority of politics and religion. What do I mean by this? Good technology doesn't care about borders; if it works, it gets used by whoever can access it. Politicians can try to regulate its use, but ingenuity and adaptability flow like water around legality.

Good business isn't limited by doctrine and idealism. Religious leaders can try to dismiss certain businesses or industries, but necessity and convenience are what drive where money is spent. These truths make tech and business unique. They are part of a culture that squeezes between the bars; they go everywhere and are hard to contain.

As a businessman living and working on the continent from late 2008 through 2014, traveling to 25+ African countries to invest in tech entrepreneurs, the energy of the time was palpable. Many great innovations emerged that changed the continent, and sometimes the world, forever.

It's this bygone era of techies, with its spirit of resilience, tenacity, and ingenuity, that I see echoing through the current generation of African entrepreneurs in 2025. The world knows Africa is resource-rich, with staggering natural resource reserves and fertile lands. What the world is still discovering is how rich the continent is with a special breed of entrepreneurs. Entrepreneurs who see past the problems and status quo because they know they have the tools, and they believe that the horizon is not that far away.

Sincerely,
Jon Gosier,
Founder, Appfrica

Appfrica was an organization founded in 2008 in Kampala, Uganda, to invest in African tech entrepreneurs. It invested in companies that are still thriving some 15 years later, including Hive Colab, Farmerline, and Apps4Africa.

Jon Gosier is a serial tech entrepreneur who EY named an Entrepreneur of The Year® 2025 winner, for "boldly disrupting markets, revolutionizing industries, and transforming lives, paving the way for a brighter tomorrow!" In 2014, he founded Audigent, a company he scaled and sold to data company Experian for $300M+. He currently runs FilmHedge[1], a fintech startup that uses artificial intelligence and data technology to mitigate risks for investors. It has raised more than $350 million to finance film and television productions globally. Jon's work at the intersection of technology, finance, and media has earned him recognition as a forward-thinking leader in emerging markets and creative economies.

---

[1] https://filmhedge.com

Preface

Seeing Opportunities

There is an art to spotting game in dense bush, where brush limits one's view to the path ahead, and an advantage in seeing wildlife before it bolts away. Bush safari novices may only see a narrow trail tunnel and the few creatures who happen to enter it, but skilled guides somehow see more. After begging one to share his secret with me, he advised me to "Look between the branches, at the spaces behind the bushes."

At first, I saw only my side of leaves and branches, which frustrated me. But I wanted to see what my guide saw, so I trusted his approach and remained focused on practicing. When we moved slowly, I could sometimes see through tiny spaces for a slightly deeper view. Then I realized that my view through these spaces changed as we moved, letting me see more breadth and depth as we passed. Encouraged by these changing perspectives, I challenged myself to look several feet deeper and was rewarded with a magical view into a large space behind the brush.

When I remained fully focused, my brain blocked out the branches and reassembled the pinpoints through the bushes into a life-sized jigsaw puzzle. The more I practiced, the more I saw through the bush barrier, as if it were a sheer fabric. Within the hour, thanks to my new superpower, I was the first to spot a large, noble, sable antelope, standing with its back to a tree and looking at me through spaces from its side of the bush barrier. The guide was impressed. I was thrilled.

Perspectives matter, as do relationships and experience. If you lack a guide you trust and who can spot things you did not know were there, how would you know you could discover a sable on the other side of the bushes?

If American news and charities portray Africa as a land of precarious chaos, why would investors bother to learn about its startups? When bestselling business authors label Africa's leading economies as "failed states," why would readers bother to challenge their perception?

Since American regulations restrict private funds from publishing their investment track records, most investors will not learn about profits from African successes. These are seriously thick branches to see through. Without a skilled guide, how would you know this sector exists, has succeeded, and has returned top-tier profits? Who can help investors see through these brush barriers?

You may wonder whether I am a skilled guide. If your metrics are longevity, frequency, networks, and outcomes, then I am among the sector's most experienced US-born investors. Many of the teams I have mentored and backed succeeded and provided profitable exits.

I've also learned what does not work, and why. Thanks to podcasters who interviewed me, I learned that people love my stories and appreciate my insights, but that sound bites and byte-sized posts are too short to clarify strategies. So, I have written this book, hoping it offers enough firsthand evidence and reliable statistics for credibility to creep in softly on cat paws amongst the stories. With practice, your perspective may shift enough for you to see between the thorns and brambles and spot the ecosystem that thrives on the other side.

You may ask whether investing in Africa is actually a thing now. If you consider $5 billion a year of investments in over 450 startup deals that were $100k or higher to be worthy, then, yes, there is enough critical mass of investment to warrant serious consideration. Astute African argonauts themselves got this ball rolling, as you will see.

Investor exits have been so exciting that many of us have recycled our profits back into the next crop of startups. This reinvestment by seasoned investors is probably the strongest validation of the ecosystem's strength and potential to grow.

In these pages, you will learn: who built the continent's tech ecosystem, how to invest well, what is not working, the dangers of not investing, and what the future offers. If you choose to join this safari and adopt best practices, I believe you will feel both challenged and rewarded.

After my 2017 Fund launch pitch during the Silicon Valley VC Unlocked program at Stanford, the Managing Partner of 500 Startups, Bedy Yang, asked, "What changed?" In my first slides, she had already seen that Africa's urbanization, middle-class growth, and youthful demographics were the obvious leading indicators of change. But Bedy was seeking insights on what I saw behind that data, as the underlying drivers of progress.

This book introduces the art of seeking African rainmakers, seeing their perspectives, and seeding the opportunities they offer. It shares the stories, strategies, and mindsets behind this sector's first investor successes. The ideas here aren't meant to inspire you to invest in these countries out of a sense of civic responsibility—they're meant to help you see high-potential opportunities that others miss.

Everything has a learning curve, but investing well in Africa has taken me a lifetime. Now that I have succeeded—and before my life force wanes—I want to share the lessons I've learned, so others can start younger and succeed faster than I did.

Urgency is a factor. Afropreneurs[TM2] need insightful investors with whom they can grow companies that create jobs for that youth bubble, remember? Time is ticking, let's get started!

Note: This book is primarily written for American investors, as it is my homeland. Although other countries are gaining ground, global metrics still rank the USA as doing 4x more startup investing than the #2 country, which is the United Kingdom.[3]

---

[2] The Afropreneur,"™ a tag name coined by Idris Bello for himself and other innovative social entrepreneurs of Africa, https://www.cnn.com/2012/09/17/tech/idris-bello-afropreneur-technology

[3] Startup Blink. *Global Startup Ecosystem Index 2025.* https://www.startupblink.com/startupecosystemreport

PART ONE
Why Bother with African Startups?

Portfolio Strategies

As we learn to look through the brush, we gain new perspectives on the question, "Why Bother with African Startups?" We all want our investment portfolios to be healthy, so let's review standard portfolio management strategies and how they relate to this question.

1. As investors wanting upside potential, we seek solutions to really big problems for a lot of people. To profit, we must find these early, while still little-known, underappreciated, and undervalued. Now, think about Africa in this context. Can you honestly think of a continent where more people have *bigger* problems, yet commercial solutions are *less* known or funded? Now, look deeper between those branches. For instance, might a mobile banking app deploying economical African innovations also be valued globally? Do we have your attention now?

2. Seasoned investors value entrepreneurs who do the heavy lifting. High-potential entrepreneurs are hungry overachievers, passionate about solving problems for people they love. They innovate ways to achieve more, in less time, with fewer resources. Now, who has more reasons to care about solving big problems and who might be more cost-efficient than African entrepreneurs? And there are plenty to choose from among the continent's billion youth.

3. If your portfolio mandate includes making the world a better place, how many sectors offer more impactful solutions that are less expensive to pilot than tech-driven startups in Africa?

4. You probably reserve some percentage of your investment portfolio for "uncorrelated" assets to add upside potential that moves independently of your existing holdings. If you study the data, you will be amazed at the difference between conventional asset valuations and the timing and dynamics of African startups. Talk about diversity!

5. Finally, from a quality of life perspective, if you are tired of reading dull data and spreadsheets that lack a soul, add some excitement to your portfolio! Get out of your office and meet aspiring young Africans who are earning degrees at a university or innovating at a tech hub near you. Then, go explore Africa with them and see for yourself! Their energy, integrity, and altruism will cheer, reassure, and inspire you. There is no downside to this strategy.

Backstory: How African Argonauts are Developing Their Continent

When the world saw through "the emperor's new clothes" of the financing industry in 2007-2009, many African-born diaspora became disillusioned with their career goals in the USA. As they left lucrative corporate careers to return to their homelands, their stunned family and friends asked why. They replied that they wanted to build a supportive ecosystem where Africa's entrepreneurs and innovators could thrive. And they did.

These African visionaries pioneered digital infrastructure, technology hubs, angel investor networks, and pan-African organizations with global reach. Investing their own savings, they piloted funding strategies that nurtured the continent's first crop of tech startups well enough to attract corporate partners and private sector capital from abroad.

This entrepreneurial approach came full circle when successful African founders used their initial profits to invest in the next crop, establishing a self-sustaining cycle. This book documents how this process began two decades ago, how it became sustainable and how it is scaling up. Now, it is time for these successes to become more broadly known, replicated, and supported at scale.

Being among the first and most active investors on the continent, interviewers often ask me and my African partners about the strategies and stories that led to our successes. By opening the curtain to explore behind media headlines, this book adds context and credibility to the ecosystem that created commercial beacons of hope for the continent.

1. Tech Startups Succeed

To go fast, go alone: To go far, go together.
—An African parable

Canada's University of Waterloo was a long way from home for one of its teenage students from Africa, but he soon found his niche on the campus where the first Blackberry devices were birthed. Iyinoluwa Aboyeji, who prefers to be called "E," grew up in a part of Lagos now known as "Yabacon Valley" or the "Silicon Lagoon."

Waterloo's entrepreneurship program is named Velocity, for good reason; E's fellow students were founding their own technology startups. When one of those ventures, dubbed BufferBox, was acquired by Google in 2012, E had an epiphany. If his classmates could succeed, then he could too. E decided that someday he would have his own "BufferBox moment."

This confidence inspired him to innovate potential solutions to the challenges he knew people in his homeland faced every day. During a school break back home, he met with local advisors, who liked his vision to create jobs for African youth via tech-driven ventures. After E shared his concept for an EdTech publishing venture, this group of local business angel investors made a small equity investment so he could test his greenfield concept.

After months of hard work and slow progress, E returned to Nigeria and apologised to his investors. He realized that the venture strategy he had asked them to back would not scale well enough to reach profitability. The Afropreneur Angel Group was led by an experienced tech entrepreneur named Idris Bello, who comforted E by saying they appreciated his honest communication and shared his priorities on scaling education in Africa.

Since the investors had used a simple equity agreement, E was not obligated to repay them. Idris and his co-investors assured E that they still believed in him as a social innovator and entrepreneur. They encouraged E to complete his schooling and bring them his next venture idea.

In 2014, E did return to the Afropreneur Angel Group to pitch a more scalable EdTech strategy with a founding team that was more diverse and experienced than before. E's team explained how their new venture would address the worldwide shortage of software development engineers by training Africa's tech-savvy youth to fill the void. This new company would set up a digital training platform and physical campuses where Africa's young techies would train and work.

Andela, so named to memorialize Nelson Mandela, would manage contracts to meet the software needs of global tech corporations and would assure the quality of their emerging African workforce. The Afropreneur Angels did not hesitate to back E again. Idris even scouted out locations for the team's first training campus in Lagos, no easy task where 20 million people call home.

E rewarded the loyalty of his investors by rolling over the value of their lost investment into equity rights in the new seed-stage venture, and making room for them to add capital in a crowded round. The next year, Andela raised $14M in its first formal round from investors who included Omidyar Network, Serena Ventures, Spark, Google Ventures, and the International Finance Corporation.

Headline news photos in August 2016 showed Mark Zuckerberg jogging the streets of Lagos, sharing computer screens with Nigerian youth, and exclaiming, "These are my people!" His newly minted private LLC, The Chan Zuckerberg Initiative, was leading Andela's $24M series B investment round to help Andela maintain its startup growth spurt.

Photo: Mark Zuckerberg walks Lagos, 2016
Source: https://www.wired.com/2016/10/zuckerberg-in-africa/

Startups Make History

This news was the first global acknowledgment of Africa's budding technology sector, and it motivated me to formally join Idris Bello and the LoftyInc team I had informally worked with since 2009. In 2017, we established one of the first Delaware-registered venture capital firms dedicated to seed investing in African tech startups.

Andela went on to raise $40M in its 2017 C-round, which included Silicon Valley-based Sales Force Ventures, TLCom, and Double Bottom Line Partners.[4] A New York Times article on October 10, 2017, quoted Andela's USA-born CEO, Jeremy Johnson, as saying, "In addition to being a major milestone for Andela, it also represents a milestone for the African tech ecosystem as it is the largest venture round ever led by an African VC fund into an Africa-based business."

---

[4] Múyìwá Mátùlukò. (2017, October 7). *Andela raises $40M series C from Omobola Johnson's TLcom and 4 other new investors*. Techpoint Africa. https://techpoint.africa/general/andela-series-c/

The African-born founders of CRE Capital made this history. Pardon Makumbe, a Wharton MBA and Princeton BSE, previously oversaw global investments at EL Rothschild after working at Bain & Company, Emerging Capital Partners, and Temasek Holdings. CRE co-founder, Pule Taukobong, previously founded Africa Angels Network and held roles at Investec, Standard Bank, and Accenture.

Al Gore's sustainability-focused private equity firm, Generation Investment Management, led Andela's $100M D-round in 2019, crediting Andela's remote work strategy for reducing the environmental impact of air travel to in-person meetings.[5] In October 2021, SoftBank's social impact fund led Andela's $200M E-round at a valuation exceeding $1B, creating one of Africa's first unicorns.[6]

Beyond this funding news and valuation numbers, in its first decade alone, Andela trained over 150,000 software developers in 175 countries, many of whom moved into senior corporate positions or launched their own ventures. In his November 2023 blog about Andela's global expansion, CEO Jeremy Johnson wrote this about Africa's tech talent trends:

"Africa still represents the soul of the company. It is where we started; three of our co-founders are from the continent, and today, it still represents over half of the talent in the Andela network. While other regions faced stagnant or declining growth in 2022, Africa remained resilient and even showed some growth in the tech sector. Even the World Economic Forum now agrees that Africa is emerging as a significant source of software engineering talent and is home to the fastest-growing population of developers.

"With millions of Africans joining the workforce each year, the continent offers a growing consumer market, and an expansive, untapped talent

---

[5] Andela.com *Andela raises $100M in series D round led by former US VP's development firm.* https://www.andela.com/news/andela-raises-100m-in-series-d-round-led-by-former-us-vps-investment-firm

[6] Andela. (2021, September 29). *Andela announces $200M investment led by Softbank.* https://www.andela.com/news/andela-announces-200m-investment-led-by-softbank

pool prepared to drive global tech innovation. For the first five years of Andela's history, we primarily connected African talent with companies in North America and Europe. Increasingly, we are seeing exciting growth from clients in Africa who are more than ever playing in the global tech ecosystem and, as such, are navigating the global talent world.

"…Global brands like Visa, Google, Meta, AWS, Alibaba Group, and Rolls-Royce have all expanded operations in Africa to tap into local talent. African engineers no longer need to rely solely on companies outside Africa for opportunities. It is amazing to see that talent and opportunity are flowing in both directions."[7]

Photo: Andela Founders
Source: https://www.builtinnyc.com/articles/andela-raises-200m-softbank-hiring

---

[7] Johnson, J. (2023, November 8). *Strengthening partnerships in Kenya and Egypt.* Andela. https://andela.com/blog-posts/notes-from-the-road-strengthening-partnerships-and-connecting-with-talent-in-kenya-and-egypt

A short history of Africa's Unicorns

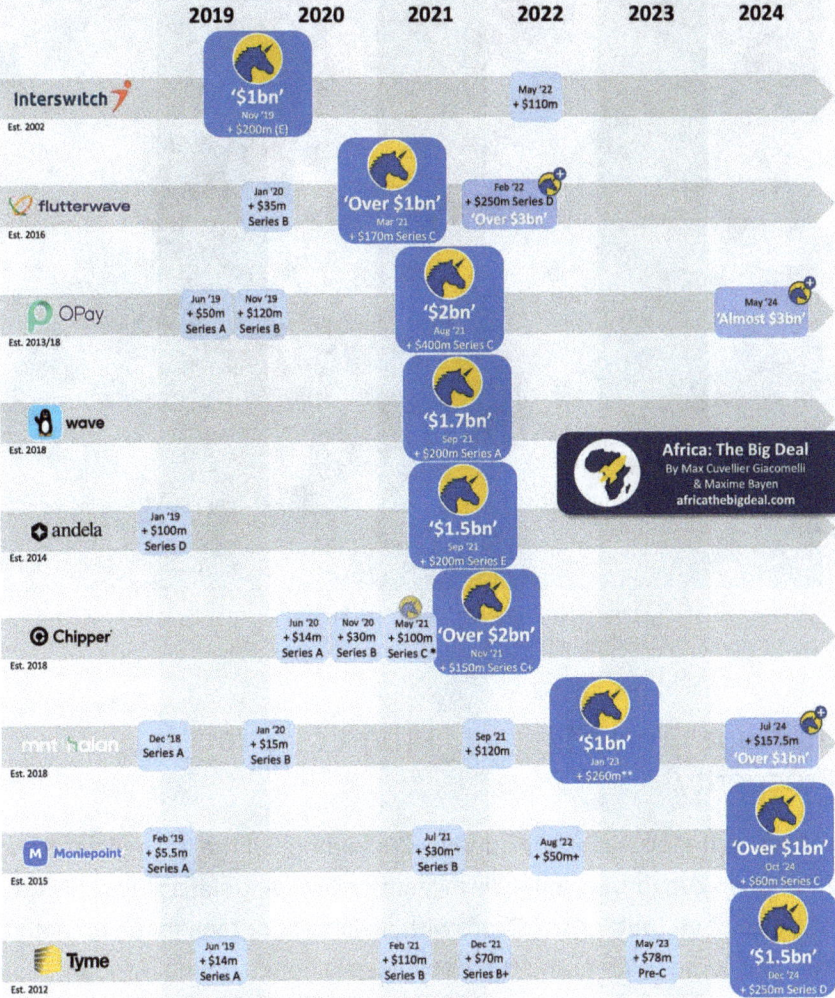

	2019	2020	2021	2022	2023	2024
Interswitch Est. 2002	'$1bn' Nov '19 + $200m (E)			May '22 + $110m		
flutterwave Est. 2016		Jan '20 + $35m Series B	'Over $1bn' Mar '21 + $170m Series C	Feb '22 + $250m Series D 'Over $3bn'		
OPay Est. 2013/18	Jun '19 + $50m Series A	Nov '19 + $120m Series B	'$2bn' Aug '21 + $400m Series C			May '24 'Almost $3bn'
wave Est. 2018			'$1.7bn' Sep '21 + $200m Series A			
andela Est. 2014		Jan '19 + $100m Series D	'$1.5bn' Sep '21 + $200m Series E			
Chipper Est. 2018		Jun '20 + $14m Series A	Nov '20 + $30m Series B	May '21 + $100m Series C * 'Over $2bn' Nov '21 + $150m Series C+		
mnt alan Est. 2018	Dec '18 Series A	Jan '20 + $15m Series B	Sep '21 + $120m	'$1bn' Jan '23 + $260m**		Jul '24 + $157.5m 'Over $1bn'
Moniepoint Est. 2015	Feb '19 + $5.5m Series A		Jul '21 + $30m Series B	Aug '22 + $50m+		'Over $1bn' Oct '24 + $60m Series C
Tyme Est. 2012	Jun '19 + $14m Series A		Feb '21 + $110m Series B	Dec '21 + $70m Series B+	May '23 + $78m Pre-C	'$1.5bn' Dec '24 + $250m Series D

Africa: The Big Deal
By Max Cuvellier Giacomelli
& Maxime Bayen
africathebigdeal.com

For all sources and more details, visit: thebigdeal.substack.com/p/unicorns2
Only 'current' unicorns included (i.e. excluding organisations that have since listed) | 🦄 indicates updated valuation since initially gaining unicorn status
* While claiming to be 'probably the most valuable private startup in Africa today' in May '21, Chipper only shared valuation data in Nov '21
** In Jan '23, valuation was estimated at 'about $1bn'; following its Jul '24 fundraise, valuation is 'over $1bn', and unicorn status assumed to have been gained in 2023

Source: TheBigDeal.substack.com/p/unicorns2

Photo: Andela CEO Jeremy Johnson with Author, 2019.
Source: Author's Archives

Startups Create Impact...Progress through Prosperity

Thanks to the publicity surrounding Zuckerberg's time in Lagos and the 2016 Chan Zuckerberg Initiative investment into Andela, a global "WAKE-UP" sign lit up, putting investors with an impact or tech focus on notice that the time had come to back inspirational young African tech founders. Only a couple of months later, E left Andela to co-found a fintech venture that fosters African employment in another way.

Flutterwave's fintech platform resolves painful cross-border payment problems. Its API-based tools enable merchants and consumers to send and receive real-time payments anywhere in Africa and worldwide, minimizing currency issues. E's co-founder was Olugbenga Agboola, or "GB," a Lagos-born software engineer and entrepreneur who earned his MBA at the MIT Sloan School of Management.

Before co-founding Flutterwave with E in 2016, GB worked in product management at Google and as an application engineer at PayPal. That year, Silicon Valley tech accelerator Y Combinator accepted Flutterwave as its second African-founded investee,[8] propelling it on a path that led it to a billion-dollar unicorn valuation, even before Andela. In 2017, Flutterwave was named Best Fintech company at the Apps Africa Innovation Awards.[9]

That status came after only five years, via a $170M C round that drew in lead investors Tiger Global and Avenir Growth Capital, investing entities that did not even exist when Flutterwave launched just five years before. The round's more experienced Fintech investors included Y Combinator's Continuity Fund (invested in Stripe), Greycroft (Braintree and Venmo), Greenvisor Capital, Omidyar Network, and Glynn Capital.[10]

By 2021, more than 290,000 businesses were using the Flutterwave platform to carry out payments in 150 different modes, including cards, mobile wallets, bank transfers, and Barter, a Flutterwave-built payment service. This offers users an inexpensive and seamless way to send invoices, receive money, and pay merchants from the convenience of their mobile phones.

Flutterwave's $1 billion valuation, unicorn-level crown, was awarded close on the heels of success by another Nigerian venture that profited from Y Combinator's Silicon Valley program and its global tech investor network.

Y Combinator's first African-led investment was in Paystack, with two young Nigerians at the helm, devoted to simplifying African payments

[8] https://www.ycombinator.com/companies/flutterwave

[9] https://dardenafrica.com/service/flutterwave-dabo-sponsor

[10] Kene-Okafor, T. (2021, March 9). *African payments company Flutterwave raises $170M, now valued at over $1B*. TechCrunch. https://techcrunch.com/2021/03/09/african-payments-company-flutterwave-raises-170m-now-valued-at-over-1b/

from anywhere to anywhere.[11] Paystack was acquired by Stripe in October 2020 for $200 million,[12] only four years after it launched, providing its seed-stage investors with stunningly high Internal Rates of Return (IRR). This acquisition also freed its devoted founders to work full-time on their core mission—to secure and amplify Africa's online payment infrastructure without wasting time raising capital for ongoing growth costs and development expenses.

What attracted Stripe to Paystack in the first place? Stripe's CEO said that during the team's YC days in 2016, they had impressed him with their focus on meaningful innovations so the company made an initial seed investment to watch what the team could do. Their innovations continued to impress him, so he invited them to come in-house.

Photo: Paystack founders
Source: https://techcrunch.com/2020/10/15/stripe-acquires-nigerias-paystack-for-200m-to-expand-into-the-african-continent/

---

[11] https://techcrunch.com/2020/10/15/stripe-acquires-nigerias-paystack-for-200m-to-expand-into-the-african-continent/

[12] Lunden, I. (2020, October 15). *Stripe acquires Nigeria's Paystack for 200M+ to expand into the African continent*. TechCrunch. https://techcrunch.com/2020/10/15/stripe-acquires-nigerias-paystack-for-200m-to-expand-into-the-african-continent/

E's sizable exits from Andela and Flutterwave, inspired him to help other young Africans solve the problems that matter to them. His survey of startup founders overwhelmingly stressed their need for funding to grow their fledgling startups. Having co-founded two of Africa's first unicorns, E had learned a thing or two about funding tech-driven startups, and he had earned the respect of global financiers. They listened when E invited them to co-invest with him in a selection of Africa's heartiest young sprouts.

E assembled a team and began his campaign by emailing investment memos, which gained traction among private investors seeking tech innovation and economic development. When his team started charging for it, their Future Africa brand was born. It evolved into a boutique investment vehicle that leverages the US-based AngelList platform[13] to manage Special Purpose Vehicles. Each SPV represents a group of investors who co-own an equity position.

Within five years, Future Africa managed $12M, and its portfolio surpassed $120M in annual revenues, raised $300M in follow-on capital, creating $1.2B of company value.[14] His personal investments of $1.5M had grown to $14M in value,[15] but more importantly, they had also created 3,000 direct and 12,000 indirect jobs.

Seeing E reinvest his profits was a momentous milestone for me because it showed a clear path to sustainability for Africa's startup ecosystem. By re-investing in other young entrepreneurs like himself, E repeated a virtuous circle of iterative support, the way Idris' investment in E had initiated years earlier. Thanks to entrepreneurial investors such as Idris

---

[13] https://www.angellist.com

[14] Partner. (2021, Augus 21). *The Future Africa Collective presents an opportunity to invest in high-growth African startups.* TechCabal. https://techcabal.com/2021/08/25/the-future-africa-collective-presents-an-opportunity-to-invest-in-high-growth-african-startups/

[15] Quinlan, N. (2021, February 1). *African capital for African innovation.* Waterloo News. https://uwaterloo.ca/news/global-impact/african-capital-african-innovation?utm_source=facebook&utm_medium=social&utm_campaign=youpluswaterloo

and E, and despite a global pandemic and economic slowdown, Africa's blossoming tech startup ecosystem attracted $5 billion in private investments in 2022.

Photo: E & Idris
Source: Idris Bello Archives

What about measuring and reporting impact? In America, where an entire new industry has grown up around tracking metrics, the process often resembles splitting hairs, which saps resources away from bootstrapping startups. But in Africa, impact metrics can be quite simple.

Every formal job supports about three Africans and spreads a safety net for many more.[16] This high-priority metric is easily tracked. Most ventures aim to increase African access to critical products and services, so the number of customers served is also relevant and obvious. The more recurring revenues, the stronger the company. Such metrics require no

---

[16] https://www.voanews.com/a/employed-south-africans-have-high-number-of-dependents/1588436.html

extraordinary effort. Burdening busy startups with overly complex tracking becomes counterproductive.

Startups Initiate Ecosystems...

At this point, you may be wondering how all this sustainable prosperity took root and how local entrepreneurs could succeed where the world's aid, loan, and charity programs failed. As the greater story of Africa's innovation revolution unfolds, you will see patterns emerge. The seeds that germinated Nigeria's blossoming technology ecosystem were planted long before E and Idris were born.

Circular migrations and technology innovations created pathways for access and connections to arise, thrive, and replicate. Personal agency and individual initiatives removed blockages; local problem-solvers became global entrepreneurs; and an emerging sense of community superseded economic status, ethnicity, nationality, gender, age, and creed...

During the 1950s, a young woman in Northern Nigeria lived as a Muslim wife with her husband and two young sons. Salamotu was concerned for her sons, because the region lacked high-quality schooling opportunities. So she bid her husband well and moved to where her mother had raised her in southwestern Nigeria. But how did Salamotu support herself and fund her sons' education while living in Abeokuta, about 40 miles outside Lagos?

Long before tie-dyed clothing became the rage in America, it was a valued art form across Asia and Africa. Salamotu was not formally educated, but she was an expert at "Adire," a Yoruba word that links "adi" (to tie) and "re" (to dye). She started out selling her fabrics in the open market, which were customized with her symbolic designs, hand-stitched. Over time, Salamotu built consumer loyalty and product demand for her fashion brand.

She bought sewing machines and employed scores of local men and women, becoming wealthy enough to build a three-story home and educate her sons well. Her customers came from countries as far as Senegal to purchase large quantities of her unique garments and fabrics. Her story was included in her half-sister's auto-biography and preserved by her protegee.[17]

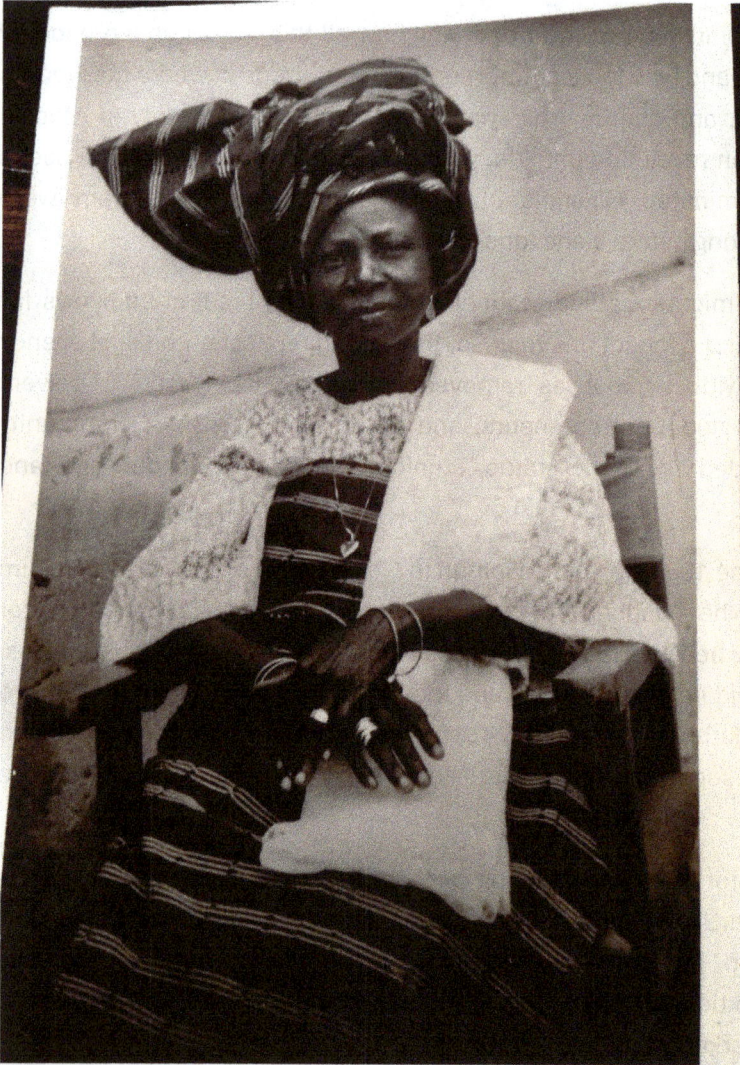

Photo: Salamotu
Source: Bello Family Archives

---

[17] The Bello family archives

Salamotu Ajoke Bello's sons became ardent young scholars, professionals and fathers. One of them fathered twin boys and one of them was named Idris Ayodeji Bello. Idris later led an African investment group that backed E's startup ventures, as cited above. How did this family move economically from selling tie-dye cloth in the open market to co-founding venture capital firms? Personal initiative, for sure.

Idris remembers many evenings as a youth, reading in a university library as he waited for his father to finish his responsibilities there. 'Never get caught without a book' became the family mantra. So, he always had a book at hand, which prepared him well.

Photo: Idris Bello
Source: Idris Bello Archives

After earning a Computer Engineering degree in Nigeria, Idris worked for Procter & Gamble's facility in Ibadan, where he reduced production costs and optimized delivery timelines. But Idris was just getting started. He moved to Texas, where he earned an MSc in Computer Science at the University of Houston, focusing on data mining techniques to improve scientific pricing analytics and execution.

Then he earned an MBA at Rice University and an MSc from Oxford.[18] Idris launched a technology startup named AfyaZima, after a Swahili word meaning complete health. Its "Blood Pressure MCuff" was lauded as one of the first low-cost, wearable telemedicine devices to monitor vital signs and manage two-way data transmissions via mobile phone.

---

[18] https://www.whtrust.org/alumni-profiles/idris-bello

In 2012, McCuff won the Dell Technology Award in collaboration with the Oxford Engineering World Health Group, MIT awarded Idris a Global Startup Fellowship, and CNN selected him as one of the Top Tech Voices for Africa.[19] When Idris sold AfyaZima, he felt inspired to invest in other young African innovators, so he combined his sale proceeds with a 401(k) he'd earned working with Chevron.

Demonstrating his characteristic drive to network, Idris built both a personal portfolio and an investing group of African professionals like himself to share deal flow, vet, and mentor young tech founders. This Afropreneurs Angel Group became an enduring organization that we will explore in more depth in Chapter Six, on funding Africa's tech ecosystem.

This multi-generational story illustrates how African entrepreneurship created a virtuous reinvestment cycle. Thanks to Salamotu's courage as an entrepreneurial mother, her grandson attained global expertise that is helping African entrepreneurs build billion-dollar corporations. These companies each train and employ thousands of African youth each year.

Investor exit proceeds are reinvested into emerging founders like E, who repeat the cycle on a grander scale. Salamotu, Idris, angel investors, and their investees put their faith in the power of entrepreneurship to transform a family, a country, and a continent. This entrepreneurial legacy created impact at scale.

> If "necessity is the mother of innovation," then
> Africans are her children– and such children she has
> raised!—Marsha Wulff

---

[19] Kermeliotis, T. (Updated 2012, October 11). *How 'Afropreneurs' will shape Africa's future.* CNN Business. https://www.cnn.com/2012/09/17/tech/idris-bello-afropreneur-technology/index.html

How Africa's Tech Ecosystem Scaled Up

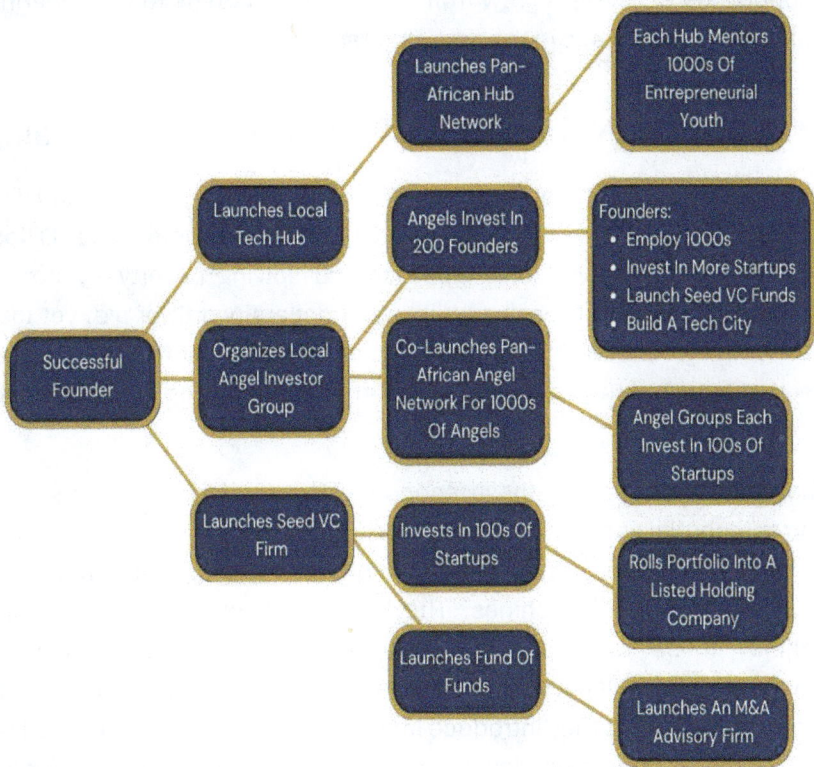

Source: Marsha Wulff 2025

In 2018, after 20 years of envisioning the potential of Africa's evolving startup ecosystem and working toward this sustainable ecosystem goal, I celebrated it coming full circle. This new development stage alerted me that my role had changed from informally pioneering a novel investing niche to establishing a formal venture capital firm. It was time to make the pioneering strategies of this fledgling movement, and its successes, known, so others would join in and scale it up. They needed to learn that they need not reinvent this wheel– it was already on a roll!

How did this ecosystem scale up? This image graphs the exponential growth from one successful founder, like Idris, who applied what he learned by co-launching tech hubs, angel groups, and a VC firm to manage seed-stage funds. This fledgling ecosystem level expanded into formal, member-backed, pan-African associations with international support; the ecosystem grew from impacting hundreds to empowering millions, as we will see in the next chapters.

Startups Lift Nations out of Poverty–like America!

In their 2019 book, *The Prosperity Paradox: How Innovation Can Lift Nations Out of Poverty*, authors Christensen, Ojomo, and Dillon challenged the conventional approach to solving poverty by noting twenty countries that received billions of dollars' worth of aid, yet lost economic ground. That development approach identified areas that needed help and then flooded them with resources, hoping some good would come of it.

The authors contrasted these economic failures with America's own entrepreneurial approach to economic development, based on "market-creating" innovations, including those of Ford Motors, Eastman Kodak, and Singer Sewing Machines. They showed how the entrepreneurs behind these companies positively impacted the economic development of at least one billion people. Their analysis becomes even more convincing as they introduce innovative entrepreneurs who led the extraordinary economic development of Japan, South Korea, India, Argentina, and Mexico.

The Prosperity Paradox team showed that innovations born of necessity solve problems and create markets. After applying exacting, thesis-driven analysis to their research, they suggested that global funders should replace their top-down, aid and debt-driven approaches with a fresh mindset about how to help the world prosper through innovative entrepreneurship.

In a 2024 article, the Nigeria-born co-author of *The Prosperity Paradox,* Efosa Ojomo applied his innovation theme to African development specifically.[20] He turned another convention in its head by pointing out

---

[20] Ojomo, E., Staples, M. (2024, November 27). *Rethinking Africa's infrastructure gap: Innovation ecosystems as the key to sustainable growth. Christensen*

the fallacy of building school, rail, and road infrastructure *prior* to developing entrepreneurial ecosystems. Indeed, America's own transition from rural subsistence farming to urban industrialization was directly linked to innovations made at Ford Motor Company, which empowered widespread, personal ownership of reliable, affordable vehicles. These incremental innovations were designed to solve the mobility problem of a society that was 96% agrarian. Mobility linked crops to markets and people to urban jobs.

As the Ford company's key owner and decision maker, Henry Ford personally drove this economic development solution, despite the failures of his two prior ventures and several earlier models. Mobility was not easy to hack. His challenges included affordability, reliability, infrastructure, and refuelling networks. Its solutions started with an innovative entrepreneur determined to solve a problem, and succeeded because he did not give up. When employees could not afford the time or money to buy and enjoy the Model T, Ford raised their salaries and shortened their work week.

He did not wait for governments to enact favorable policies or to build supportive infrastructure. Interstate highway systems and gas station chains *followed* the adoption of the Model T, as did interstate commerce policies and traffic control laws. Policies and infrastructure cannot predict the timing or direction in which innovations will take new markets or pin-point where market demands will spur progress.

Development success is an iterative process between innovations, investments, and markets—not infrastructure, loans, and regulations.

Institute. https://www.christenseninstitute.org/blog/rethinking-africas-infrastructure-gap-innovation-ecosystems-as-the-key-to-sustainable-growth/

2. Startups Drive Economies

Shall we repeat the mistakes of the past or innovate a better future? This is the question.

Imagine being a well-rounded teenager with academic and entrepreneurial successes under your belt, but you have expenses. Today, you heard that a local company wants to hire a few entry-level people, so you showed up to apply. But literally thousands of other youths like yourself were also in line. Your heart sinks.

Fortunately, your chicken eggs are in demand at the local market, and you made enough sales last year to pay your school fees and expand your chicken coops. This year, several steady customers bought your eggs, so you started paying your younger brother's school fees and bought an inexpensive smartphone to manage poultry supplies, egg orders, and deliveries.

Ten years later, instead of thousands of youths applying for each job offered, there are tens of thousands. Job contenders' frustration bursts into fury, as they have been job-hunting for years. Now they need to help their parents with health care costs and want to marry someone they love. Job-hunting becomes a full-contact sport, which leaves the winners with no leverage for negotiating a living wage or job security.

Good thing that your chicken business has grown! Now you have 50,000 laying hens roosting in covered, open-air coops that efficiently collect not only eggs, but also manure sold as fertilizer for your nation's rapidly expanding agriculture industry. You have your pick of competent workers eager to prove their worth. You love being an entrepreneur.

But you want to help with youth employment, so you organize a group of seasoned entrepreneurs to mentor young people who have entrepreneurial goals of their own. You think some of them are ready to get startup businesses off the ground, so you invest small amounts in your favorite young entrepreneurs. They remind you of yourself at their age.

Now you want to start an informal investor group to share the work of choosing ventures and mentoring teams, to be partners who can share in their success. But there are millions more promising youths across your country, whose ventures could also thrive, if only they knew the right investors.

Some have tech-driven innovations that might attract global markets and make the world a better place. They could use bigger checks and broader networks. You see the potential for more efficient investing to scale startups like these, and you feel compelled to act, but what's the first step?

This is Africa today, in a nutshell.

As you return your thoughts to your life in the US, you may feel your mindset shift. As cynicism creeps back into your psyche, you may ask, "Why should I care about African startups?" After reading Chapter 2, I hope you will respond, "Enlightened self-interest!" But first...

Africa's Youth...Treasure Chest or a Ticking Bomb?

One billion young people under the age of 30 now live in Africa, thanks to successful immunization and disease control programs. These have prevented enough childhood deaths to create an extraordinary demographic youth bubble where over ten million new workers enter a job market each year that only creates room for three million.

Although African women today have half as many pregnancies as they had sixty years ago, newborns are four times more likely to survive childhood, and life spans have lengthened, retaining job holders longer.[21] Ideally, immunization programs would have built in job creation, but they were not. Net result? One billion youth will soon need jobs.

Africa's entrepreneurs are not waiting for governments and charities, and are creating jobs for youth themselves, often via low-cost, high-growth technology startups. Their efforts have already built a middle class that is using its clout to improve governance and shared services.

Demographically speaking, the timing is perfect for Africa's development bubble. As industrialized societies face population declines and mass retirements, they are seeking growth sectors for their retirement investments. Simultaneously, African youth are maturing with the energy, enthusiasm, and creativity to build a better future via entrepreneurship. One billion tech-savvy youth can innovate all kinds of solutions, sell them, and afford to consume them, upgrading their lives at the speed of investments in startups, employment creation, and new market development.

Almost all African youth have informal jobs, often several at once, to compensate for uncertainties in their lives. Most have "side-hustles" because they must buy food and pay school fees, but they feel underemployed and hunger for opportunities to progress via formal employment. Entrepreneurship is plentiful, but investment capital is almost nonexistent for even the best ventures to grow sufficiently to provide stable employment. We will explore this problem later, in Part Three: What's Not Working.

Startups Create Jobs...

Theoretically, if each new venture creates one hundred new jobs, then Africa will need one million new entrepreneurial ventures each year for

---

[21] ECA. (2024,July 12). (Blog) As Africa's population crosses 1.5 billion, the demographic window is opening; getting the dividend requires more time and stronger effort. https://www.uneca.org/stories/(blog)-as-africa's-population-crosses-1.5-billion,-the-demographic-window-is-opening-getting

the next decade to sustain its maturing youth without mass emigration. Since new businesses mostly compete with non-consumption, the opportunities to create new markets are extraordinary. But...you may well argue, these new ventures will need an army of astute founders to launch them, mentors to guide them, and investors to seed-fund them.

Where will all this seasoned talent and funding come from?

Fortunately, Africa already has an entrepreneurial army in place—formally organized, fully committed, and operational. Twenty years ago, grass-roots leadership started establishing a pan-African ecosystem that now supports startup founders and investors alike. Each year, it refines best practices, deepens capacity, and scales up impact. It trains entrepreneurs, welcomes co-investors, and partners with corporates. Its members reinvest profits back into the next crop of rising entrepreneurs, scaling and sustaining a virtuous cycle.

Who built this startup ecosystem? How did it handle infrastructure and all the other challenges of Africa? Does it have investment success stories? Yes, it does, and "Part Two: What's Working" introduces the wider world to this thriving grassroots ecosystem that Africans have built, with a bit of American encouragement.

This is an amazing story of shared values that drove unique collaborations between visionaries, pioneers, builders, entrepreneurs, investors, strangers, and friends. It shares the lessons they learned from their successes, failures, and challenges. But first, I invite readers to consider a fundamental question about economic development.

From an historic perspective, what approach has most often lifted people out of poverty? Was it government aid, non-profit charity, or personal initiative? Which mechanism is validated as most effective against poverty? This quest will guide us toward optimal, data-based strategies.

Accordingly, I cite below the work of a dedicated team of researchers, whose publications authoritatively lit this path for seekers like us to follow. One World Bank team asked 60,000 people who had risen out of extreme poverty around the world, how they had done it. After a decade of amassing copious data, the team's findings were statistically consistent and overwhelmingly conclusive.

The *Moving out of Poverty*[22] research team explained their startling findings this way...

"The successes usually required a level of freedom to claim project ownership and having no one block their way forward. Sometimes the best way to help development is to NOT block, limit, or restrict entrepreneurs from access, opportunity, or ownership. In other words, the single most important thing for governments, charities, and investors to do is to stay out of the way of entrepreneurs on a mission. This means not trying to dominate or control them by way of investment strategies that we will explore later.

"The key to poverty reduction lies in the intersection of initiative and opportunity. Again and again, our respondents told stories of overcoming obstacles by using their freedom to seize opportunities. They see maintaining their own freedom and power as essential to finding their way out of poverty...they see hard work and initiative as the means to achieve that future."[23]

---

[22] World Bank Group. (2009). *Moving out of poverty: success from the bottom up.* https://openknowledge.worldbank.org/entities/publication/8ccfe651-e7ff-556b-a503-fa0b941b1b4d/full

[23] World Bank Group. (2009). *Moving out of poverty: success from the bottom up.* pg 339 https://openknowledge.worldbank.org/server/api/core/bitstreams/f00c122d-af1e-5557-80b7-af80738a9155/content

Photo: World Bank Study "Moving out of Poverty"

In other words, personal initiative is what moves people out of poverty toward sustainable self-sufficiency. Period, full stop. The study learned that poor people attempted to launch their own initiatives as often as the rich, but that the rich more often succeeded. Poor people most wanted equal opportunities to attain economic self-sufficiency—to use their own ingenuity to provide solutions that other people need. They wanted to be entrepreneurs so they could support themselves and hire others. Why? Because that is what works.

Their astonishing discoveries were published in four carefully worded volumes, including *Success from the Bottom Up, Concluding Reflections*, which says: "Movers most frequently cite personal initiative as the reason for their move out of poverty. People most often cite new jobs, new agricultural initiatives, and new businesses as routes out of poverty. All these solutions reflect the decisions of people who took the initiative to resolve their own problems."[24]

So we have a definitive answer to our question about the optimal approach to development. But, are these conclusions being implemented? Maybe we should take a closer look at how emerging market startup businesses are funded, and by whom.

---

[24] World Bank Group. (2009). *Moving out of poverty: success from the bottom up.*
Page 20 Figure 1.2
https://www.google.com/books/edition/_/VwPFvoxyXwoC?hl=en&gbpv=1&pg=PA336&dq=%22The+key+to+poverty+reduction+lies+in+the+intersection+of+initiative+and+opportunity.%22

Since people want to be self-sufficient, the wisest path from poverty to prosperity is to empower entrepreneurs. The best founders do not want handouts; they want to solve problems, support themselves, and create jobs. They do not want governments restricting entrepreneurship with complex, unhelpful regulations or charities competing with their business ventures. They want entrepreneurial investors who believe in them and mentors to advise them.

Moving Out of Poverty

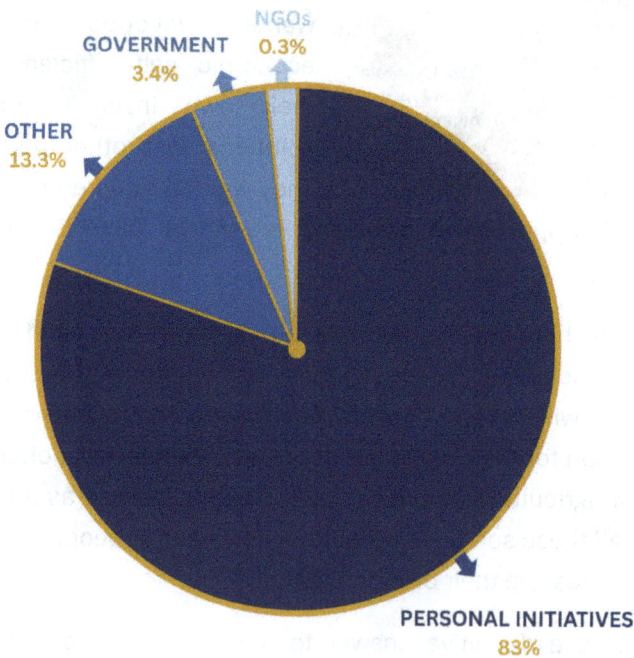

GOVERNMENT
3.4%

NGOs
0.3%

OTHER
13.3%

PERSONAL INITIATIVES
83%

Startups Empower Economies...

Tony Elumelu was a hungry teenager in Africa. Tony excelled at schools he could afford and jobs where he could sell. He turned around a failing bank and leveraged it into a pan-African force. Now, he is wealthy and has backed thousands of aspiring young Afropreneurs.

Why does he use his wealth to encourage entrepreneurship? "I've long questioned the traditional approach to development, where donors and governments fund access to basics, hoping that beneficiaries will become self-sufficient. While all assistance is to be acknowledged and appreciated, we need to give from the perspective of empowering the recipient rather than making them dependent.

"I have so much belief in the potential of nascent and budding African entrepreneurs that I [am]... committing $100M to support the next generation of African entrepreneurs. [We] will identify 1,000 African entrepreneurs each year for the next 10 years and provide them with seed capital to realize their business ideas...Our target is the creation of one million jobs and $10B in additional revenue on the continent.

"If we support people in a more sustainable way – by increasing access to economic opportunities – they can afford to pay for those same basic goods and services that governments and donors sometimes struggle to provide. When we invest in jobs and economic opportunity, beneficiaries will lift themselves out of poverty.

"This approach fosters the spirit of enterprise and decent work and will preserve dignity and reinforce self-reliance. It also enhances social stability because minds are constructively engaged. I call this approach Africapitalism."[25]

Startups Scale-up Development

> *"The reasonable man adapts himself to the world:*
> *the unreasonable one persists in trying to adapt the*
> *world to himself. Therefore, all progress depends on*
> *the unreasonable man."*
> —George Bernard Shaw

---

[25] Elumelu, T. (2016, May 19). Africapitalism: empowering people works much better than giving them aid. *The Guardian*.

Historical records for impacting development at scale are currently being broken almost every year by tech startups now named Alphabet, Amazon, and Apple. These entrepreneurial corporations are out-innovating institutions that were once considered essential to the USA, from public libraries to the US Postal Service.

African entrepreneurs are doing the same thing. The US National Space Administration had all but ground to a halt, abdicating space exploration leadership to Russia, until SpaceX challenged the conventional notion that rockets were too expensive for private enterprise to build. That defeatist assumption held back a generation of US-born entrepreneurs until one audacious African reversed the trend. Now, the recycling innovations and productivity of SpaceX propel the US to the leading edge of interplanetary travel.

It also leverages that effort to install infrastructure for a new era of rapid computing via global satellite networks. These satellites orbit not only over me in California but also over Michael's offices in Abuja and Teddy's tech hub in Kampala. These African-born, US-educated entrepreneurs empower thousands of aspiring local entrepreneurs to seize economic opportunities for their communities. They put their names on the Starlink waitlist years before I even knew it was coming.

This is vital tech development at scale, initiated by one entrepreneur born and raised in Africa to parents who were also raised in Africa. Yet Elon somehow achieved what US-born innovators did not. This inconvenient truth alone should spur American investors' curiosity.

How did this African-born boy gain the confidence, credibility, and capital he needed to succeed? The same way that anyone else does, by achieving one small success at a time and never giving up. And, because quitting in Africa is a luxury that few can afford.

12 year-old Elon created a video game and sold it to a computer magazine. The Britannica states that young Elon was driven by exactly the same things that *Moving Out of Poverty* cited: personal initiative, economic opportunity, and freedom, which in this case involved an escape from mandatory military service that enforced apartheid.

American venture capital investments into his first three ventures bridged Elon's path from frustration to sustainability. At PayPal, he joined other aspirational entrepreneurs who founded and became famous for recycling what they learned to create other impactful technology startups in the US.

The number and complexity of challenges that average African entrepreneurs face daily pre-condition them to juggle several projects at once. When the power grid quits, your phone battery recharging service stalls, so go sell your chicken eggs. If your chickens were frightened by a hawk, they may not lay eggs for a while, so you dig a ditch with your brother, or help your mother make a wedding cake. Survival demands personal initiative.

> *"Why would you even bother with an African biotech's pediatric antimalarial, when Novartis is in phase three trials for theirs?"*

The Executive Director of Medicines for Malaria Ventures (MMV) asked me this in 2006 at the Global Health symposium in Palm Springs. He ran a nonprofit that the Gates Foundation had recently funded with $200 million and had clearly missed my presentation. Hoping to secure his help was one reason I had accepted the invitation.

I wanted to reply, *because investing in African problem solvers resolves more than just their malaria problem; it empowers sustainable economic development—that's why!* But how to persuade him of this strategy's wisdom, in an elevator pitch? On behalf of a Ghanaian MBA with a ScD in BioChem from MIT, I had asked the MMV head for access to a testing device that would condense a required two-year product shelf-life stability test into a few weeks. That was the last step before marketing the product for African kids with malaria.

Dr Gbewonyo's career at Merck had been in pharmaceutical development,[26] and his innovation could start saving kids' lives almost immediately. His powdered Artemisia leaves in combination with other

---

[26] https://www.linkedin.com/in/kodzo-gbewonyo-65445012/

active ingredients was already blessed by the World Health Organization. It would be an affordable, convenient, shelf-stable sachet, like other successful local products. His young daughter had taste-tested and selected the banana flavor, so he knew sick kids would swallow it.

Did this MMV leader not care that prolonging the practice of crushing bitter adult pills into smaller portions condemned reluctant kids to preventable deaths by malaria? They would rather die– and they were, by the millions. If the goal was to start saving kids' lives asap, there was no need for years of expensive, brand-protecting trials.

But full FDA approval, based on phase three human trials, would protect a branded drug from competition for the lucrative PEPFAR contracts being awarded by the US government. That product would create a more expensive, branded monopoly with a supply chain problem. The Novartis strategy would not create thousands of local jobs for Africans who were ready to scale up crops of Artemisia plants and other nature-based health products.

Why would I bother with an African biotech's pediatric antimalarial? The more pertinent question was, *why would he withhold the use of one of the idle machines donated by the Gates Foundation?* This needless barrier to a more rapid and embraceable solution that would have built local capacity tilted the scale toward an already wealthy foreign corporation, whose costs were being covered by charity, while Dr Gbewonyo's product development was being bootstrap funded.

Since over 58,000 African kids were dying of Malaria every month, you would think this guy would have cared about speeding a more affordable product to market. Instead, he protected a major pharmaceutical's path, and asked me why I bothered with an embraceable African solution. He refused to share his equipment. That product never made it to market.

Traditional mindsets represent a prior era, when Africa and its resources were "owned" by others. The continent had few MIT doctors of science with Merck drug development expertise returning home to build businesses that resolved poverty and its debilitating effects. A lot of things are different now, or they could be...

Startup Innovations Solve the Poverty Trap

The presentation that the MMV head missed at the Global Health Symposium was similar to those I'd made in 2005 at the "Financing Global Health" workshop in Cambridge and at the United Nations in New York City, highlighting potential roles for the African diaspora in lifting Africa out of poverty. It was like the one I presented in 2007 at Stanford's first African Business Forum to demonstrate the path for investors to commercialize the continent's innovations.

It echoed the first seven years of my work, but it was not rocket science. Titled *"Collaborative Commercialization,"* my presentation contrasted the conventional institutional development model prevalent in Africa with the product innovation model that had built developed nations like the USA in the first place.

The European age of exploration and empire-building had relied on venture-specific collaborations. Monarchs led militaries that needed funding from merchants. Merchants paid for this military protection, but they also needed merchandise to trade. Explorers discovered products that traders purchased and mariners transported to markets, all of which were financed with venture capital. Each of these agreements shared risks, resources, costs, and rewards specific to the venture. Stakeholder interests were aligned to provide value and profits.

The product development model below shows how products, like the Novartis pediatric anti-malarial discussed above, are commercialized across Africa, from health products to jewelry. This value chain ensures that developed nations own the juiciest value addition stages, leaving Africa with only the potential for a few wage-generating jobs. These crumbs offer little wealth-building potential, despite their large market. This approach is a poverty trap.

Conventional Product Development Model

Value Creation	Developed Nations	African Nations
Product Discovery and Innovation	x	
Intellectual Property Rights	x	
Regulatory Licenses	x	
Product Development/Refinement	x	
Market Research & Planning	x	
Manufacturing/Processing	x	x?
Sales & Distribution	x	x?
Corporate Ownership	x	

On the other hand, when African innovators develop their own products, their ownership embeds the right to benefit from every subsequent value-adding stage in the commercialization process. Innovators can negotiate from a position of empowerment to collaborate with others in the value chain. Its effects are demonstrated in the chart below, where ownership shifts from one column to the other.

Proposed Collaborative Commercialization Model

Value Creation	Developed Nations	African Nations
Product Discovery and Innovation		x
Intellectual Property Rights	x?	x
Regulatory Licenses	x?	x
Product Development/Refinement	x?	x

Value Creation	Developed Nations	African Nations
Market Research & Planning	x?	x
Manufacturing/Processing	x?	x
Sales & Distribution	x?	x
Corporate Ownership	x?	x

This local product commercialization model avoids the poverty trap and creates local empowerment.

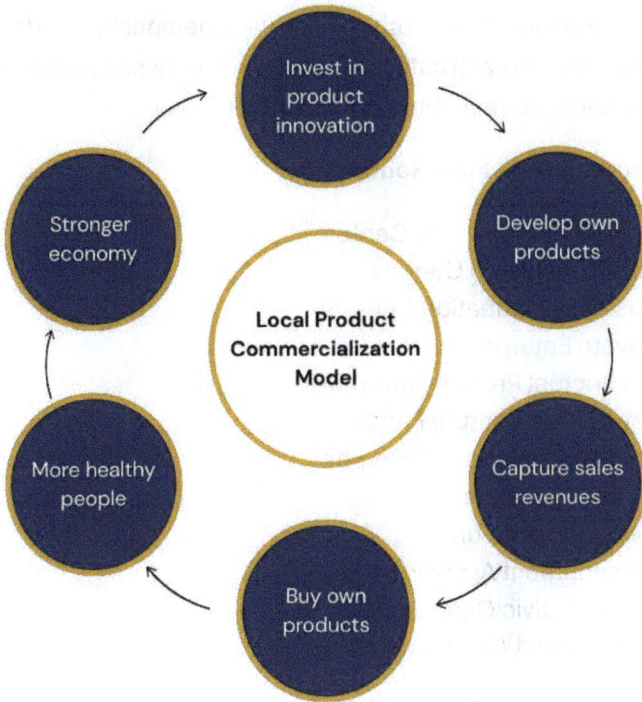

This solution to Africa's poverty trap seemed obvious to me, so why do development funders not support it? If they do see it, and their organization's mandate is to help with Africa's sustainable development, then why is this collaborative ownership model not being widely implemented? Perhaps because management is hired to fulfill bureaucratic jobs, not to empower sustainable entrepreneurship, and they are not incentivized to work themselves out of a job? Perhaps private investors fear the risks? Perhaps too few people understand startup investing? And even fewer know qualified African entrepreneurs with viable startups?

While working one-on-one with African innovators, I had seen ample opportunities for collaborative venture capital strategies to launch African innovations. Those who worked from "ivory towers," had not. Where could they have looked for emerging innovations?

The list below of African innovation sources is from a slide in my 2007 presentation to the first African Business Forum at Stanford. During a decade of independent research I had already personally interfaced with African leadership in each category and been impressed with their world-class potential as sustainable deal flow resources.

African Product Deal Flow Sources:

- University Innovation Centers
- Public Research Centers
- Business Incubation Centers
- Private Enterprise
- Intellectual Property Attorneys
- Seed Stage Venture Funds
- Trade Associations & Co-ops
- Licensing Agents
- Development Funds
- Development Agencies
- NGOs & Civic Organizations
- Professional Associations

If all these provide viable deal flow, what barrier prevents product innovators from creating markets? In every case, the constriction point for product development was at the commercialization stage. Each innovation resource lacked venture capital funding for startup teams that were passionate about bringing innovative products to market.

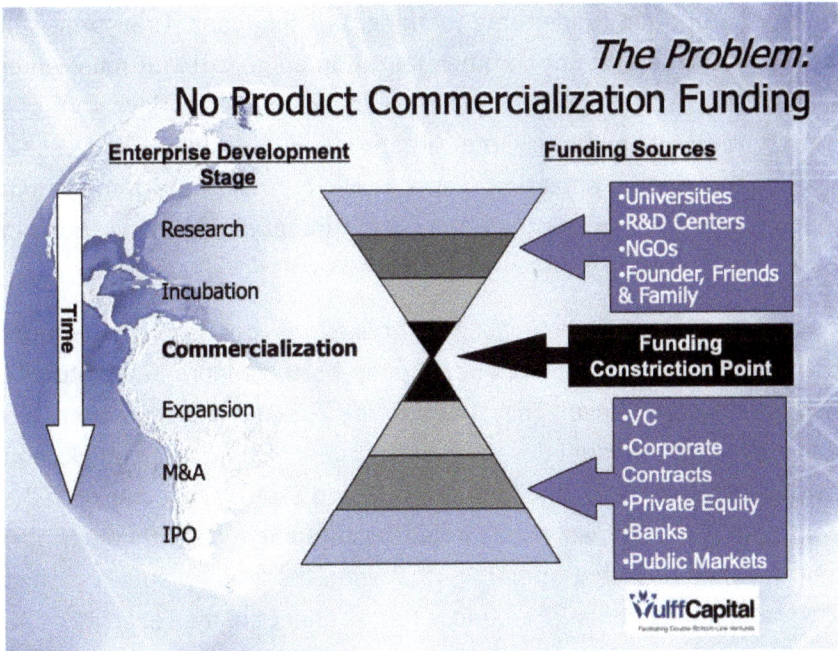

The Problem:
No Product Commercialization Funding

Enterprise Development Stage	Funding Sources
Research	•Universities •R&D Centers •NGOs •Founder, Friends & Family
Incubation	
Commercialization	**Funding Constriction Point**
Expansion	•VC
M&A	•Corporate Contracts •Private Equity
IPO	•Banks •Public Markets

Time

WulffCapital

So I kept rattling the cages...

To their credit, the Bill & Melinda Gates Foundation launched the Grand Challenges Explorations (GCE) program in 2008, with $100,000 grants–far more digestible initial increments for pilot innovation projects at the time. Teams that progress may qualify for a $1 million grant, which may enable further progress. The Global Health Labs may then engage to carry it further, and Gates Ventures may finance the later stages toward product-market entry. As this research report explained, "GH Labs is a nonprofit corporation fully funded by Gates Ventures, the private office of Bill Gates. It partners with the Gates Foundation and other cross-sector leaders to develop health technology solutions for low- and middle-income countries, where many lack access to sufficient health care."[27]

---

[27] Martin, S. (2024, November 12). *HemaChrome collaborates with Global Health Labs to enhance its mobile health technology to test blood hemoglobin.* Purdue University. https://www.purdue.edu/newsroom/2024/Q4/hemachrome-collaborates-with-global-health-labs-to-enhance-its-mobile-health-technology-to-test-blood-hemoglobin/

Private foundation funders are learning, but this capital resource still stalls out at the product commercialization stage, when it must enter target markets. This is when private entrepreneurs and investors can morph product potential into enterprise sustainability and scale distribution across emerging markets. No one will care more about market delivery success than local entrepreneurs, including those in Africa.

What has changed since 2007 to make this collaborative product commercialization start working? African-born diaspora have returned home to lead change: They have earned robust degrees from top universities, led product development at major firms, built networks and established their own firms, universities, and sector ecosystems on the continent. Crucially, advancements in communication technology now enable efficient global interaction between these argonauts and their international networks. The world is more connected than ever.

Meanwhile, established corporations in developed nations have grown too top-heavy to innovate low-cost products in-house, so executives purposefully build "war chests" to engage in acquisitions of more entrepreneurial firms. Many of these acquisition opportunities are in emerging markets, where most growth opportunities await. Corporations are learning to appreciate the potential for bottom-line profits from building markets at the *Bottom of the Pyramid*, as explained by C.K. Prahalad in 2004.[28]

This product commercialization model requires major corporations to collaborate with local entrepreneurial ventures to create branded products for vast, untapped markets. No one knows the needs and desires of local markets better than local entrepreneurs. Collaborative commercialization resolves systemic poverty.

As emerging markets develop economic strength, they can afford to buy their own health products. Their improved health promotes more

---

[28] Prahalad, C.K. (2004). The fortune at the bottom of the pyramid: Eradicating poverty through profits. Wharton School Publishing.

economic development. This self-sufficiency breaks the cycle of regional poverty. Personal empowerment promotes social, political, and economic stability. Problem solved, via collaborative commercializations.

But wait! There is another problem to solve. Who is funding African innovations? Primarily, grant funders, but grants are for research, not commercialization. This creates a funding gap at the commercialization point, as depicted in the slide below from the 2000s. Bridge funding that understands risks, rewards, and new product introductions is required, and scarce.

What do we call this kind of funding? Startup capital! On a spectrum that starts with no revenues and no viable product, pre-seed stage angel funding appears on the far left. As a product starts to sell, first revenues may attract bigger angel tickets and early venture capital–lumped together as "seed stage" funding.

Surprisingly, many people believe banks should fund product commercializations, but banks are structured to lend money for incremental growth, not invest in creating the future. Loans require borrowers with ample recurring revenues to repay them; equity shares both risks and rewards.

In practice, pilot funding for product commercialization usually comes from sector professionals who understand specific markets and how to structure startup funding, either as angels or VCs. In the USA, corporate VCs tend to hover near innovation hubs like San Francisco, Boston, and Triangle Park.

Seed stage funding used to be structured as promissory notes to be either repaid or converted into equity when the venture matured. But over the past decade, Silicon Valley tech hub Y Combinator has refined a category of "SAFE" documents for this purpose. S.A.F.E. stands for "simple agreements for future equity."[29] At this early stage of value

---

[29] Levy, C. (n.d.). *Safe financing documents.* Y Combinator. https://www.ycombinator.com/documents

creation, innovators cannot yet verify the value they envision creating, so funders postpone this decision, agreeing to general parameters, such as what value their early backing would earn, relative to later-stage investors.

Seasoned startup investors have grown comfortable with this process. And the end game makes the effort worthwhile, if the upside potential benefits are eminently scalable.

The final slide below depicts how funders empower indigenous health industries to thrive. Startup investors have pioneered these value additions in Africa for over two decades.

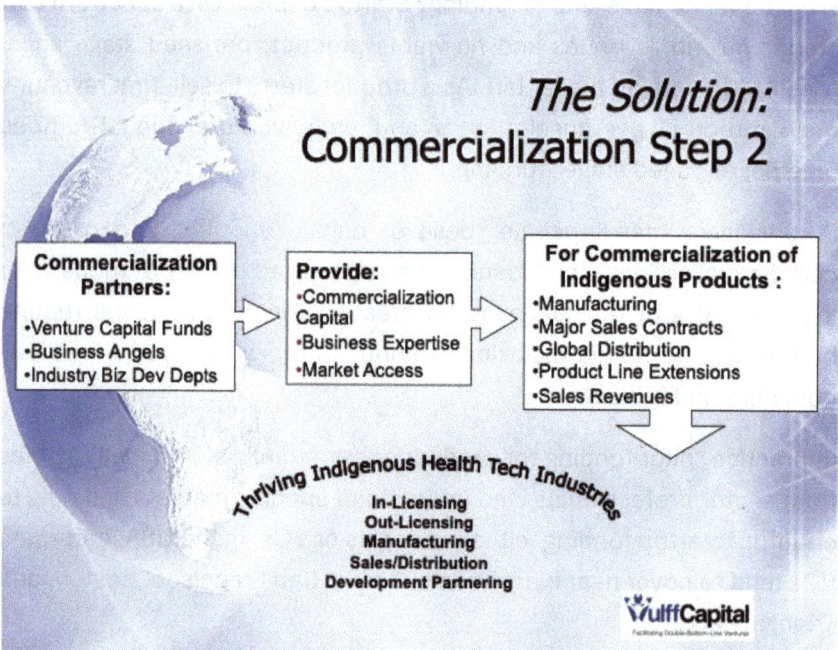

Wrap-up: Why bother with African startups? Enlightened Self-Interest

Speaking frankly, institutional approaches crafted for Africa by donors, debtors, and militaries have failed, so why not try an entrepreneurial investing approach that has worked? Trillions of USD have been wasted, without reducing American risks or African poverty.

However, a few billion USD of private investments into tech-driven startups have already produced self-sustaining, scaling, prosperity. Co-investing with African entrepreneurs who are building their own viable, impactful, and profitable ventures is the only approach that has proven overwhelmingly effective for creating personal wealth, national strength, and global stability. As individual investors and as a nation, Americans will get more bang for our buck by investing in African entrepreneurs who are hell-bent on helping their loved ones thrive.

What do *we* get out of this approach? As collaborative equity investors, we can co-own African successes. For instance, some early Flutterwave investors walked away with over 100 times what they invested. In truth, many of us reinvested our profits back into the next crop of startups. Some ventures will inevitably fail, as E's early venture failed, but portfolio successes can more than compensate for those. Meanwhile, investors learn lessons that make our next investments better; we build personal friendships that enrich our lives; and we expand our opportunities to learn more.

On the impact side, the innovations, products and services that succeed also empower Africans to pay for their own food, healthcare, education, and security. This not only reduces global terrorism, but it also reduces the risks of rampant pandemics, crime, corruption, and poverty. Americans have already benefited from African ingenuity in healthcare, logistics, entertainment, sports, and high fashion.

> *"Africa's true wealth is not under our feet, but above*
> *our shoulders."*
> —Michael Oluwagbemi, LoftyInc

In *Part Two: What's Working*, we delve into how African ingenuity is succeeding. Who built the tech ecosystem that is supporting African startups? What drove those pioneers? Where did they get their funding? How was it structured? Even more importantly, we will learn what our role is, or could be, as American investors in this grassroots-powered, entrepreneur-led Africa.

PART TWO
What's Working?
Afropreneurs are...

*"In today's world, paradoxically, it is the boldest
action that is often the safest. Remaining where you
are in a world that is changing so rapidly is, in fact,
the most dangerous of all places to be."*
—Hakeem Belo-Osagie,
Chairman of Metis Capital Partners

3. Afropreneurs are Returning Home

If necessity is the mother of innovation, then Africa is her nursery.—Marsha Wulff

The Edge of Ingenuity

Thanks to modern genetics linking geologic, anthropologic, and paleontological findings, the record is clear: 500,000 years ago, when our homo sapiens species began emigrating out of Africa, our ancestors dominated Earth's other eight human species. The species our ancestors encountered in Asia and Europe were stronger, such as Neanderthals, but we were more curious.

Homo sapiens' edge was our ability to innovate, adapt, and migrate when advantageous.[30] It still is. When the Northern hemisphere warmed, homo sapiens migrated further and wider, following coastlines, hunting game, and populating the world. Can this innate ingenuity be nurtured?

Professors at elite MBA schools often test their students' ability to creatively solve problems. One test, named the Duncker candle problem, presents each student with a candle, a pack of matches and a box of tacks, then tells them to attach the candle to a cardboard wall, so the candle burns properly, not dripping wax on the table or the floor, and does not set the wall on fire! In the USA, at Northwestern University's Kellogg School of Management, they learned that students who had lived

---

[30] Wong, J., Hendry, L. (n.d.)*The origins of our species*. The Natural History Museum. https://www.nhm.ac.uk/discover/the-origin-of-our-species.html

abroad did better at this novel-use test than those who had only lived in America.

At the INSEAD business school in France, where more students have lived abroad, the students who had truly adapted themselves to a foreign culture innovated this solution more rapidly. Because the solution involves the ability to imagine atypical functions for an object, students who had adapted well to new tools in novel surroundings were faster at envisioning new uses for simple tools from unrelated contexts.

One study's lead author concluded that "experiences abroad are critical for creative output, making study abroad programs and job assignments in other countries that much more important, especially for people and companies that put a premium on creativity and innovation to stay competitive."[31] During the heat of difficult business negotiations, their logic implies, such students could adroitly pioneer pathways around mountain ranges of opposing stances.

Think of Marco Polo and the Silk Road's impact on Eurasian prosperity. Merchant traders innovated the double-entry accounting solution while creating the wealth of Venice. These international trading experiences gave empires insights that led to competitive advantages during the colonial period.

How does mobility relate to Africa?

In 2000, about 20,000 of the USA's college and university students were from sub-Saharan Africa.[32] This more than doubled by 2023 to 56,780 students from 51 nations.[33] Nigeria sent almost a third, at 20,209. Ghana ranked second, with 9,394 and 4,507 were from Kenya. Ethiopia, South

---

[31] Hamilton, A. (2009, April 23). *Living outside the box*. Kellogg Northwestern. https://www.kellogg.northwestern.edu/news_articles/2009/galinskyresearch.as px

[32] Institute on International Education's Open Doors publication. https://nces.ed.gov/programs/digest/d21/tables/dt21_310.20.asp#:~:text=Table %20310.20.%20Foreign%20students%20enrolled%20in%20institutions,selecte d%20countries%20of%20origin:%20Selected%20years%2C%201980%2D

[33] https://opendoorsdata.org/data/international-students/all-places-of-origin/

Africa, Zimbabwe, the Democratic Republic of the Congo, Rwanda, Tanzania, Uganda, and Côte d'Ivoire each had more than 1,000 students studying in the United States.

Time and again, conditions at home spurred migrations and innovative funding strategies to support them. For instance, the British system of retaining land ownership under the first son encouraged younger progeny to leave home, discover new lands, commercialize novel products, and establish optimal trade routes.

These pioneering adventures required investment innovations to be born out of necessity. Strategies that succeeded laid the financing foundations for modern corporations, whose ownership structure even now reflect that of the Dutch East India Company. These "chartered trading companies" became more powerful than their original patrons and investors.

They were launched with co-ownership financing, structured as joint-stock that could be bought and sold privately. The historic commerce of India, China, South America, North America, Australia, and Africa is strategically linked back to Europe through this shared-risk, shared profits investment process.

Respective colonizing governments issued– "chartered"-- official rights for emerging companies to conduct commerce; these rights were defended by the State's military might. If the companies succeeded, the governments shared in the profits via taxation, as did private owners who had invested in the ventures and also shared commercial losses. Private investors mitigated their risks by spreading their stock ownership across portfolios of such ventures, which diversified across vessels, captains, locations, products, and markets.

Innovative weapons and naval strategies played major roles in defending trade routes from pirates and foreign government forces alike. Sometimes while abroad, ship captains found themselves commercially aligned with parties considered enemy agents back home. Such shifting alliances in new lands encouraged innovative financing and investment strategies that suited unforeseen scenarios in which stakeholders found themselves.

These entrepreneurial investment innovations helped shape successful venture strategies, relationships, and the deal terms in agreements we see working for African tech startups today.

Brain Drain or Regain?

The keynote speaker at Stanford's Africa Business Forum in 2016 was introduced by the Knight Business School Dean as if he were a Cardinal alumnus, but during his presentation, Patrick Awuah admitted earning his MBA from UC Berkeley. I was not interested in that rivalry; as an investor, I wondered why someone who founded a school in Ghana merited a business leadership spotlight.

Patrick was Ghana-raised, earned a scholarship to Swarthmore, became a Microsoft engineer, program manager, a millionaire by 30, married and started a family, retired young, and returned home (with the family) to establish a university focused on ethical leadership and critical thinking.[34] But how he financed Ashesi was what made this goal a reality.

Leveraging his personal net worth, it took five years from retirement to opening the doors to its first 30 students in 2002. Then another seven years passed before Bill and Melinda Gates honored Patrick in their Integral Fellows program[35] as a Microsoft Alumnus who had made a meaningful difference.[36]

Since then, the Microsoft Foundation has thought highly enough of him to donate tens of millions in scholarships, supporting his dream. This confidence attracted other backers. Now, a large percentage of the

---

[34] Maguire, K. (2010, January). *A new model of leadership for Africa*. Swarthmore College Bulletin. https://www.swarthmore.edu/bulletin/archive/wp/january-2010_a-new-model-of-leadership-for-africa.html

[35] Microsoft Alumni Network. *Ashesi University Foundation*. https://www.microsoftalumni.com/s/1769/19/interior.aspx?sid=1769&gid=2&calcid=1612&calpgid=447&pgid=550&crid=0

[36] Ashesi University. (2009, November 19). *Patrick Awuah receives Microsoft Alumni Foundation Integral Fellow Award*. https://ashesi.edu.gh/patrick-awuah-receives-microsoft-alumni-foundation-integral-fellow-award/

Ashesi student body is able to attend on scholarships, just as Patrick did at Swarthmore.

One Ashesi scholarship recipient arrived in 2011 from Liberia. There, Kpetermeni had no access to university courses in Computer Science, which was his passion in life. Ashesi awarded him a scholarship because, earlier that year, Kpetermeni demonstrated his potential as an innovator and leader. After his country's elections, the government had closed down the internet to squelch protests. Kpetermeni and his fellow Liberians leveraged a digital tool originally developed during Kenya's 2008 post-election violence, which we will study in Chapter Five. They also established a Liberian tech hub.

At Ashesi, Kpetermeni and his classmates learned new tools from a Google team that visited the university to introduce their student ambassadors program. These permitted Kpetermeni and his colleagues at iLab in Liberia to offer resource-challenged Liberian students open access to learning materials for students who previously had no internet available in the country.

During his third year at Ashesi, as Ebola spread across Liberia, Kpetermeni reached out to colleagues back home looking for ways to help from in Ghana. After learning that health workers were struggling to track and store data on Ebola cases, he built and helped deploy tools for the Liberian Ministry of Health, so medical experts became more efficient at managing Liberia's progress towards becoming Ebola-free.[37] This was not easy to do. In contrast, the USAID failed to deliver Liberia's health supplies during its Ebola outbreak, as you'll see in Part 3: What's Not Working.

When Kpetermeni graduated from Ashesi in 2015, he returned home to work at the tech hub he had co-established. At iLab Liberia,[38] he served

---

[37] Rustche, P. (2015, March 25). *How did Ebola volunteers know where to go in Liberia? Crowdsourcing!* NPR. https://www.npr.org/sections/goatsandsoda/2015/03/25/394266190/how-did-ebola-volunteers-know-where-to-go-in-liberia-crowdsourcing

[38] Chhabra, E. (Updated 2015, April 29). *iLab, a tech refuge in Liberia's capital, finds solutions to Ebola crisis.* Forbes.

as its Director of Innovation so he could empower African youth to solve their own problems, believing this to be the best way forward in the long run. "Ebola has shown that we need to start looking at local solutions. People were just waiting for help to come from outside. That left the entire country vulnerable," he said. "Imagine how different the Ebola story would have been if more Liberians, Sierra Leoneans, and Guineans had opportunities like I did to develop skills through education." Indeed! But Kpetermani's level of impact also required entrepreneurship and investment capital.

Photo: Patrick and Kpetermani
Source: https://ashesi.edu.gh/kpetermeni-siakor-15-profile/

Migrations of educated entrepreneurs, like Patrick and Kpetermani, are often depicted as a binary, with "brain drain" written on the homeland side of a door, and "brain gain" on the other side. But longer-term insights into the realities of revolving door migrations add the dimensions of "brain regain" and of "circular brains." These more complex and recurring interactions empower multi-migrators to become even more innovative, speed their learning curves, and encourage them to be more assertive about what works and what does not, both within their homelands and abroad.

While living in foreign places, migrants see the same problems they had back home being solved differently. Their neurons grow new branches, they envision new pathways, and they get excited. Returnees do not simply transplant what they saw; they modify foreign solutions in novel

---

https://www.forbes.com/sites/eshachhabra/2015/04/28/ilab-a-tech-refuge-in-liberias-capital-finds-solutions-to-ebola-crisis/

ways that local markets can more readily adopt culturally and cost-effectively. These are not blind, mindless, plug-and-play solutions. African ingenuity creates value via novel intellectual property and trusted brands. These are assets they can own, trade, lease, and sell.

Palaeontological research shows us that even in prehistoric times, more effective hunting and gathering innovations were rapidly embraced from one region to another, and adapted to make use of regional materials, flora, and fauna. Early culinary innovations, weapons of war, and construction designs spread across different territories through a combination of migration, trade, cultural exchange, and adaptation to environmental changes. Of course, they did not share these innovations on the internet, but now entrepreneurs can and do, speeding mutual adoption of innovations across long distances.

E-commerce, for instance, is a modern Golden Fleece that tech startup investors have embraced, as it augments market creation, brand building, product distribution, and cost efficiencies. It facilitates financial transactions that are made more secure and hassle-free via technology. One recent study put it this way, "...the economies of developing countries can benefit in terms of economic growth through technology transfer of their nationals [who live] in the North, including remittances, links to international trade and foreign investment, and diaspora networks. Also, another advantage is the physical return of nationals."[39]

When people learn about uber-talented Africans who live abroad, they tend to worry that this is a loss that will permanently undermine Africa's viability. However, historic examples in other regions show beneficial outcomes over time, such as the heroic Argonauts of ancient Greece, who sought their Golden Fleece. Asian diaspora from China and India returned to manage their countries' commerce.

---

[39] Samet, K. (2013). Circular migration between the north and the south: Effects on the source southern economies. *Procedia- Social and Behavioral Sciences, 93.* Pp. 2234-2250.
https://www.sciencedirect.com/science/article/pii/S1877042814038610

In 1975, mutual friends brought 19-year-old Kunle Odumade to my home for lunch the day after he arrived in America. He had come from Nigeria to pursue a degree in civil engineering at Cal Poly. He was on a "bursary," a scholarship intended to prepare him to return home to build airports and roads, but Kunle stayed and retired here after a career as a city engineer. That was then...

In 2010, a mutual friend brought a twenty-something Nigerian engineering student in Texas to my home for a dinner meeting. Over the years, Michael Oluwagbemi and his Nigerian friends established businesses, earned advanced degrees, secured excellent jobs in the US, and became US citizens. However, they returned home, created jobs, and contributed to building their local economies.

Although research data reports do not yet reflect this reverse migration as a trend, it is. African returnees often maintain dual citizenship, with homes and family members in both the US and their birth countries, which makes these data harder to track.[40] They are creating new markets by linking local and global marketplaces. They have also built healthy economic interdependencies between most of Africa's 54 emerging national markets.

Africa's diligent middle class has also been growing, urbanizing, and inspiring their offspring to excel in schools and secure scholarships at foreign universities, hoping they will land career positions abroad so they can send money home. And they have. Roughly 200 million Africans living outside their countries of birth now send home over $100 billion a year. Most funds the living expenses of loved ones, however, about $25 billion is invested locally. Most of these migrants still live inside Africa, just across a border or two, but the over two million African immigrants in the US have an outsized impact on their homelands, due to the relative strength of the US dollar.

---

[40] Tamir, C., Anderson, M. (2022, January 20). 1. The Caribbean is the largest origin source of Black immigrants, but fastest growth is among African immigrants. Pew Research Center.

African Development Funding Sources, 2021

1. African Diaspora US$95 Billion

> **From:** 160 million Africans living outside their countries of birth.
> **For:** 75% daily needs of over 200 million, 25% went into savings or investment

2. Foreign Direct Investment (FDI) $88 Billion

3. Official Development Assistance $35 Billion

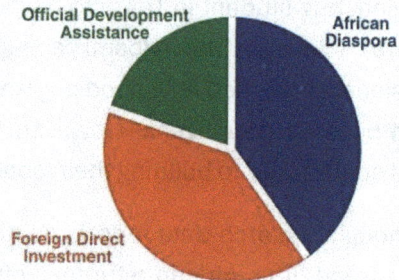

Source: African Development Bank

This chart shows that Africa's diaspora sends the lion's share of Africa's development funding. And that lion is growing.

In the past, jobs in finance were a significant draw for African immigrants to the US; however, the global financial meltdown of 2008 was an "Emperor's New Clothes" moment for the world's most developed nation. Attractive finance jobs evaporated due to the fallout from institutional fiscal mismanagement on a massive scale, causing the allure of a finance career abroad to lose its luster for aspirational Africans. Although they had earned global accolades for their academic and career achievements, many members of the African diaspora started returning home, where they saw more opportunities.

These African returnees from the US offer unique opportunities for Americans who have befriended them, because these returnees are frequently tapped for African leadership positions or empowered to launch their own ventures with global expansion potential. This phenomenon is not novel to economic development. Asia's diaspora returnees have significantly boosted their homelands' economies, lifting one billion people out of poverty in a decade by attracting commerce and investments.

A prime example is Taiwan's TSMC, a critical semiconductor manufacturer on which the US heavily relies for its most advanced chip fabrications. TSMC's founders, Morris Chang and Shang-Yi Chiang, gained experience in the US before returning to Taiwan to establish the company. Their multi-national insights led to TSMC's robust contributions to regional job creation and global tech leadership. This case illustrates the positive impact of 'circular migration' and predicts a similar vital development in the African diaspora's countries.

4. Afropreneurs are Building Tech Infrastructure

Telecom Infrastructure

Photo: Mo Ibrahim

Source: https://www.lemonde.fr/en/economy/article/2024/01/13/mo-ibrahim-oil-money-is-like-a-honey-pot-it-attracts-wasps_6428375_19.html#

Mo Ibrahim was born in a remote part of Sudan in 1946 and raised modestly in Egypt with several siblings. He credits his mother for instilling in him the notion that the only decent way out of poverty is through education. The hero posters on his bedroom wall depicted scientists.

He grew up respecting professionals and assuming that businesspeople were not to be trusted. After earning a BSc in Electrical Engineering from the University of Alexandria, Mo worked in Sudan's telecom department before moving to England. There, he added an MSc in Electrical Engineering and a PhD in Mobile Communications to his CV.

As the technical director of a British Telecom subsidiary in 1989, Mo knew he was at the vanguard of mobile communication development when he launched the UK's first cellular network. But he felt stifled by the bureaucracy's view that limited mobile tech to emergency services, so he left BT to start his own network design firm. At Mobile Systems International, or MSI, Mo still considered himself a sector expert who did research, advised corporate telecom clients, and designed their communication systems; he was not a businessperson who made deals.

Mo claims he had no idea how to run a business when he launched MSI—yet somehow, he grew it into Europe's largest independently owned technology company. He says running a business is mostly about common sense and honesty. One of the most important lessons he learned was not to pretend that he knew everything. Accordingly, he became known for encouraging his managers to ask questions, and he did the same.

As an industry advisor to leading telecom executives, Mo saw his clients pay skyrocketing prices for cellular licenses. They were paying millions of dollars to secure national licenses that they could get for free in African countries, where cell use was still limited to urban areas of South Africa and Zaire. Across the entire African continent, only a few urban elites even had landlines, and expanding that antiquated, hard-wired technology made no sense, now that cell networks were gaining market share. Mo began asking his telecom clients the logical question, *Why aren't you going to Africa?*

Western ignorance about African opportunities no longer surprised Mo at this stage of his career, but sometimes the knowledge gap was shocking. Once, he advised a telecom executive to take advantage of an opportunity in Uganda. Mo thought its youth demographics were a compelling factor, as they promised high technology adoption rates. However, this otherwise astute CEO replied, "You want me to go to my board and say I want to start a business in a country run by this crazy guy, Idi Amin?"[41] Mo was stunned, as Amin had left Uganda fifteen years earlier!

> *"Whenever there's a big gap between perception*
> *and reality, there's a wonderful business*
> *opportunity."*
> —Mo Ibrahim

Being born and raised in Africa, Mo was not afraid of doing business there himself. He knew what its people needed, how to provide solutions, and why Africans would pay for them. Mo personally understood how much Africans care about communicating with family members back home. He had seen anxious people negotiating with vehicle drivers over the cost of carrying messages to family members in another area, and wondered how often those were not even received. Surely, they would pay to actually hear the voices of loved ones.

Thus, Mo asked himself, since his clients did not understand the opportunity that he saw, why not follow his own advice? There were challenges, of course. Although he was respected as a top designer of cellular networks, Mo was not someone who actually built and managed them, regardless of their location.

He would have to hire a specialized operating team to secure licenses, lease land, build roads, and hire helicopters to install thousands of towers before he could even market cellular services. Then he would need to set up a fintech system to bill and collect payments from Celtel's first customers. Even after this huge cash flow problem was solved, there was still the issue of getting daily power to all those off-grid towers via generators, backup generators, and then batteries to back up the generators. He would also need to hire and manage local people who

---

[41] Ibrahim, M. (2012, October). *Celtel's founder on building a business on the world's poorest continent.* Harvard Business Review. https://hbr.org/2012/10/celtels-founder-on-building-a-business-on-the-worlds-poorest-continent

would reliably refuel those generators, recharge the batteries, and protect them from theft and abuse. Who would organize and maintain all these operations?

But the gap between Africa's cellular network supply and its potential market demand created an opportunity that was too great for him to ignore—and this was only part of the potential. Because landlines had barely made a dent on the continent, African cellular networks would not even face competition from conventional phone services, as they did in more developed markets.

An even more lucrative opportunity awaited any African network robust enough to offer money transfers. All those Africans working away from home needed more reliable ways to send cash back to loved ones. The fact that people were now entrusting cash to strangers demonstrated the extreme urgency felt by Africans, whose only alternative was to shoulder the more expensive combined costs of missing work and physically traveling for several days to check on loved ones or to deliver funds.

Accordingly, in 1998, Mo launched an exploratory project with five employees as a sideline to his existing consulting business, MSI. This project evolved into the African cellular network entity, dubbed "Celtel." Meanwhile, his consulting firm continued humming along nicely, with the credibility of 800 employees and a respected board of directors who understood the African opportunity. They included Sir Gerry Whent, Vodafone's first CEO; Sir Alan Rudge, a former deputy chief executive of British Telecom; and Salim Ahmed Salim, a former prime minister of Tanzania, an early leader of what would become the African Union.[42] With their help, Mo built a specialized management team and track record that won licenses fair and square, as African regulators and telecom ministries trusted them to deliver on their assurances.

---

[42]Ibrahim, M. (2012, October). *Celtel's founder on building a business on the world's poorest continent.* Harvard Business Review. https://hbr.org/2012/10/celtels-founder-on-building-a-business-on-the-worlds-poorest-continent

Africa's reputation for corrupt business practices seemed to be the main reason telecom players and investors avoided the continent, so Mo's Board devised processes and procedures that ensured transparency. For example, Celtel required the signature of every board member for expenses that exceeded $30,000. The Board only accepted licenses won in an open bidding process, never accepting an under-the-table offer or one made at a dining table with a prime minister, which is why they did not do business in Guinea or Angola. If an African official still indicated that a side bribe was expected, Mo's directors would tap into their networks, depicting the request as an embarrassment to Africa and a practice that would impede its development. As their management team built this level of credibility, it also added value to the company in other ways.

Celtel's initial target markets were in countries that offered free network licenses, or nearly so. In its first year, Celtel acquired licenses in Malawi, Zambia, Sierra Leone, and Congo, as well as a minority stake in Egypt. In 1999, the company bought licenses in Gabon, Chad, and the Democratic Republic of Congo. It then made acquisitions in Burkina Faso, Niger, Sudan, Tanzania, and Kenya. Wars were raging in these regions, often over ownership rights to natural resources, which discouraged conventional business development by outsiders. But Mo empathized with Africans who craved reliable communication, especially during times of unrest.

Although consumer demand in these markets was high, their ability to pay was limited, so Mo's team innovated payment methods that suited their needs. The team deployed prepaid "scratch" cards in small denominations with a hidden code that buyers could reveal by scratching off an opaque layer and keying the code into their handsets for cellular services on demand. These were crucial to onboarding their customers, who usually worked away from home and lacked a permanent address, phone number, or credit card. These pre-payments also provided reliable cash flow for Mo's fledgling networks, which was essential, as startup financing was scarce for African telecoms, whose revenues could not begin until a network was built.

Celtel's indirect impact on African economies was also profound. Service-providing businesses sprang up to support cell phone users. Thousands of African entrepreneurs hired tens of thousands of youth to manage branded kiosks on street corners where millions of retail customers paid for phone charging services and scratch cards. Subcontractors were employed to build out Celtel's network and logistics businesses, which serviced their telecom towers.

When it came to financing African startup ventures like his, Mo saw funders for African cellular networks stall more than they did on projects located elsewhere. Even financiers with aligned mandates to finance development made their terms more restrictive for him.

By 2000, Celtel's management and investment growth demanded Mo's full focus, so he split it off from MSI as an independent entity, then sold MSI itself for over $900 million to Britain's Marconi group. This financial liquidity was a relief for Mo, who had spent most of his time during Celtel's early years trying to raise funding for it from wary sources. Now, Mo could fund more of Celtel's aggressive growth himself, and he did.

In 2005, I attended a dinner in Washington, DC that the IFC hosted for investors. That evening, IFC leadership introduced Mo Ibrahim as their keynote speaker and Celtel as one of their best investments ever. Mo illustrated the market demand for African mobile phone connectivity by sharing this story:

"We would be inside the office of a new branch working 16-hour days, setting up service in a country, and people would already be waiting outside, queued up all around the building, wanting to sign up. Sometimes a civil war was going on right outside where we were working, and people were pounding with their fists on our door wanting to get in and sign up so they could start using our services."[43]

Mo announced that he had just sold his seven-year-old African company to the Kuwait-based Mobile Telecommunications Company, now Zain,

---

[43] Author notes

for $3.4 billion. He made a personal commitment to allocate over half of his net worth to causes that could help Africa develop. He established the Mo Ibrahim Foundation in 2006 to track, publish, and reward good governance and exceptional leadership on the African continent. Dr. Ibrahim also founded Satya Capital Limited to invest in the growth of other African ventures like Celtel.[44]

However, the title, "Father of African Telecommunications," probably belongs to another innovative entrepreneur who also illustrates the edge that circular migration brings to innovation.

Photo: Miko Rwayitare
Source: https://iafrikan.com/miko-rwayitare-the-man-who-built-africas-first-ever-mobile-network/

Miko Rwayitare is Rwandan-born and Zaire-educated. He earned his engineering degree in Germany in 1970. Because he understood the needs of the local mining industry, Miko was able to sell satellite-linked

---

[44]Ibrahim, M. (2012, October). *Celtel's founder on building a business on the world's poorest continent.* Harvard Business Review. https://hbr.org/2012/10/celtels-founder-on-building-a-business-on-the-worlds-poorest-continent

mobile phone handsets, initially to Zaire's government, at $3,000 a unit. His TeleCel company was established in 1985. At its prime, TeleCel had 15 telecommunications licenses and operated in 14 countries across Africa.[45]

After building it for fifteen years, Miko sold TeleCel for about $213 million in 2000. Five years later, Miko exemplified the Brain-Drain-Regained concept when he bought the Hôtel des Mille Collines, a five-star hotel in Kigali, Rwanda, which had become famous for being a refuge for 1,268 people during the 1994 Rwandan genocide.[46]

By 2020, mobile technologies and services generated more than $130 billion of direct economic value addition (8% of GDP) to Sub-Saharan Africa. The GSMA estimates this sector will reach $155 billion by 2025.[47]

Broadband Infrastructure for East Africa [48]

...Built by Argonaut Bitange Ndemo

Kenya largely owes its dynamic leadership in building East Africa's digital infrastructure to Bitange Ndemo. Although born in southwestern Kenya in 1959, Bitange earned his BS in Management from the University of Minnesota and his PhD in Industrial Economics from the University of Sheffield in the United Kingdom. He then took a job in the US as a financial systems analyst at Medtronic, a prominent medical device

[45]Mohapi, T. (2022, June 1). *The man who built Afrika's first-ever mobile network.* iAfrika. https://iafrikan.com/miko-rwayitare-the-man-who-built-africas-first-ever-mobile-network

[46] Miko Rwayitare. https://en.wikipedia.org/wiki/Miko_Rwayitare

[47] GSMA. (2021). *The mobile economy: Sub-Saharan Africa.* https://www.gsma.com/solutions-and-impact/connectivity-for-good/mobile-economy/wp-content/uploads/2021/09/GSMA_ME_SSA_2021_English_Web_Singles.pdf

[48] Ndemo, B., Weiss, T. (Eds.). (2016, August). *Digital Kenya: An entrepreneurial revolution in the making.* Palgrave MacMillan. https://www.researchgate.net/publication/299469062_Digital_Kenya_An_Entrepreneurial_Revolution_in_the_Making

company, whose value was built upon digital innovations. This period coincided with the rise of powerful applications from companies like Microsoft, which Ndemo incorporated into his daily work.

Photo: Bitange Ndemo
Source: https://en.wikipedia.org/wiki/Bitange_Ndemo

Meanwhile, back home, Telkom Kenya held a monopoly on infrastructure for landline and international telecom services. The entire country shared a single dial-up international telephone line connection. One megabyte of data cost $3000 and comprised the total capacity allocated to the entire University of Nairobi, where students waited in lines to access data.

During his holiday visits to Kenya, Ndemo recognized the unmet demand for internet bandwidth and opened a cyber cafe in Nairobi to address it. There, he experienced firsthand the challenges of high-cost bandwidth and the pressing need for email access. After he became deeply concerned that Kenyan youth needed access to the internet for research, skill-building, and commerce, Ndemo returned home with a passion to see what technology could do for his homeland.

This passion led him to assist political aspirants in understanding the benefits of tech opportunities and to communicate potential approaches during their campaigns. A presidential candidate, Mwai Kibaki, tapped Ndemo to write his manifesto, outlining policies and strategies for national development. Upon winning the 2002 election, Kibaki appointed Ndemo as the Permanent Secretary of Kenya's Ministry of Information and Communication.

From 2004 to 2013, Ndemo led Kenya's development of undersea cables. His goals were to increase access to connectivity and data via lower-cost services, bringing transparency to government and efficiency to the public and private sectors. Broadband internet would also create jobs, initially via the call center outsourcing industry. Kenya's nascent call center business had grown from employing 200 people in 2004 to 3,000 in 2005, despite relying on expensive satellite communications. To attract more companies, Kenya needed to increase its bandwidth to 500 megabits per second and subsidize satellite costs until a submarine fiber-optic cable was operational.

A 2005 UN task force found that 90% of calls between African countries were routed through Europe or North America via satellites, costing $400 million annually. This arrangement offered low-quality calls at high costs. However, it confirmed Kenya's market need, which would flourish with lower-cost, higher-quality fiber optic links via subsea cables. At that time, the eastern seabed of the Indian Ocean, off the coast of East Africa, was the last frontier for submarine telecom infrastructure.

Kenya urgently needed fiber optic cable services. Ndemo grew frustrated with the slow progress of the Eastern Africa Submarine Cable Systems (EASSy) project, a consortium of southern, central, and eastern African nations. Conflicts of interest caused delays over ownership and funding, with the World Bank, the International Finance Corporation (IFC), and the Development Bank of Southern Africa expected to finance construction.

Kenya promoted universal, inexpensive access, while Telkom South Africa threatened to withdraw if its return on investment was not similar to its monopoly profits. At that time, email downloads in South Africa cost around $40 per session, compared to $2 in the US. Ndemo pushed for lower-cost telecommunication services, requiring African nations to bring more funding if they rejected the South African agenda.

The funding problem was complicated by differing views on the potential impact and demand for internet connectivity. The World Bank believed Africa only needed a single fiber optic cable, reflecting ignorance of the growing demand. This misperception led to investment terms requiring 22 African countries to collaborate under one agreement. Many African representatives also doubted the technology's potential and its worth.

A 2006 editorial highlighted the tensions, noting Kenyan frustration with delays and monopolistic tendencies suggested by some consortium members. In May 2006, Ndemo issued an ultimatum for an implementation date for the Sh15 billion EASSy project, threatening to pursue a parallel project connecting Mombasa to Djibouti.

After years of stalled progress, Ndemo acted on his threat. He secured presidential permission to partner with the United Arab Emirates' telecommunications company, Etisalat, to build Kenya's own fiber optic cable. The government would invest 15% and have a board seat, launching The East African Marine Systems (TEAMS) project.

Ndemo, who sat on the board of Safaricom, persuaded his fellow directors to invest in the Kenyan cable, and the government followed. An escrow account was created, and companies were invited to bid on laying the undersea cable between Mombasa and Fujairah. Alcatel-Lucent won the $79 million contract in October 2007, and construction began three months later.[49]

Two years later, East Africa's first cable landed in Mombasa. The final ownership structure of TEAMS was a blend of Kenyan government, private, and publicly listed entities, as well as UK and UAE interests. By mid-2009, the cable arrived amidst fanfare, with President Kibaki comparing its significance to the Kenya-Uganda railway line.

Near Kibera, the Horizon Contact Centres building prepared to ramp up its call center business. Its CEO expected call costs to drop 80% from satellite levels. The company's first job posting attracted 6,000 applicants, most of whom held college degrees, and planned to expand from 80 to 1,200 employees within a year. The Kenya National Bureau of Statistics cited the average salary in the formal sector as $407 per month, with English as the most common language.[50]

---

[49] Submarine Cable Networks. (n.d.). *TEAMS*.
   https://www.submarinenetworks.com/en/systems/asia-europe-africa/teams
[50] https://www.knbs.or.ke/wp-content/uploads/2023/09/2009-Economic-Survey.pdf

By the time TEAMS went live, Safaricom had launched M-Pesa. Prodded by Ndemo's success, EASSy completed its launch a year later. Multiple cables proved crucial, as by 2014, M-Pesa spurred an explosion in mobile phone-based financial transactions, amounting to 50% of Kenya's GDP.[51] Bitange Ndemo helped capture much of this digital development story in *Digital Kenya*, published in 2016.

Broadband Infrastructure for West Africa

... Built by Argonaut Funke Opeke

Photo: MainOne CEO, Funke Opeke. Source: https://blog.equinix.com/blog/author/funke-opeke/

In 2018, Forbes honored Funke Opeke as one of "The World's Top 50 Women in Tech" for her significant contributions to empowering online banking, e-training, and e-commerce in Nigeria, Africa's largest economy at that time.[52] Funke's journey toward this recognition began with a strong educational foundation. While earning her B.S. in electrical engineering from Obafemi Awolowo University in Nigeria and her M.S. in E.E. from Columbia, Funke was aware of being one of the few women and people of color in tech infrastructure leadership.

Still, her focus remained on doing her best and enjoying her work, which made others comfortable collaborating with her.

---

[51] Center for Public Impact. (2016, 21 March).*Mobile currency in Kenya: The M-Pesa*. https://centreforpublicimpact.org/public-impact-fundamentals/mobile-currency-in-kenya-the-m-pesa/#:~:text=The%20public%20impact,person%2Dto%2Dperson%20transactions

[52] Forbes. (2018). Profile: Funke Opeke. https://www.forbes.com/profile/funke-opeke/

One professor at Columbia made a snide remark, questioning the affordability of the systems she was studying for her fellow Africans. This remark served as a challenge for Funke, motivating her to prove that such systems could be deployed and utilized in Africa. But first, Funke spent 20 years working in the U.S. telecom industry, rising through the ranks to become a New York-based executive director of Verizon.

Despite holding this prestigious position, she chose to pursue her vision of developing robust telecommunications infrastructure in her home country, returning to Nigeria in 2005 as MTN's Chief Technical Officer. In 2008, she joined NITEL, the state-owned telecommunications company, as Chief Operating Officer, tasked with leading its privatization. During her time at NITEL, she witnessed corruption and fought for the rights of junior staff, who were often exploited.

Seeing the underemployment of young Nigerians and their limited internet access, she recognized the need for infrastructure to bring the internet to her people. After working at the top levels of both private and public entities, she believed the private sector could best address this development need. Funke's entrepreneurial juices kicked in.

At an African Development Bank conference in Shanghai, Funke shared her vision and received encouragement and pledges of funding and support from global funders and contractors. Recognizing her ability to bring technology to layperson applications, Funke named her professional telecom services company Main Street Technologies. It spearheaded the development of the MainOne Company, whose primary goal was to bring West Africa's first privately owned, undersea, high-capacity cable from Portugal.

She recruited Fola Adeola, the executive who had previously lured her to NITEL, to help launch her new venture. She also invited corporate lawyer Asue Ighodalo to co-found MainStreet. Funke invited Asue and Fola to bring their wives to hear her plan, wisely seeking their approval before risking their families' financial futures. One thing they could count on was Funke's organizational skills and dedication, which ensured the company met all deadlines, even during challenging times.

Financing the MainOne cable proved to be the most difficult challenge. After pledging her personal savings, Funke faced mountains of in-depth foundational work, including feasibility studies, business plans, and technical plans. Dealing with the African Development Bank was particularly challenging, but she persevered.

With support from multiple financing entities, including the Africa Finance Corporation, the Pan-African Infrastructure Development Fund (PAIDF), and Nigerian banks, MainOne secured $240M in funding.

MainOne became West Africa's leading communication services and network solutions provider, building the first privately owned, open access undersea high-capacity submarine cable from Portugal to West Africa, with landings in several countries. Funke Opeke's efforts sparked a digital revolution, enabling young Nigerians to leverage broadband access for tech startups and improving access to essential services.

From the outset, Funke's goal was not only to build an efficient data center and connectivity solutions provider but also to ensure a profitable exit for her investors, who had shared the risks with her. Together, they had not only built a 7,000 km submarine cable and a 1,200 km terrestrial fiber network in southern Nigeria but also established a data center business, office facilities, and secured land for future expansions. MainOne investors had enjoyed years of strong dividend income growth, making them hesitant to sell.

In 2022, a company founded in Silicon Valley named Equinix expressed interest in making MainOne its first African investment. Equinix is a publicly listed REIT whose US tax-advantaged structure attracts mostly institutional ETFs, mutual and pension funds such as the Vanguard Group, BlackRock, and State Street. It trades on exchanges around the world, focusing on global internet infrastructure and AI data center development in high-growth areas.[53]

---

[53]DCF Modeling. (n.d.). *Equinix, Inc. (EQIX) How it works and makes money.*
https://dcfmodeling.com/blogs/history/eqix-history-mission-ownership#:~:text=Understanding%20this%20structure%20is%20key,Equinix%2C%20Inc.'s%20Leadership

Twelve years after Funke launched MainOne, it sold for $320 million USD. Equinix retained Funke as the head of the company's 500+ well-trained employees, whose operations were generating $60 million in annual recurring revenues.[54] This success brought Funke's leadership and competence wide acclaim. Among them were interviews with Harvard Business School, Forbes, and Al Jazeera, which highlighted her calm, trustworthy demeanor and expertise in the telecom industry.

Funke's story is particularly noteworthy because American media often overlooks positive stories about African leaders. Her global competence, rooted in her Nigerian upbringing, is a testament to her family's tradition of education and integrity. Her father, who earned a PhD in the UK, also returned to Nigeria to become the first Nigerian director of the Cocoa Research Institute of Nigeria. Her mother was a teacher who rose to the top administrative levels in several Catholic schools. Academics were central to her family life, and she and her six siblings shared chores and educational opportunities regardless of gender. Ethics were also paramount, with a strong sense of community responsibility in Ibadan, where she grew up.

Scaling Infrastructure Funding

Photo: Adebayo Ogunlesi
Source: https://en.wikipedia.org/wiki/Adebayo_Ogunlesi

When he addressed Wharton's African business luncheon in 2004, Adebayo Ogunlesi was already a prominent figure in global finance. This Nigerian-born graduate of Oxford and Harvard embodied success. But Bayo's message to hundreds

[54] Equinix. (2022, April 5). *Equinix enters Africa, closing the US $320 million acquisition of MainOne.* https://www.equinix.com/newsroom/press-releases/2022/04/equinix-enters-africa-closing-the-us-320-million-acquisition-of-mainone

of African students and alumni that day was as unexpected as it was impactful.

Despite his successful career as the head of Global Investment Banking and Executive Vice Chairman at Credit Suisse First Boston, Bayo advised his audience of elite, ambitious youth against following in his footsteps. "Go home," he urged them. "Africa needs you!" Because he had not followed his own advice, Bayo's call to action seemed inauthentic at the time, but the past 20 years have proven it prescient.

Bayo's plea would resonate, as US finance jobs soon evaporated during the debt crisis, tilting opportunities in favor of Africa's cash-based, emerging economies. China's growing demand created African trade surpluses, and Africa's fintech innovations created a vibrant niche for global investors. Africa would become increasingly attractive, potentially reversing the "brain drain" of talent leaving the continent.

Two years after his Wharton speech, and shortly before a global financial collapse, Bayo co-founded Global Infrastructure Partners (GIP), an independent firm focused on investing in, owning, and operating large-scale, complex infrastructure projects. GIP launched with $1.5 billion in funding from Credit Suisse and General Electric. Over the next 15 years, the firm grew to manage $81 billion in assets, significantly influencing the investment landscape by establishing infrastructure as a distinct and viable asset class for endowment and pension fund portfolios.[55] One of GIP's first acquisitions was London's Gatwick Airport. While infrastructure in the United States is often considered a government domain, many countries, including the United Kingdom, Australia, Germany, Switzerland, and China, have privatized airports and other infrastructure.

How is this working out? A 2023 study reported that private equity acquisitions roughly doubled airport operating incomes. Under Ogunlesi's

---

[55] Swiss Info. (2024, March 22). *Former Credit Suisse APAC head Low joins private equity firm GIP.* https://www.swissinfo.ch/eng/former-credit-suisse-apac-head-low-joins-private-equity-firm-gip/73749258#:~:text=GIP%20was%20founded%20by%20Chairman%20and%20CEO,digital%20infrastructure%20and%20water%20and%20waste%20management.

leadership, Gatwick hired operations experts who implemented innovations, such as increasing the size of security checkpoint tubs. This reduced security wait times and increased retail sales as passengers had more time to browse. Gatwick's processing rate increased by 20 million passengers annually, accompanied by a corresponding rise in job growth. The low correlation of infrastructure with other asset class valuations, such as loans and public stocks, is attractive to institutional investors. Infrastructure also offers attractive returns, averaging 10-12%, with inflation-protected revenues, and mature funds achieving net returns of 17-19%.[56]

Revenue-generating projects advance more swiftly than government-led infrastructure, as complex government approvals slow infrastructure timelines, increase costs, and deter construction firms. The American Society of Civil Engineers now gives US infrastructure a C-minus rating.[57] While a $550 billion infrastructure legislation allocated $55 billion per year, this falls short of the trillions of dollars the government projects its annual needs. This creates opportunities for private funding, ownership and operations.

In this book's final section, we will see how Bayo's positive mindset and private investment strategies are bringing this private infrastructure engine of development back to his homeland, at scale.

African Argonauts have brought a transformational impact to the continent's digital economy. Its professional diaspora, exemplified by Mo Ibrahim, has bridged commercial gaps that required both knowledge and trust, empowering African economies to emerge and expand. Their work has established internet service, university programs, supply chains, and global validation that have endured the test of time. What else are Africans doing to help themselves?

---

[56] https://www.nber.org/digest/20231/privatizing-infrastructure-evidence-airports

[57] American Society of Civil Engineers. (2025, March 25). ASCE report card gives US infrastructure highest-ever 'C' grade, stresses need for sustained investment to support economic growth. https://www.asce.org/publications-and-news/civil-engineering-source/society-news/article/2025/03/25/asce-report-card-gives-us-infrastructure-highest-ever-c-grade

5. Afropreneurs are Founding the Tech Ecosystem

*"...instead of shying away from chaos, [success is]
about stepping into chaos, because that is the most
creative place to be."*—Grant Shuttleworth, 2002

Pioneering Innovation Centers

Photo: Mamphela Ramphele

Despite Apartheid's oppressive restrictions on educating black individuals, Mamphela Ramphele somehow earned her PhD while also being an activist in the anti-Apartheid "Struggle." Three years after apartheid was democratically voted out and Mandela was voted in, she became the Vice Chancellor of the University of Cape Town (UCT).

In South Africa in 1997, shortly before James Wolfsen hired Mamphele to be a Managing Director of the World Bank, she challenged me to help attract "foreign direct investments." She asked, "Where else can you wake up in the morning knowing you can change history every day?" She shared my enthusiasm for technology-based innovations and, 20 years later, would be named an African Academy of Sciences Fellow.[58] But that year, she introduced me to Dr. Mike Herrington, the Founding Managing

---

[58] The African Academy of Sciences. *Ramphele Mamphela Aletta*.
   https://aasciences.africa/fellows/Ramphele-Mamphela-Aletta

Director of The Centre for Innovation and Entrepreneurship (CIE) at UCT's Graduate School of Business (GSB).

When he arrived in South Africa with his family in tow, Mike was a Zimbabwean refugee with $100 in his pocket, but he had a PhD in biochemistry and an entrepreneurial mindset. He built a successful women's hosiery manufacturing business and sold it to Hanes Hosiery, then retired to establish the CIE.

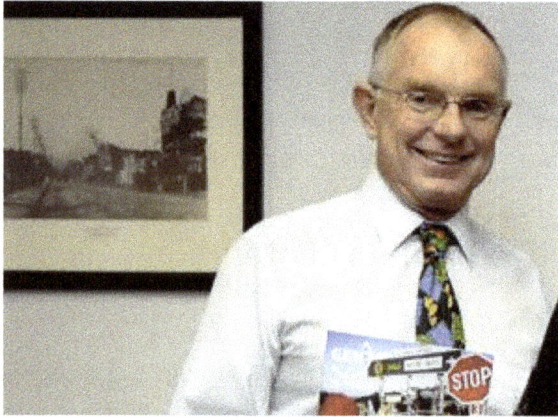

Photo: Mike Herrington
Source: https://www.news.uct.ac.za/article/-2008-05-26-uct-study-spotlights-youth-entrepreneurship

Besides attracting professors and creating a curriculum, Mike convinced UCT's business school to require its MBA students to spend time assisting local township entrepreneurs in growing and formalizing their businesses. This initiative supported existing entrepreneurial spirit within the communities and provided customized support for growth.

Simultaneously, UCT itself was generating globally groundbreaking innovations. Mike's team categorized these as "Globally Viable Ventures" and paired them with experienced entrepreneurial mentors. For context, UCT's medical school performed the world's first successful heart transplant and pioneered both medical CAT Scan and MRI technologies. The engineering and physics departments were making significant strides in bio-fuels, aquafarming, and prosthetics. For example, a UCT team engineered prosthetic intellectual property that Mike introduced to

Smith & Nephew, a British medical equipment company, and they acquired it.

Optimism about venture exit opportunities for local innovations during the early 2000s was largely spurred on by a young South African techie who invented something most Americans have probably used for decades without knowing it. Mark Shuttleworth had launched Thawte, a company that developed cybersecurity innovations for financial transactions. By 1999, Thawte had captured 40% of the international internet security market and was sold to Verisign for $575 million.[59]

Following the Thawte sale, Shuttleworth redeployed his colleague, Julia Fourie, to pioneer an investment fund focused on South African technology startups, named HBD (Here be Dragons). This fund evaluated thousands of applications, further encouraging the nation's tech scene. Julia and Mark also launched HIP2B^2, a nationwide marketing program to promote scientific innovations among students. Mark's own space travel served as an inspiration and symbol of defying limitations, reinforcing the message that Africans could achieve anything.

Photo: Mark Shuttleworth
Source: https://www.liysf.org.uk/liysf/principal-lectures/mark-shuttleworth

Shuttleworth's success demonstrated the potential of African tech startups on a global scale. He later founded Canonical, the company behind Ubuntu's open-source software, which would help quell post-election violence in Kenya and empower that country's technologists to create their own tech hub.

Julia and Mark also initiated the African Venture Capital Association, AVCA, in 2000 to support startup venture

---

[59] SERIANU. (2017). *Uganda cybersecurity report 2017*.
    https://www.serianu.com/downloads/UgandaCyberSecurityReport2017.pdf

capital investing. Though later renamed the African Private Equity and Venture Capital Association to embrace larger ticket writers, the initial focus on innovation-stage, equity-based funding was pivotal in fostering the early ecosystem. It retains the use of AVCA, for short.

Meanwhile, other South Africans were establishing formal technology hubs and innovation centers. In Cape Town, the Bandwidth Barn was founded in 2001, becoming a regional hub for tech innovation. Other initiatives, such as the Acorn incubator for medical innovations and Blue Catalyst in Johannesburg, further contributed to the growing ecosystem. These efforts underscored the drive of Africans to build their own infrastructure for innovation and entrepreneurship, independent of external reliance.

Building Tech Hubs

Ghana's BusyInternet

I started my African investment journey in South Africa because I was told that 80% of the commerce of the rest of the continent flowed through South Africa. While working in South Africa from 1997 to 2004, I thought I was learning on the frontlines of Africa's digital revolution, from the continent's first and most progressive technology entrepreneurship centers and innovation hubs.

I now doubt both perceptions.

In Bitange Ndemo's *Digital Kenya*, a chapter by Eric M.K. Osiakwan reveals that Africa's early digital crusade was more robust and widespread than many know.[60] This alerted me to dig into an amazing story of tech collaborators who converged in Ghana. The idea germinated in the back seat of a New York City bus, where a Welsh-born tech entrepreneur envisioned extending the tech immersion opportunities he

---

[60] Osiakwan, E. M. (2017). The KINGS of Africa's digital economy. *Digital Kenya*, 55-92.
https://www.researchgate.net/publication/310498148_The_KINGS_of_Africa's_Digital_Economy

was experiencing in the Big Apple to less developed countries. He'd heard that the government in Ghana was laying out a red carpet.

Mark Davie's idea of celebrating the new year in 2001 was to move to Accra, Ghana, where he set up a mixed-use space to incubate tech startups. He named his for-profit venture BusyInternet. Mark was already a successful entrepreneur who had developed and sold his Digital City Guides entity in the US, known as Metrobeat and Citysearch. His new fascination was Africa's development potential, and he had local investors helping him.

Photo: Mark Davies, BusyInternet Founder
Source: https://www.ghanaweb.com/GhanaHomePage/business/Keeping-the-Internet-busy-in-Ghana-85268

Destined to become a leading brand in Ghana, BusyInternet became Africa's largest internet cafe within two years[61] and it shaped Ghana's digital economy for 14 years. Open 24/7, Busy offered a blend of shared office space, conference facilities, and a copy center with over 100 public access terminals. While Busy was charging $1 an hour for internet use, and half-price at night, I was paying $40 for a single download of my emails in South Africa, perhaps thanks to Southwestern Bell's monopoly.[62]

Mark's co-working incubator hosted the very early conversations of African tech entrepreneurs, topping 1,400 visitors daily at its peak. And it was Busy that hosted the Ghana New Ventures Competition, one of the

---

[61] Pambazuka News. (2003, June 2). *Busy Internet Accra: A case study*.
   https://pambazuka.org/index.php/security-icts/busy-internet-accra-case-study
[62] Mail & Guardian. (2007, September 3). *Study in botched reform*.
   https://mg.co.za/article/2007-09-03-study-in-botched-reform/

many successful tech startup ecosystem events and entities led by Eric Osiakwan, Ghana's own high-energy Argonaut.

Eric went on to support Bitange Ndemo's TEAMS submarine cable roll-out in East Africa. In 2013, he also co-founded the Angel Fair Africa[63] and the Chanzo Capital[64] venture funds in 2014 to invest in high-tech startups and scaleups in Kenya, Ivory Coast, Nigeria, Ghana and South Africa. He dubbed these nations "the KINGS" of Africa's digital economy at the time. Eric is also a fellow of Stanford, MIT, Harvard, TED, and Poptech.[65]

Photo: Eric Osiakwan
Source: https://africasharedvaluesummit.com/speakers/eric-osiakwan/

The Wennovation Hub, Nigeria

"Michael Oluwagbemi was born in Ibadan, Nigeria to a school administrator mother, and a public health practitioner father, who also published books, lectured at tertiary institutions, and worked at Shell." In 1998, when Michael was 14 years old, he would sit on the schoolyard grass with his friend Wole Odetayo[66] and dream of what they would do with their lives.

They made a solemn vow to each other to create jobs for Africa's entrepreneurial youth by leveraging technology and the magical innovations that it could enable. To attain this goal, they knew they would need careers that could help them finance the costs of pioneering their goals and a bigger team to add diverse skill sets.

---

[63] https://allafrica.com/stories/202504150009.htm

[64] Chanzo Capital. https://www.chanzocapital.com/#abt

[65] PopTech. https://poptech.org/community/

[66] *Wole Odetayo*. LinkedIn. https://www.linkedin.com/in/wole-odetayo-69277a2a/

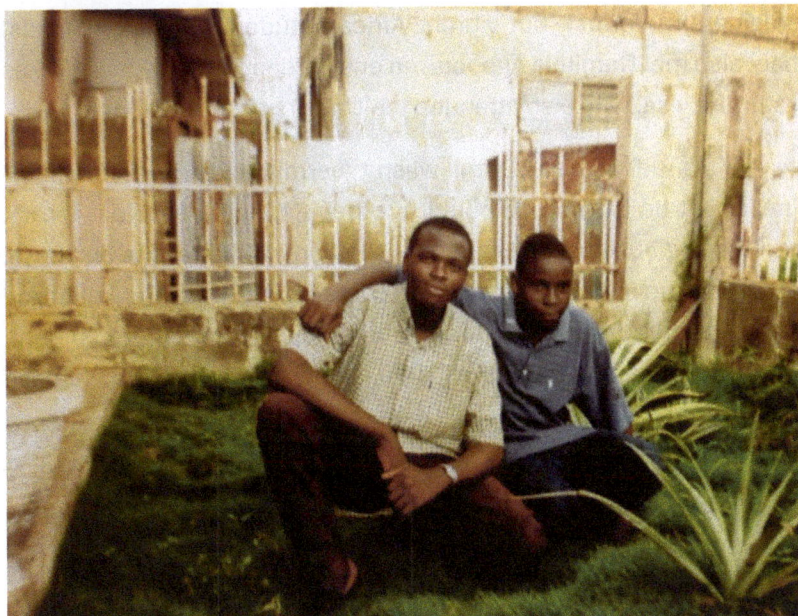

Photo: Michael Oluwagbemi at 14, with Wole Odetayo
Source: LoftyInc Archives

Wole set his sights on medicine, while Michael set his sights on engineering. They decided to establish a technology hub where they would train tech-savvy youth of Lagos on how to launch ventures. Through a series of chance meetings, their dream would become a reality, the kind of chance that favors prepared minds. Their youthful determination led them to positively impact tech hubs across the continent.

When I met Michael in 2010, he was leveraging his Master of Electrical Engineering from the University of Houston to build energy projects for WorleyParsons. His Kenyan girlfriend introduced us via email, and we began communicating regularly regarding our various African projects. We met in person thanks to the Kenya Development Network Consortium's conference in Dallas, where I was their keynote speaker. I was impressed with Michael's vision for impacting Africa's entrepreneurial youth. Although I had international business and investing strengths, he had African, project management, and engineering insights I would never fathom.

Leveraging an informal, but vibrant African student network in Texas, Michael also met Damilola Agboola, an entrepreneurial Nigerian in Texas on a student visa, who also attended the University of Houston.

While on a student visa, Dami wasn't permitted to work for a US business, but he learned he could hire people, so he set up a formal office-cleaning business in Houston while earning degrees in business. Dami signed up office buildings as customers, hired and managed personnel to perform the janitorial work, while he rented equipment, handled all billing, and paid taxes. This is how Dami supported himself through university in the US.

LoftyInc Allied Partners Limited
Michael Olubusayo Oluwagbemi · May 9, 2010 · 🌐   •••

L-R: At Nigeria Bond Seminar, Houston on May 8, 2010 LoftyInc Exec Partner, Michael Oluwagbemi, Marsha Wulff of Wulff Capital/Project Diaspora, and Associate, Hendrik Mason — with **Bola Onipede**.

👍 Like   💬 Comment   📨 Send   ↪ Share

Photo: Michael & Marsha 2010
Source: LoftyInc Archives

Dami already knew Idris Bello, whom I introduced in Chapter One as an early investor in E's successful ventures. Dami introduced Idris to Michael. All three 20-something men worked in technical areas of large multinational corporations, while also continuing to build their academic and professional qualifications. For example, when Michael introduced me to Idris, Idris was working at Chevron, having completed a master's in computer science from the University of Houston and was pursuing a Master of Business Administration at Rice University. We met briefly during an airport layover, but years would pass before we would fully appreciate each other's potential to contribute to our common goals, which Michael had envisioned all along.

Dami and Idris shared the same values and goals for Nigerian youth as Michael and his childhood schoolmate, Wole. Meanwhile, Wole had earned a degree in medical surgery to fulfill his mother's dream, but he never lost his passion for helping innovative entrepreneurs. In 2009, Michael and Wole co-founded Loftyinc Allied Partners, Ltd. (LAPL) with the goal of generating revenues from consulting and project management.

Within months, Dami and Idris joined LoftyInc as co-founding partners, sharing the costs and workload on top of their other responsibilities. Initially, salaries from their corporate jobs went into traveling between the US and Nigeria and supporting the Nigerian team, as they developed ways to help young African entrepreneurs. Their plan was to launch a tech hub like Y Combinator to nurture technology-based innovations that create sustainable jobs. LoftyInc was set up to be "an innovation development company that supports start-up teams, innovation enterprises and social impact projects in Africa."[67]

The team chose the name "LoftyInc" to represent the partners' goals to merge high ideals with efficient business operations. This was set up as a for-profit project management platform that leverages the team's diverse skill sets for various digital services related to African economic

---

[67] LoftyInc. https://loftyincltd.biz

development. Their staff has stabilized at about 75 local young people who work on projects, such as bringing transparency to government infrastructure projects by digitizing and posting public reports of all stakeholders, dramatically reducing the prior costs of self-dealing and graft.

In 2010, Michael, his team, and his ecosystem were heading in the right direction, but were not yet ready for what I envisioned as an American investor. It was another decade before we formally established LoftyInc's first seed-stage venture capital firm to manage funds for African-born founders innovating digital solutions to the continent's biggest challenges.

In 2011, the LAPL team launched its first tech hub location in Lagos, among the first few tech hubs operating in Sub-Saharan Africa. Although they would be quick to credit others with contributing to their success, I can verify that this team led their hub's planning, financing, operating, and management.

Because their first cohort consisted of young Lagos entrepreneurs who had not yet built a team, the partners realized that team building was the first strategy they needed to focus on. This priority gave the LoftyInc partners the idea to name their tech hub, the "Wennovation Hub", to remind aspiring entrepreneurs to replace the "I" in innovation with a "We" for teams. "WeHub" welcomed the curriculum development help of a Nigerian graduate student at the Massachusetts Institute of Technology in the United States, who was their age and also working with MIT's university technology hub. He dedicated his summer to teaching Wennovation Hub and its young entrepreneurs in Lagos.

That year, as if they were not already busy enough, I invited LoftyInc partners to join me in helping the business school dean of the Institute of International Studies (now the Middlebury Institute of International Studies) to set up a new graduate certification program at their Monterey campus in California. The purpose of the Frontier Market Scouts program was to train intermediaries on how to match impact investor goals to the financing needs of social entrepreneurs building ventures in frontier markets. Somehow, Michael, Dami, and Idris did join me as adjunct professors and taught courses enthusiastically enough to recruit a group of graduate students who enlisted to help WeHub roll out new programs for young entrepreneurs in Lagos.

WeHub has grown to serve tens of thousands of young African entrepreneurs across multiple countries. LoftyInc's African returnees never gave up on their goals. Instead, they have consistently worked to transform entrepreneurial dreams into sustainable organizations. Every year, these pioneering partners continue to roll out new and vital components to Africa's tech startup ecosystem.

To their credit, the same partner group has enthusiastically shared management responsibilities and their friendship for over a decade, despite all life's changes and challenges. For years at a time, they have not only resided in different countries but also on different continents, rarely seeing each other in person. They often had to revise their strategies, but they never lost sight of their shared goals.

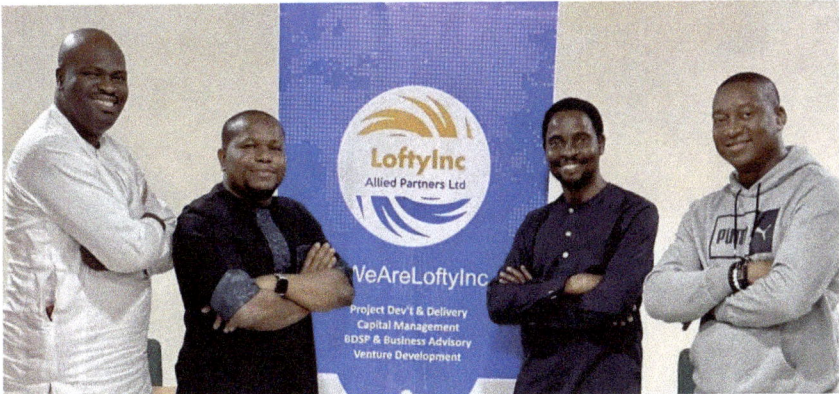

Photo: LoftyInc Allied Partners, Michael, Idris, Wole and Dami, 2021
Source: LoftyInc Archives

Photo: LoftyInc Allied Partners, 2018, Lagos, Nigeria
Source: LoftyInc Archives

Photo: Michael and Wole Celebrate 10th Anniversary of
LoftyInc Allied Partners, 2019
Source: LoftyInc Archives

The iHub, Kenya

Pioneers supersede challenges by innovating solutions.

After prior peaceful administrative transitions, Kenya's 2007 disputed presidential election erupted into violence. The shock and dismay that Kenyans living in the US felt prevented those I worked with from being able to focus on our shared projects. They thought their nation had evolved beyond this level of behavior. Americans who were troubled by the 2021 Trump followers' assault on Capitol Hill may identify with this feeling.

Kenya's diaspora feared for the safety of loved ones back home. Those who had sent emergency funding wanted to ensure it was received, without endangering recipients. A descending curtain of silence suppressed their ability to stay connected. Meanwhile, an ad hoc team of tech-savvy Kenyans was innovating a remarkable resolution to their own crisis.

Photo: Ory Okolloh, Co-founder of the Ushahidi platform and iHub, Nairobi, Kenya

A young Kenyan blogger, known for championing economic development through entrepreneurship, had built a loyal following while earning her JD from Harvard Law School in Cambridge, Massachusetts. Ory Okolloh[68] challenged the software developers on her blog to help her hack an emergency solution to the government's communications shutdown that was preventing the world from knowing the violence being perpetrated within Kenya. Working around the clock, Ory's ad hoc team of Kenyans built an open-source platform and rolled it out in just a handful of days. They aptly named it Ushahidi, which means "testimony" in Swahili.

---

[68] Ory Okolloh https://www.linkedin.com/in/ory-okolloh/

Ushahidi empowered anyone who could send a text or email to post eyewitness reports of violence. The Ushahidi platform automatically tagged each report with its location on a Google map using GPS. Although this solution may seem novel today, it was deemed ingenious at the time, and it instantly went viral. Eyewitness testimony to cruelty was quickly verified by trusted international media, government sources, and NGOs. Reports flowed out, and effective assistance flowed in.

This level of timely visibility brought violence out of the shadows, directed rapid responders to where help was needed, and spotlighted perpetrators who could no longer hide their abuse. The opposing political factions soon agreed on a ceasefire and a restructured government that shared power and restored peaceful transitions. The Ushahidi team reached national hero status.

Then the global awards started rolling in. The Silicon Valley-based Omidyar Network invested US$1.4 million in 2009 to support the continued growth of the Ushahidi platform, which won the Global Adaptation Index Prize in 2012 and the MacArthur Award in 2013.[69] But this was just the beginning of the impact the Ushahidi team would have on their country and the world at large. Their emergency app and its open-source platform have been upgraded and adapted time and again for crisis responses around the world, from natural disasters to terrorist attacks.

Ory Okolloh walked away from six-figure income career options in the US to return to her country and become Ushahidi's first CEO. From there, she managed Google's policy development for Africa, which laid the foundation for the rapid, progressive development of Africa's tech sector. Then she helped the Omidyar Network influence the digital revolution to share "power, prosperity, and possibility."[70] Ory's own Mzalendo Trust is a foundation that holds African Parliamentarians accountable to the citizens who voted them into office. Ory also serves

---

[69] https://en.wikipedia.org/wiki/Ushahidi

[70] Omidyar Network. https://omidyar.com/who-we-are/

on the boards of several corporations active in developing Africa's tech ecosystem, including Deloitte Africa and Thomson Reuters. She is now a partner in the Verod Keppel Africa venture capital fund, which invests in African tech entrepreneurs.

Erik Hersman[71] was another Ushahidi co-founder who became "The White African" icon of the tech industry. He was born in Sudan to an American missionary couple, who were friends and former schoolmates of mine. Erik learned digital proficiency from an early age because his parents were linguists whose work required computers. He was educated in Kenya at a boarding school where he lived with boys who were primarily from Kikuyu families, known for their entrepreneurial spirit. His schoolmates' approach to innovative problem-solving fascinated Erik, so he soon merged this new entrepreneurial mindset with getting into the back end of games and building websites.

Erik's skillset was rare for the time and for an African, so he became an early thought leader, blogging about ways that technology could accelerate businesses in general and, more particularly, how it could resolve challenges in Africa. By the time Erik joined the Ushahidi development team, he had already built a reputation as a tech blogger and was known on the continent as "The White African." Erik was named a Fellow by both Pop!Tech in 2008 and TED in 2009.

Meanwhile, Ndemo was linking Kenya to fiber optic capacity and enabling East Africans to leapfrog from landlines to mobile phones. In 2009, his TEAMS submarine fiber optic cable landed on Mombasa beaches, about 500 kilometers east of Nairobi. The EASSy cable arrived the next year, spurred by Ndemo's progress, bringing even more capacity for tech startups. These communications resources sparked a digital coming together, providing a boost to the idea of creating a Kenyan tech hub. Ushahidi was the only organization that came forward to provide funding for setting up the iHub with a mission to help Kenya's upcoming startups.

---

[71] *Erik Hersman*. LinkedIn. https://www.linkedin.com/in/erikhersman/

Erik had tried moving to the US, where his parents had retired, but while watching from afar as cell phones and the internet took root in Africa, Erik recognized the huge opportunities emerging there and returned to his African home, where he grew up. "Whether it's in fintech, edtech, or insurtech, you can name your space and there's just lots going on here and a lot that can be done," he pronounced in an interview. He knew that coming together and collaborating was a big part of Africa's culture, which also drives innovation.

The phrase, "I am because we are," conveys the power of alliance, encapsulated in the word "Ubuntu." Ubuntu was the cohesion that propelled the development of Ushahidi. Now it was the impetus for establishing African technology hubs.

"There's a lot of people in tech here, but we were just not coming together," Erik reminisced during an interview.[72] "We asked, 'What if we have a place of our own?'" Ushahidi's global notoriety had attracted offers of support from global tech giants, who instantly saw the potential of a tech hub to commercialize software being produced by a billion tech-savvy youth. But the Ushahidi team was leery of becoming dependent upon powers that might inhibit African sovereignty over their own innovations.

"So, we built this little space," he remembers. "It's 1,500 square feet or 2,000 square feet. Within a year, we had 12,000 members, and then we grew to 17,000 members, and we grew to four floors in the building. And you realize that there are so many people who want to solve things together.

---

[72] Hersman, E. (n.d.). *Episode 14. Erik Hersman: The white African*. Michael Redd. https://michaelredd.com/erik-hersman/

Photo: iHub Founders (from top left, clockwise): Ory Okolloh, David Kobia, Juliana Rotich, and Erik Hersman

Source: Harvard Projects, ©2014 Initiative on Violence Against Women

https://projects.iq.harvard.edu/files/carrcenter/files/ushahidirichasehgal_0.pdf

New companies are coming out of the woodwork, just because one guy met this other guy at the coffee bar on the fourth floor.

"And investors are now dropping in because this is the rich hunting grounds for good deals. Media people are showing up because this provides them with a rich target to find a good story. All of a sudden, there's acceleration in a space that was already active, but didn't have a nexus point, didn't have a nerve center yet... It's that community, it's that network of people that actually makes you successful here. It's not normally ever done alone."

Uganda's CoHive Lab

Teddy Ruge was a young entrepreneur, Uganda-born and US-educated. When a mutual friend introduced us at a house party in 2007, all I knew was that Teddy had a commercial photography business and that he loved his mother, who lived in Uganda. He desperately wanted to learn how to help her and her community of farmers develop a cash crop.

Over time, I learned his corporate clients included the law firm where my angel investor group met each month, and the Dallas Cowboys. Every year, Teddy visited the homes of the players from this NFL football team to photograph them and their families as they cooked and ate their favorite foods. He compiled their stories into attractive recipe books that the team sold to raise funding for their favorite charities.

The first time we chatted about my work, Teddy was totally overwhelmed to learn that Africa's diaspora had networks that supported economic development on the continent. I gave him a list of organizations to study that he consumed like a ravenous cookie monster. Being an effective communicator who loved staying on the edge of technology development, Teddy began writing blogs, participating in think tank sessions, accepting speaking engagements, and attending conferences. In short, within the Afro-Tech community, Teddy soon became famous. I could not keep up with the network he was building.

In October 2008, while I was attending X-Prize and Barcamp Africa meetings at Google headquarters in Silicon Valley, Teddy was in Johannesburg for some tech-focused immersion at events named MobileActive[73] and Barcamp Jozi. In California, I met David Kobia from Nairobi, a co-founder of Ushahidi with Erik. I was thrilled to make this connection, but it got even better.

He told me Erik was speaking at the same tech events in South Africa that Teddy was attending. So I asked him to tell Erik to watch for Teddy, and I

---

[73]Gosier, G. (2008, October 12). *This week in Appfrica (Oct. 5-11, 2008)*. Appfrica. https://appfrica.wordpress.com/2008/10/12/this-week-in-appfrica-oct-5-11-2008/

reached out to Teddy to tell him to find Erik. But I need not have worried, as Erik and Teddy had already connected and were discussing collaborations. This was amazing! Africa's tech network was already working, across the globe, and it was being led by social entrepreneurs I knew!

This convergence was even broader and deeper than I knew at the time. During that year, Erik's *White African* site posted about a dozen event notices occurring across Africa,[74,75] as well as in Europe and the US, as did BarCamp's own site for Africa.[76]

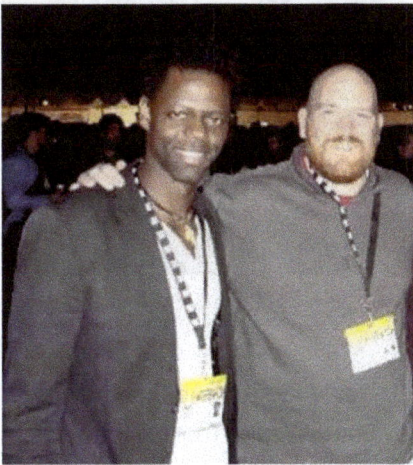

Photo: Teddy & Erik
Source: Author Archives

Topics discussed at these meetups ranged from how to post geolocation data for developers of apps like Ushahidi to updates on digital infrastructure expansions. They also asked themselves hard questions. Why were most of them developing web apps for Africans that were designed to be used on computers, when most Africans used mobile phones, as this would limit their app adoption rates?

One blogger wrote, "As African developers, we often develop for the West, or for the few really tech-enabled people in Africa—small markets. Lots of opportunities exist in the bulk of the population—but we develop for the fringe. Question: Why do we do this? Why don't we develop for the

---

[74] White African. (2008, June 13). *Upcoming technology events throughout Africa.* https://whiteafrican.com/2008/06/13/upcoming-technology-events-throughout-africa/

[75] White African. (2008, July 24). *5 More African Conferences.* https://whiteafrican.com/2008/07/24/5-more-african-conferencesevents/

[76] BarCamp Africa Day Media. http://barcamp.org/w/page/400202/BarCampAfricaDayMedia

bulk? Some answers from the crowd: we've always lived from a computer screen, not a cellphone screen—this means we think differently and can't see the opportunities."[77]

To their credit, they already saw substantial tech opportunities on the horizon, including this: "Mobile currency: major hole, but some people [are] trying to fill it."

Photo: Erik, Jon and Teddy (out of frame) sat on SXSW Panel, Austin, Texas, 2009
Source: Teddy Ruge Archives

In March 2009, out-of-the-box thinkers converged in Austin, Texas, for inspiration and networking at "South by SouthWest." There, Teddy sat on an African Tech panel with Erik and was sufficiently inspired by the Ushahidi platform's successful example to establish his own non-profit named Project Diaspora to more formally connect Africa's diaspora to their homeland.

An American Black entrepreneur named Jon Gosier also sat on that panel with Erik and Teddy at the SXSW event in Austin, Texas. Jon already knew of 'the White African', and he considered Teddy a famous tech blogger from Africa.

---

[77] Cook, P. (2008, October 12). *BarCampJozi 08 Day 1*.
https://paulcook.me/2008/10/12/barcampjozi-08-day-1/

Photo: Erik Hersman and *Jon Gosier*, SXSW, Austin, Texas, 2009
Source: Jon Gosier Archives

When Jon arrived in Kampala, he immediately saw tech opportunities through the eyes of a serial entrepreneur, investor, and philanthropist. While living there for three years, he launched a unique technology consultancy in 2008 and named it Appfrica.[78] Well-located near Makerere University, Appfrica attracted top local talent, who Jon hired to develop technical software and design solutions. His tier-one tech corporate clients were entering African markets and included Google, Facebook, and Twitter. For instance, Appfrica helped Google Africa translate its landing page for Ugandan audiences. Jon's model may remind you of E's startup, Andela, which would launch in Lagos a few years later.

With Jon's guidance, his young African team was capable of building whatever tech platform solutions his clients envisioned. They could also innovate tech solutions to overcome the local economic development

---

[78]https://en.wikipedia.org/wiki/Jon_Gosier#:~:text=SwiftRiver%20at%20Ushahidi.-
.Appfrica,in%202008%20in%20Kampala%2C%20Uganda.

barriers they experienced daily in Kampala. Fittingly, Jon dedicated one day per week for his employees to use their office resources to work exclusively on their own innovative ideas for a brighter future. He also dedicated capital to finance their most promising pilot projects.

Appfrica was founded as a hybrid corporate entity, with innovation, project finance, and job creation built into its DNA. But soon Jon and his team cast a wider net, inviting non-employee innovators to enter annual Apps4Afrika tech competitions, then investing in the winners. The US State Department covered the costs of marketing and travel for contestant finalists.

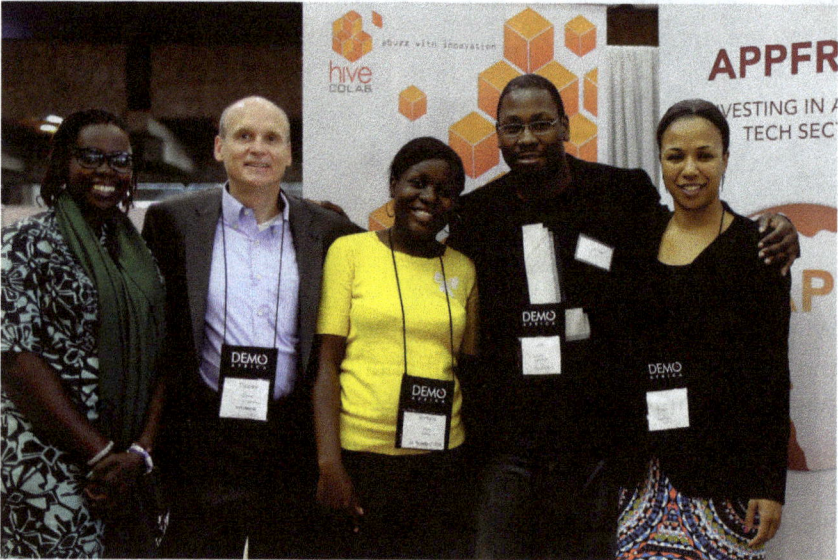

Photo: Jon Gosier and Barbara Mutabazi of Appfrica, with the Apps4Africa team
Source: Jon Gosier Archives

Jon says that the best decision he made was to hire Barbara (Birungi) Mutabazi as Appfrica's country manager. Though still young, she was already a champion of Africa's technology sector, believing that it offered young women their best chance at career equality. Her collaboration with Jon empowered the personal initiatives and passions of his team, driving them to unexpected levels of productivity and excellence—a legacy that lives on today in the continued success of the businesses Appfrica co-founded, largely due to Barbara Mutabazi's leadership.

Her passion for leveling the playing field for young women via technology also drove her to co-found, with Teddy Ruge and others, Kamplala's Hive Colab working space and to raise grant funding to support its programs. It turned out she was really good at managing both Appfrica and Hive CoLab. In 2010, after the digital-forward Appfrica team chose to work remotely from diverse locations, Jon Gosier graciously donated Appfrica's internet-enabled office space to Hive Colab. Appfrica's for-profit operations and CoLab's non-profit tech hub have thrived under this arrangement.

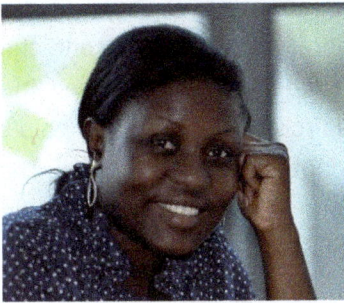

Photo: Barbara Mutabazi at Hive Colab, Kampala, Uganda
Source: Jon Gosier Archives

With the benefit of hindsight, we can now see that 2010 was a watershed year for the mid-continent's tech hub ecosystem. Teddy was in Uganda, helping Jon and Barbara set up Hive CoLab in Kampala. In April, he attended my pre-conference salon dinner in Dallas, where he met Michael and Dami, who were setting up LoftyInc's Wennovation Hub in Lagos.

That same year, Bitange's cable went live in Kenya, where Ory's Ushahidi team was building out the iHub in Nairobi. Funke came online in Nigeria, as Michael's LoftyInc team was founding Wennovation Hub in Lagos, and Rebecca, who we'll get to know soon, was opening the doors of Cameroon's ActivSpaces.

Over the next two years, rapid-fire developments continued concurrently, resembling a jumble of dominoes being connected. For example, because I moved to California in 2010, I reached out to the graduate business school in Monterey, now named Middlebury Institute of International Studies (MIIS). Because the Dean, Yuwei Shi, was excited by what I told him about Africa, the LoftyInc partners and I taught the first cohort of the Frontier Market Scouts program, which grew popular among ardent impact investing pioneers.

Photo: LoftyInc team co-teaching the first Frontier Market Scouts Program in Monterey, CA,
Source: 2010, LoftyInc Archives.

Teddy formally aligned his Project Diaspora with both MIIS and the University of Lagos to organize a conference. Teddy also linked the female managers—Ory and Barbara—of Nairobi's iHub and Kampala's Hive CoLab to bring the Frontier Market Scouts program their way. The Ushahidi team in Nairobi hired Appfrica's Jon in Kampala to help build out their open-source platform, making it robust enough for a plethora of first-responder users globally. Early collaborations such as these laid the foundation upon which a pan-African startup ecosystem was built.

AfriLabs

These early tech hub founders, along with many more like them from coast to coast, soon felt the weight of the responsibility they had assumed. Youthful demand for startup services was strong—outsized relative to the resources available. Local mentors stepped up to help with training, local professionals began forming ad hoc investor groups, and Africans living abroad made extra trips home to contribute. Still, more needed to be done.

Curricula needed to become more comprehensive, trainers needed to be trained, funding needed to be raised to pay for internet access, equipment to share, a safe space, and full-time management. Accordingly, Hub supporters formalized training curricula, enlisted program sponsors, and opened their own pockets to help. They aspired for their ad hoc training and investing efforts to be world-class and scalable enough to meet the needs of hundreds of millions.

To this end, Africa's first tech hub pioneers banded together to lay the groundwork for a pan-African entity that would formally network emerging local hubs. These African leaders hailed not only from Kenya, Nigeria and Uganda, but also from hubs in Senegal and Cameroon. In direct response to the needs of these first innovation hubs, a new, pan-African entity was intentionally birthed.

AfriLabs was founded in 2011 and structured as a non-profit membership association to build a supportive ecosystem around the rapidly emerging technology hubs, providing innovation spaces where developers, entrepreneurs, and investors could meet and network. Its founders' main focus was to organize programs and events for knowledge sharing and collaboration between hubs. By helping each other attain global best practices, members now stand together in offering cohesive partnerships to leading tech corporations of the world.

It has supported the continent's emerging technology hubs by providing financing, mentoring, networking opportunities and other capacity-building resources. In 2018, for instance, I was moderating a panel discussion between high-profile technology startup founders at the African Diaspora Investment Symposium, on the stage of Silicon Valley's Computer History Museum. After I stepped away from the podium, an African man approached me from the audience with a sense of urgency. He introduced himself as Dèjì Akómoláfé, a Silicon Valley-based Solutions Architect with a corporation that wanted to scale up the use of its cloud infrastructure on the African continent.

VMware had assigned Deji to establish train-the-trainers programs for young African technologists to learn cloud infrastructure construction and management. Deji was seeking pipelines of astute talent he could train, courtesy of his employer, and he basically had a blank check to do so. His problem, he admitted sheepishly, was that he had no idea how to get started; he had been living away from his Nigerian homeland for too many years.

AfriLabs was my first thought, and Deji immediately recognized the advantages of partnering with a pan-African organization. I introduced him to Anna, AfriLab's astute and personable Executive Director, and left them to negotiate. Because LoftyInc co-founder Michael Oluwagbemi was chairing AfriLabs' board at that time, I alerted him to the training opportunity and was relieved to learn that AfriLabs directors had already agreed upon standardized terms and a pricing structure for this very eventuality. Although Deji initially feared the terms may have been inflated by potential corruption, he eventually became comfortable and reached a mutual agreement.

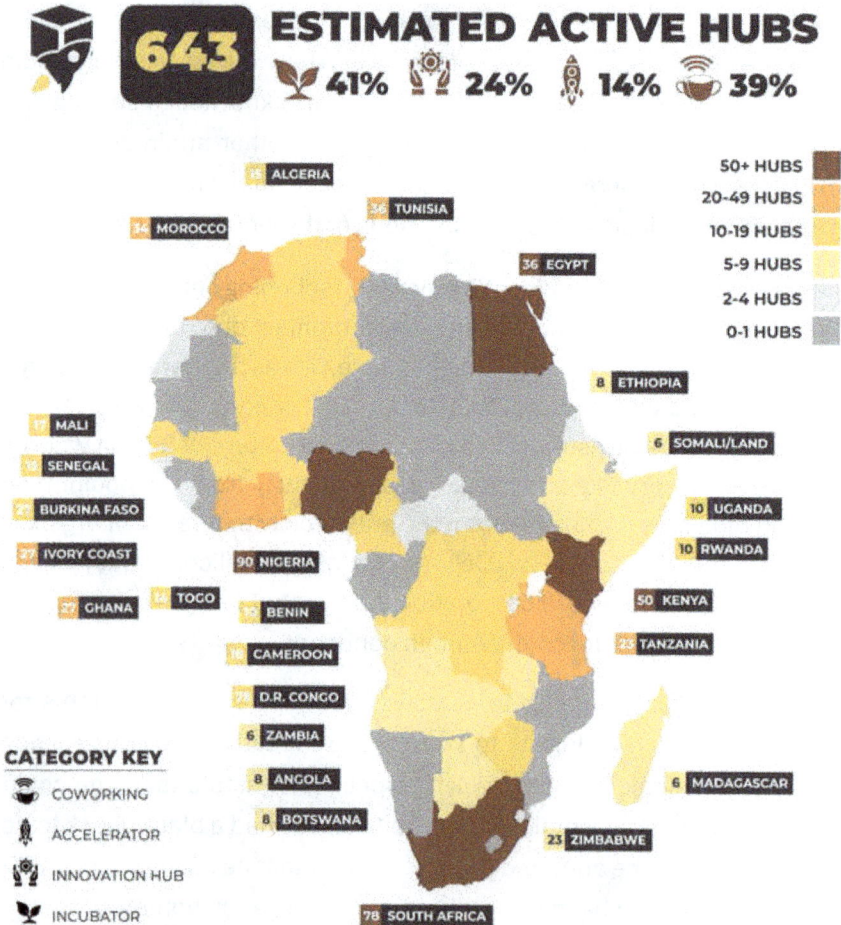

643 ESTIMATED ACTIVE HUBS
🌱 41% 🤲 24% 🚀 14% 📶 39%

Legend:
- 50+ HUBS
- 20-49 HUBS
- 10-19 HUBS
- 5-9 HUBS
- 2-4 HUBS
- 0-1 HUBS

Map labels:
- 15 ALGERIA
- 36 TUNISIA
- 34 MOROCCO
- 36 EGYPT
- 8 ETHIOPIA
- 17 MALI
- 6 SOMALI/LAND
- 18 SENEGAL
- 10 UGANDA
- 22 BURKINA FASO
- 10 RWANDA
- 27 IVORY COAST
- 90 NIGERIA
- 50 KENYA
- 12 TOGO
- 27 GHANA
- 13 BENIN
- 23 TANZANIA
- 10 CAMEROON
- 75 D.R. CONGO
- 6 ZAMBIA
- 8 ANGOLA
- 6 MADAGASCAR
- 8 BOTSWANA
- 23 ZIMBABWE
- 78 SOUTH AFRICA

CATEGORY KEY
- 📶 COWORKING
- 🍶 ACCELERATOR
- 🤖 INNOVATION HUB
- 🌱 INCUBATOR

Within eight years of its founding, AfriLabs had already mapped 643 active tech hubs across the continent.
Source: AfriLabs and Briter Bridges (2019).

A 2023 CNN report highlighted AfriLabs' accomplishments as having grown to serve nearly 500 member hubs across 261 cities in 53 countries, plus other regions where diaspora members reside.[79] In reality, many hubs operate in several locations, typically empowering thousands of youth annually, which means that AfriLabs easily touches over two million entrepreneurial African aspirants per year.

The importance to the ecosystem of creating this centralized tech hub component cannot be overstated, as validated by news reports and impact metrics. It not only reached but surpassed its impact goals to establish a network organization that's "committed to driving innovation and entrepreneurship on the continent by bringing together technology hubs, startups, investors, and other key stakeholders in the ecosystem."[80]

AfriLab's news reports indicate the organization's reach and collective wisdom. For instance, AfriLabs recently announced a one-year collaboration with the investment arm of a Moroccan university's funding vehicle to collaborate on scientific innovation and entrepreneurship initiatives in Africa. Another announced a new learning track that was launched at the AfriLabs Annual Gathering 2024 at the Cape Town International Convention Centre. It is designed for entrepreneurs building Africa's creative arts digital economy. This reflects the network's flexibility to embrace sectors emerging from the continent's rapidly rising fashion, film, and music industries.

Other news underscores the level of credibility that AfriLabs has built among mainstream funders. Meta (Facebook) and the Bill & Melinda Gates Foundation funded their Impact Hackathon to foster AI innovations that address social impact issues across Africa. Participants

[79] Busari, S. (2023, November 10). *How Afrilabs is powering Africa's tech revolution through community.* CNN. https://edition.cnn.com/2023/11/10/africa/how-afrilabs-is-powering-africas-tech-revolution-through-community/index.html

[80] Jackson, T. (2024, August 26). *Hub network Afrilabs welcomes 18 new hubs.* Disrupt Africa. https://disruptafrica.com/2024/08/26/hub-network-afrilabs-welcomes-18-new-hubs/#:~:text=AfriLabs%20is%20a%20network%20organisation,key%20stakeholders%20in%20the%20ecosystem.

"collaborate in cross-disciplinary teams to address inclusivity and diversity in digital content, while also focusing on economic development, science & innovation, public services, or education and skills development using Meta's Llama AI technology."

Incentives for entrepreneurs to participate include grants up to $100,000 to further their projects and the possibility of $500,000 in seed funds through a subsequent global competition. The hackathon offers a provision that outsiders rarely think of on their own, which indicates AfriLab's level of expertise in program management... "To facilitate in-person participation, travel costs will be covered for all selected participants to attend the Hackathon in Kigali, Rwanda." The best participants are often youth who are also working their way through school.[81]

To connect more female founders to funding, AfriLabs often spearheads gender-based programs, including this news that it "is leveraging its large network of incubators, accelerators, and investors on the continent to implement the RevUp Women's Initiative, funded by Visa Foundation. The initiative targets early-stage women-led startups in Africa. The pilot phase of the programme will focus on supporting 500 female-led startups across the 5 regions of Africa."[82] Wennovation Hub recruited mentors for this program's local participants.

In 2020, Wennovation Hub was selected to run a pre-incubation program for AfriLabs. Dubbed Ideas to Business, it won an AfriLabs Capacity Building Program award for incubating 50 women entrepreneurs in Lagos and Ibadan over a four-month period, culminating in a Demo Day presentation event. See photo below.

---

[81] Afrilabs. (2024). *AfriLabs announces Llama 3.1 Impact SSA Hackathon for AI Innovators, Funded by Meta and the Bill & Melinda Gates Foundation.* https://www.afrilabs.com/afrilabs-is-thrilled-to-announce-the-llama-3-1-impact-african-hackathon-for-ai-innovators-a-pan-african-project-funded-by-meta-and-bmgf/

[82] Afrilabs. (n.d.). *Why we need to pay attention to supporting female entrepreneurs in Africa.* https://www.afrilabs.com/why-we-need-to-pay-attention-to-supporting-female-entrepreneurs-in-africa/

Wennovation Hub Demo Day for Women Afropreneurs, 2020
Source: LoftyInc archives

Why has this organization worked so well? AfriLab's remarkable contributions to Africa's tech startup sector inspire us to explore the strategies and sentiments held by its founders and early funders. Who were the visionaries behind it, and how did they set it on a viable path to succeed?

Rounding out AfriLabs' diverse team of initial co-founders was a young American, Ben White. Equally smitten with the vision of a tech-driven continent, he spent his career co-launching additional components of the continent's tech startup ecosystem from his base in Amsterdam. He started in 2007 building VC4A, a trusted digital platform that empowered venture founders, investors, and institutional development funders to convene, research, and finance African tech development.

In 2011, Ben was able to bring AfriLabs one of its first financial backers, Hivos, which stands for the "Humanist Institute for Development Cooperation" (Dutch: Humanistisch Instituut voor Ontwikkelingssamen werking). Hivos was founded in 1968 by a Dutch association of humanists who believed that development work should be secular, "as true cooperation presumes respect for differing beliefs." In its first brochure, Hivos founders wrote that *"necessary changes should spring from communities themselves – from people at the base of society."*[83]

This mindset empowered AfriLabs' local management to fulfill the highest and best mutual interests of their own ecosystem. Grassroots enfranchisement by a global funder used to be rare in Africa, yet it has proven itself massively significant. It encouraged AfriLabs to evolve via African commitment and collaboration, based upon a foundation of pooled resources, common goals, and shared ownership.

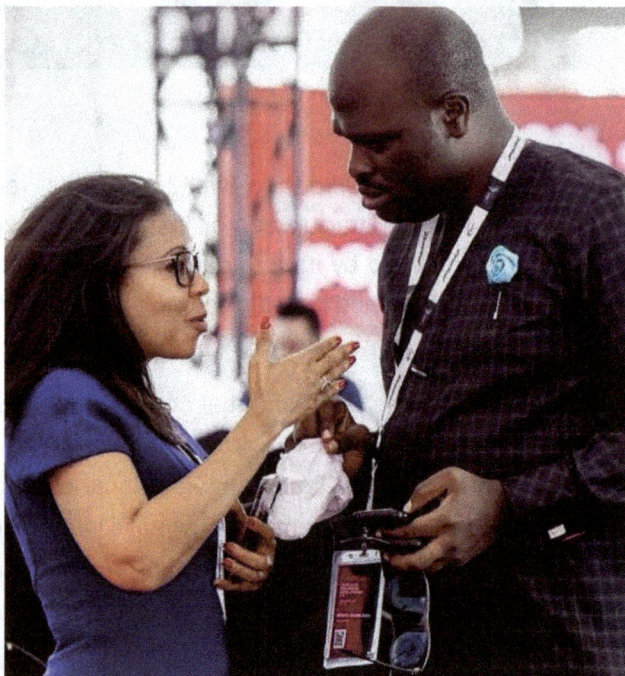

Photo: Investors Rebecca Enonchong, Cameroon, and Michael Oluwagbemi, Nigeria, at Afrilabs' pan-African conference in Tanzania, 2018.
Source: LoftyInc Archives

But all those new ventures need funding, and local angel investors provide their best hope for survival. So...

---

[83] Wikipedia. *Hivos.* https://en.wikipedia.org/wiki/Hivos

6. Afropreneurs are Funding the Tech Ecosystem

Building Local Investment Groups

Meanwhile, LoftyInc founders were not standing still. Idris had earned his MBA from Rice University in Houston and an MS in Global Health from Oxford, where he had launched a digital MedTech venture and gained global accolades. Throughout, he was also serving as Wennovation Hub's Program Director with in-person training and mentoring engagements in Lagos.

Photo: Crop2Cash Agtech Award, thanks to FCMB Bank and Wennovation Hub, Source: Wennovation Hub Archives, 2018

Michael earned an MBA from London while leading the turnaround of an energy corporation in Nigeria. Dami built a career in Cost Accounting at Google, and Wole managed the programs and growth of WeHub. With their Lagos tech hub humming along, the partners were mostly concerned about helping their best entrepreneurs access capital. Local banks did their best, but what they needed most were well-organized local angel groups to do pre-seed investing before the first revenues began to flow.

Even in Silicon Valley, startups rely on angel groups to nurture development from ideation to a viable product stage. Examples include the SandHill Angels, the Band of Angels, the Tech Angels, and the Keiretsu Forum, each of which has organized investors into the hundreds or thousands, and refined their processes for collaborating on pipelines, vetting, investing, nurturing and exiting startups.

America's special interest investing groups formed for the same reasons, but were structured for nationwide participation: Impact investors formed the Investors' Circle, and female founders pitched to the Golden Seeds. The IndUS Entrepreneurs, or "TiE" organization, connected American investors to Indian founders. And each network was gathering momentum.

The same dynamic was emerging in Africa. Gone were the days when students could aspire to cushy government jobs. Budgets had been cut, and schools were churning out graduates with nowhere to look for a job. New businesses needed to be built. Young people loved tech and had already seen successes that encouraged them along the path of entrepreneurship: But they'd need more angel investors.

The first angel group LoftyInc helped establish was to be named LoftyInc Angel Networks, or LAN, but this group became so popular and broadly supported that the Lagos Angel Network name better suited its inclusive base. LAN soon became the continent's most active investing group, led by Tomie Davies, a seasoned technopreneur and African argonaut returnee. Idris and the other young LoftyInc partners wondered how they might personally fund more startup teams. They discovered something interesting: although they were only twenty-somethings, they already owned retirement accounts that had built up nicely with the matched funding from their large corporate employers, like Chevron. They decided to invest this capital into the best of the hundreds of African founders they were working with.

In 2012, Idris et al. formally registered another angel group to focus more on the opportunities generated by LoftyInc and Wennovation Hub, naming it the Afropreneurs Angel Group (AAG). They invited Nigerian professionals who were mentoring local young entrepreneurs to join them. One of their first investing commitments was to Iyinoluwa Aboyeji, whose initial venture failed, but his next team founded Andela, which would mature into a billion-dollar valuation.

The AAG tested strategies using their own capital, so they learned quickly that the best way to invest in startups was to do so in small sums over time, across several ventures and sectors, to diversify risks and improve their opportunity of finding a winner to scale up. AAG now numbers about 200 investors, has made about 200 investments, and has realized exits. This is the basis upon which LoftyInc's first venture funds were built.

Other local groups have formed and flourished as well, as we will see in more depth in the Pan-African Angel Investing section below. This strategy of casting a wide net worked even better as large numbers of local groups banded together to share not only venture funding needs, but also deal pipelines, diligence vetting, founder mentoring, expert advice across many sectors, and global networks. Does this intentionality of AfriLabs' supporters remind you of the 2009 World Bank report, *Moving Out of Poverty?* It highlighted personal initiative and ownership as the driving forces that lift nations out of poverty.

Why does personal initiative matter? Because entrepreneurial success lifts nations out of poverty. Teams that are empowered to "own" projects by selecting their own milestones and strategies are far more invested and committed to superior execution and are rewarded when they succeed. This path to success is well-known in business management. Incentives impact outcomes.

Those of us who have raised teenagers can also attest to the wisdom of similarly empowering our offspring to set their own goals and consequences. Instead of wasting their abundant youthful energy on resisting controls imposed on them, it is rewarding to see them choosing to focus on achieving longer-term goals they care deeply about.

AfriLabs' success reflects this same autonomy, born of the sovereignty and positive energy that accompanies ownership. It is also referred to as personal agency and is central to development success. But what does it look like in practice? How does this concept translate into practical day-to-day operations?

Ushahidi was built in Kenya by a team that held personal agency dear. They were individuals who dedicated themselves to solving transparency issues during post-election violence. When they opened the doors of Wennovation Hub in Lagos, Michael, Wole, Dami, and Idris felt they were herding cats, each of whom valued personal initiative. But this was a positive trait they could guide. This was how the LoftyInc team itself had begun, and the basis upon which tech ecosystems were built.

This drive for self-determination is how the seeds of economic opportunities germinate, take root, gather resources, and magically sprout into sustained economic development. It inspires enterprise development worthy of investors willing to share both its risks and rewards.

African Business Angel Network

Tomi Davies was the techno-angel investor who shepherded the fledgling Lagos Angel Network to an active investment role on the continent. A US-educated Nigerian returnee with a gold-star track record, Tomi's passion for pan-African networks has seeded over a thousand ventures across the continent and trained as many investors.

Tomi has become the continent's de facto *Father of African Angel Investing*, co-founding the pan-African angel network, ABAN, the African Business Angel Network. His heart for entrepreneurs is obvious in his recent book, *Investment Worthy Startup*, in which he explains that "Startups are innovative commercial ventures built for rapid and even explosive growth. This means they are continuously in need of capital."[84]

---

[84] Davies, T. (2023). Investment worthy startup: Building business ventures investors want to fund.

Rebecca Enonchong was born in Cameroon to a barrister who founded that nation's Bar Association. Her life decisions have reflected a focus on truth, justice, and establishing viable, related organizations. After moving to the US as a teenager, Rebecca proved herself a competent student, entrepreneur, and leader. Her early work at an international development bank and then as an Oracle consultant gave her insights into the gaps that entrepreneurial tech companies can fill, so she founded a firm that innovated solutions.

This was no easy task for an African female founder in 1999. But she was an innovative entrepreneur who carried her office in her briefcase and slept on the couches of friends. As every bootstrapping founder knows, you cannot hire a full management team until you have robust sales, and robust sales require a full team. Rebecca's solution was to fill as many roles as needed herself, so she used a generic title on her business card until she could afford to hire a team.

AppsTech, the company she founded, now operates in over 40 countries, is a Platinum-level partner of Oracle, and has remained relevant to enterprises worldwide for decades. Within three years, Rebecca was recognized at the World Economic Forum of Davos, Switzerland, as a "Global Leader for Tomorrow," on par with other tech entrepreneurs, including co-founder Larry Page of Google and CEO Marc Benioff of Salesforce.com.[85]

Rebecca went on to co-establish vibrant tech hubs in both Washington, D.C., and Cameroon, offering technology tools and entrepreneurial support to youth with limited resources. Since then, Rebecca has championed every major component of Africa's evolving tech startup ecosystem for entrepreneurs, investors, and global partnering. Although she has maintained this extraordinary level of impactful leadership with courage and elegance, it has not been easy.

---

[85] Quartz. (Updated 2022, July 20). *Cameroon detained an influential tech figure for African entrepreneurs.* https://qz.com/africa/2046701/cameroon-has-detained-rebecca-enonchong-on-unknown-charges

Fearing threats to its four-decade reign, Cameroon's political leadership shut down its citizens' internet access more than once, hence undermining its own economy. During the Covid pandemic, Rebecca's staunch support for African access to technology brought her a summons to meet the Cameroonian head of police at the Legion of Gendarmerie. There, she was detained without formal charges.

With lightning speed, two African networks demanded her release: AfriLabs, where Rebecca was serving as Board Chair, and the African Business Angel Network, which Rebecca had co-founded with Tomi Davies. Because these organizations represented hundreds of tech hubs and thousands of African investors living across the continent and in the diaspora, their voices were heard at the highest levels around the world.

Under the *#FreeRebecca* hashtag, the world at large was alerted to her dilemma. We learned that the Cameroonian Attorney General had been personally "outraged" at Rebecca's stance on access to technology and had verbally demanded the Gendarmerie Legion arrest her, despite filing no formal charges. The Attorney General was not only Rebecca's accuser, who had ordered her arrest, but also would be the one who would determine both her guilt and her punishment.

This situation was decried by Ambassadors from the US and France, as well as the United Nations. On the third day, Rebecca was released and freely resumed her leadership positions. Such is the power of the ecosystems that African argonauts have built.

Eight years before Rebecca Enonchong was detained, the idea of a pan-African Angel network was first discussed at the 5th EU-Africa Forum held in Brussels. Organized by the European Commission, the African Union, and associated business organizations, key ecosystem attendees decided to organize an initial African angel investor summit that would bring together various investor groups to explore the creation of a formal Pan-African network. In September 2014, Ben White's VC4Africa and Tomi Davies' Lagos Angel Network (LAN) hosted the first pan-African Angel Investor Summit as part of the DEMO Africa 2014 event in Lagos, Nigeria, where wealthy Africans were already slated to participate.

For example, Tony Elumelu was attending. He had retired from banking and established a holding company named Heir Holdings. It bought Nigerian assets worth billions of USD from global energy, insurance, and health corporations. It also committed US$2.5 billion to the Power Africa initiative spearheaded by US President Obama, making Heir Holdings the program's largest private sector donor. Elumelu set up a foundation that pledged $100 million to fund 10,000 young African entrepreneurs in a decade. By 2024, it had funded "20,000 young African men and women, who have created more than 400,000 jobs and generated US$2.5 billion in revenue. We've also provided access to training to more than 1.5 million young Africans on our digital platform, TEFConnect."[86]

Tony's commitments align with his philosophy, which inextricably links development with self-sufficiency. "Africapitalism," he said, "sees Africa's private sector, particularly every young entrepreneur, as instrumental in driving the continent's social and economic transformation.[87]

"We believe that philanthropy must be catalytic, combining traditional tools, like grants and donations, with business acumen to advance self-sufficiency for communities and generations. Such catalytic philanthropy can equip our youth with the resources, opportunities and visibility not only to create livelihoods for themselves but also to drive job creation and community development. Entrepreneurship offers the most transformative vehicle to reshape our continent's narrative within our lifetime—to create jobs and generate revenue, while pursuing sustainability, inclusion and social impact."[88]

Rebecca Enonchong co-led the 2014 pan-African Angel Investor Summit, joining diverse ecosystem stakeholders who expressed their common

---

[86] Tony Elumelu Foundation. (2024). *A decade of impact.* https://www.tonyelumelufoundation.org/wp-content/uploads/dlm_uploads/2024/03/2024-selection-fact.pdf

[87] Tony Elumelu Foundation. (2019, June 24). *What is Africapitalism?* https://www.tonyelumelufoundation.org/news/what-is-africapitalism

[88] Chris-Asoluka, S. (2024, August 1). *Africapitalism and the Tony Elumelu Foundation.* PANL Perspectives. https://carleton.ca/panl/2024/africapitalism-and-the-tony-elumelu-foundation/

desire for an organized structure through which they could connect with counterparts across the continent and around the world.

Also, that year, many of the 20,000 members of the European Business Angel Network gathered at their conference held in Helsinki, Finland, where the EBAN President announced the launch of The African Business Angel Network (ABAN). There, Candace Johnson said, "The opportunity to create African-European entrepreneurial and innovative companies through co-investment by European and African angel investors is one of the most exciting initiatives that we have ever undertaken."[89]

ABAN #1 L-R Alexandra Fraser (So. African Angel), David S. Rose (co-founder New York Angels), Candace Johnson (President, European Business Angels Network (EBAN)) Tomi Davies and Rebecca Enonchong in Helsinki, Finland, November 2014, when they agreed to form ABAN.

---

[89]White, B. (2014, November 19). *African Business Angels Network (ABAN) launches at EBAN 2014*. VC4A. https://vc4a.com/blog/2014/11/19/african-business-angels-network-aban-launches-at-eban-2014/

ABAN#2: Front L-R Peter Jungen (Founding President of EBAN), Rebecca, and Tomi with Ben White and David Van Dyke of VC4A, behind L-R, at the same event.

ABAN was formally established in early 2015 as a Mauritius Foundation. The organization was co-founded by six African angel networks, including the Lagos Angels Network (LAN), Cameroon Angel Network (CAN), Ghana Angel Investor Network (GAIN), Venture Capital for Africa (VC4Africa), and Silicon Cape. As of November 2024, the site said, "Today we count over 56 member networks in more than 40 African countries and the Diaspora."[90]

ABAN's annual investment surveys are a treasure trove for wannabe investors who wonder what kind of people are investing, where, in what, and how much. Its readable case studies add valuable insights from Africa's most active and well-informed investors. Newbies learn how to get started in Africa, and what to expect when they do. ABAN even provides clean document templates for angel investors. The 2023 ABAN Survey of its members even compares the results of US-based angel investors who have also invested in Africa.

For instance, ABAN's data show that Africa's angels are unusually motivated to invest for a positive impact (96%)—principally for economic development. This makes sense. Investors care about the people they know. Since one-third of the population lives at or below the poverty line

---

[90] ABAN. https://abanangels.org/about-us/

of $2 per day, more African investors are likely to know entrepreneurs who are innovating solutions vital to economic development.

The McKinsey consultancy predicts that the female economy is the world's largest emerging market, with the potential to add US$12 trillion to global GDP by 2025.[91] Much of that potential may emerge in Africa because African angels invest in a higher proportion of female founders than US angels. This is consistent with data showing that a higher percentage of Africa's angel investors are female, hold advanced degrees, and are entrepreneurs themselves.

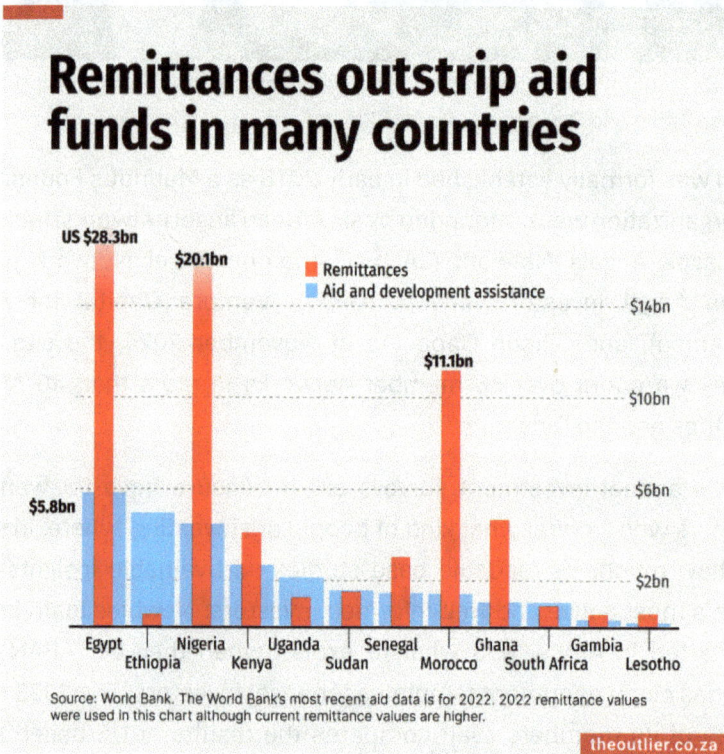

Remittances outstrip aid funds in many countries

Source: World Bank. The World Bank's most recent aid data is for 2022. 2022 remittance values were used in this chart although current remittance values are higher.

theoutlier.co.za

[91] Kimeria, C. (2025, January 31). *World Economic Forum 2025: Takeaways on emerging markets.* Delphos. https://delphos.co/news/blog/world-economic-forum-2025-takeaways-on-emerging-markets/#:~:text=Gender%20Parity%20and%20Inclusion%20Efforts&text=Closing%20gender%20gaps%20in%20emerging,can%20drive%20innovation%20and%20productivity.

The African Development Bank reported that the highest proportion of female entrepreneurs globally is in sub-Saharan Africa, where about 26% of women are actively involved in starting or managing a business; this is also reflected in their growing presence on corporate boards, where women in the region hold over 24% of seats.[92] The 2018 Mastercard Index of Women Entrepreneurs globally showed that the countries with the most female entrepreneurs are Ghana and Uganda.[93]

Most angels also invest in young startup founders, thereby investing in their energy, zeal, and potential careers. Because two of every three Africans are under 25 years old, it is the world's youngest continent. This makes Africa the most likely source of cutting-edge innovations and startups.

In summary, Africa's innovation-based startup sector is booming, and African diaspora returnees have supported the vision and enthusiasm of African entrepreneurs. Often the magic happens when both founders and funders are argonauts who engage in circular migrations, connecting insights and resources.

Global Remittances

One dramatic example of this ecosystem is the amount of funding the diaspora sends home. Very few people know that these "remittances" exceed any other source.

---

[92] African Development Bank Group. (n.d.). *Why AFAWA?* https://www.afdb.org/en/topics-and-sectors/initiatives-partnerships/afawa-affirmative-finance-action-for-women-in-africa/why-afawa

[93] African Studies Centre Leiden. (Updated 2023, November 13). *African women entrepreneurs.* https://www.ascleiden.nl/content/webdossiers/african-women-entrepreneurs#:~:text=By%202018%2C%20the%20Mastercard%20Index,in%20the%20MIWE%202021%20report.

Global Remittance Flows Outpace Other Funding Sources

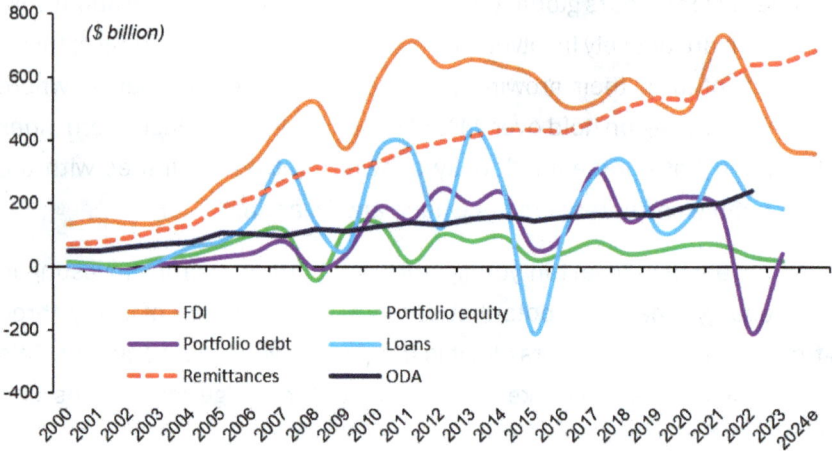

Source:[94] Authors' estimates, World Development Indicators, IMF Balance of Payments Statistics

Notes: FDI = foreign direct investment; ODA = official development assistance. "Officially recorded remittances to low- and middle-income countries (LMICs) are expected to reach $685 billion in 2024. The true size of remittances, including flows through informal channels, is believed to be even larger."

The above chart shows global remittances sent by individuals consistently outpace other major sources of external funding, including foreign direct investment (FDI), loans, and official development assistance (ODA). For over twenty years, the two most stable and growing development funding sources were both from the private sector– Foreign Direct Investing[95] and remittances.[96]

---

[94] Ratha, D., Plaza, S., Kim, EJ. (2024, December 18). In 2024, remittance flows to low- and middle-income countries are expected to reach $685 billion, larger than FDI and ODA combined. World Bank Blogs. https://blogs.worldbank.org/en/peoplemove/in-2024--remittance-flows-to-low--and-middle-income-countries-ar

[95]https://trendsresearch.org/insight/foreign-direct-investment-in-africa-trends-and-prospects/?srsltid=AfmBOoonVeUhcUgzUE7J7affms2Kw2lX0CBU5zMhmLNNc1V5HApLlwJ-

[96] Remittance Inflows and Outflows. https://drive.google.com/drive/folders/1vrGXeAf_6VH64kTC_plsHNvHfQyyocYj

Both sources represent personal initiative and ownership, but only diaspora remittances have grown steadily, without the wild volatility swings of all other sources. For example, when Covid hit, instead of stepping up to meet the needs, foreign development institutions cut their funding for African ventures in half, sending those reliant on it into tailspins.

Many assume that aid and government funding are Africa's primary financial resources, however, remittances are–Africans backing Africans–and they have remained Africa's most stable and growing source of capital over the past two decades. Unlike the volatility of portfolio equity or debt, remittances provide steady, direct support to families and communities. This highlights the critical role of diaspora contributions in driving financial resilience across the continent.

Growing gap between aid and remittances in Africa

Remittances to African countries was $37-billion more than aid donations in 2022

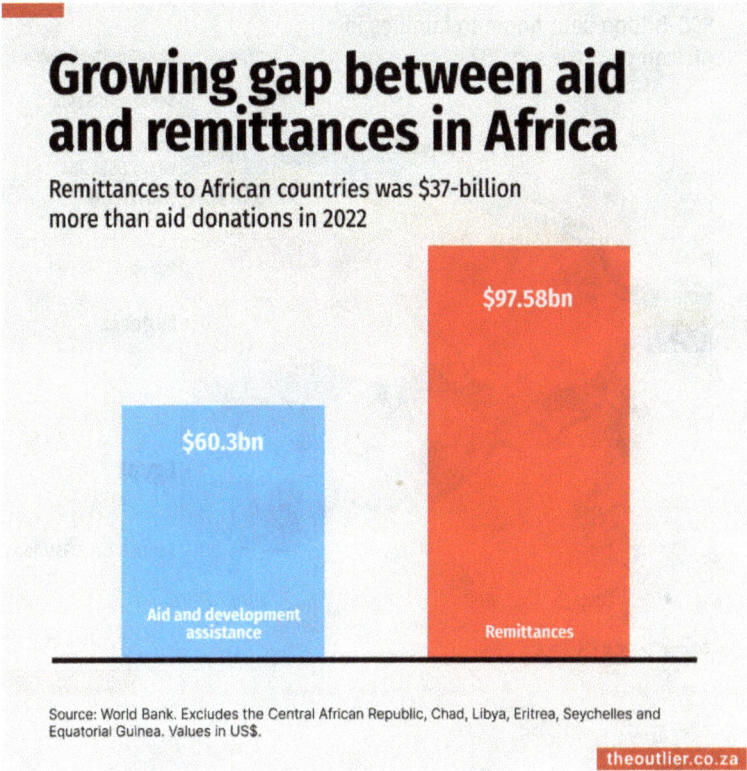

$97.58bn

$60.3bn

Aid and development assistance

Remittances

Source: World Bank. Excludes the Central African Republic, Chad, Libya, Eritrea, Seychelles and Equatorial Guinea. Values in US$.

theoutlier.co.za

In 2023, remittances to African countries surpassed $90 billion. Nigeria, for instance, received over $20 billion from its diaspora in 2022 alone, which accounted for 7% of its GDP and was equivalent to $91 per capita. Six African countries had higher levels than this on a per capita basis, including Egypt, whose diaspora sent over $28 billion home that year.[97] As impressive as this data is in demonstrating the importance of remittances, it only represents the funds that flow through formal channels, while most remittance funding is sent informally.

Although most remittances are spent on the health, education and welfare of loved ones, about 25% is invested locally, and this number has grown significantly, as aid and donor funding are being replaced by private capital.

African inflow balloon

$90-billion sent home to families in African countries in 2023

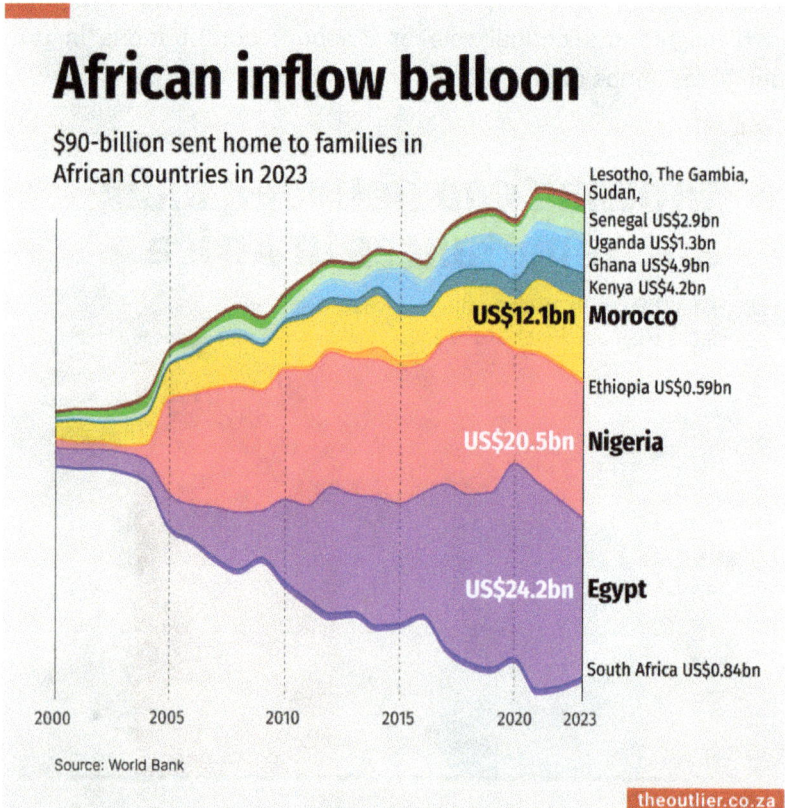

Lesotho, The Gambia, Sudan,
Senegal US$2.9bn
Uganda US$1.3bn
Ghana US$4.9bn
Kenya US$4.2bn
US$12.1bn **Morocco**

Ethiopia US$0.59bn

US$20.5bn **Nigeria**

US$24.2bn **Egypt**

South Africa US$0.84bn

Source: World Bank

theoutlier.co.za

[97] Outlier Editor. (2024, October 28). *African remittances surpass $90bn a year.* https://outliereditor.co.za/index.php/2024/10/28/african-remittances-top-90-billion-in-2023/

7. Afropreneurs are Honing Successful Strategies that Reduce Risk

Informing World Funders...

In 2013, Jon Gosier, the American entrepreneur behind Appfrica and Hive CoLab, spoke to the UN General Assembly at the invitation of its President.[98],[99] This august group included UN Ministers, Ambassadors, staff, civil society, academia, and business. They wanted to hear how Jon and other twenty-somethings had achieved so much African development with so few resources, so rapidly. They hoped to learn success strategies they could replicate in their homelands.[100]

Surveying that vast cathedral, the energy from the array of diverse leaders made Jon feel both powerful and insignificant. Africa's tech ecosystem was still nascent, yet Jon was already on the world stage debating its strategies and successes. He began by explaining the tech innovations and entrepreneurial mindsets that his teams had deployed on the continent.

"The jobs my companies created have kept people all over Africa employed and their families fed," Jon later wrote in his memoir about this

---

[98] Email to Jon Gosier Re: High Level Thematic Debate on Entrepreneurship for Development, from Simonne Levav, Social and Economic Affairs, United Nations Jun 12, 2013

[99] https://docs.un.org/en/E/2013/95, Page 7

[100]https://www.un.org/en/ecosoc/newfunct/pdf13/amr_tanzania_programme.pdf

event, in his book, Code Switch.[101] "These companies are still operational and scaling across Africa. It was the elusive outcome every entrepreneur hopes for. Successful companies created jobs that lifted people out of poverty."

This is how economies grow," Jon told his UN audience. *"Africa doesn't need more philanthropists or aid money from the countries represented in this room. Africa needs more investors."*

But why were these jobs so tech-oriented, some wondered. A woman with a Sierra Leonean accent asked how her country's fishermen and farmers fit into this grand future. She wondered how all this would work if schools had computers with no power and people had mobile phones but no money for cell service. Jon acknowledged Africa's "tale of two economies," but as the world's agrarian and industrial economies transition toward being knowledge-based and service-centered, most new jobs will be technology-driven.

"Tech jobs won't employ everyone," Jon conceded, "but for each technology job created, we've found that five traditional jobs and twenty unskilled jobs are created." He explained that formally employed people spend money in ways that create opportunities and growth across the employment spectrum. The lifetime value of each tech job is over half a million dollars to an economy. And his company was operating in 30 countries.

"For every one dollar my company has invested across the continent, we estimate that $220 of value was created overall. Over the past five years, our little company from Uganda has created an estimated $110 million of impact...Not by investing in Africa's past, but by investing in its *future*. These jobs gave people the advanced skills needed to make them relevant in an increasingly global business community."

"When I started my company, there were one or two like ours. Now, there are hundreds like us...that's tens of billions of dollars of new wealth, across the continent." Jon spoke of this exponential growth a dozen years

---

[101] Gosier, J. (2023). *Code switch: A memoir.* Misfit Press.
https://www.codeswitchbook.com/

ago. Since then, tech ecosystem pioneers have bridged the continent through robust collaborations that have enlivened African startups. These were launched with the shared goal of jump-starting tech ventures, led by local youth who have succeeded, garnered global awards and trained tens of thousands of African entrepreneurs.

History was being made across the continent. As startup seeds like these germinated and sprouted into plants of opportunity, the excitement grew.

> *"'That's how it's always been' is never a good*
> *enough reason for how it should stay."*
> —Ahmed Adeagbo

Although many people avoid investing in Africa, successful risk mitigation strategies are not complex. Mindsets are the bigger problem. Diverging from the status quo to negate widespread ignorance, fear, and bias takes courage. But the successful investing strategies are fairly simple, straightforward, and logical.

In the prior pages of this book, you have seen the most effective approaches in action. Next, we'll explore case studies to clarify the strategies that ultimately impacted the numbers depicted in related graphs. By then, you will understand what strategies were deployed and why they work.

Startup Strategies

Thomas Edison learned that 2,774 materials would not work as light bulb filaments before he successfully twisted and baked cotton filament that stayed lit. If a conventional debt holder had foreclosed on his home and laboratory after Thomas' first 2,700 tries, how much longer would it have taken for the light bulb to have been commercialized? If Thomas was penalized for his efforts, who else would have tried again?

Remember when "E" was still in school in Canada? He asked business angels he knew to back his first venture. Idris, who had lived a similar life to E but was older and more experienced, structured that investment as equity. He used a Simple Agreement for Future Equity, known as a

"SAFE" agreement. Y Combinator created this document for their portfolio of tech startup investments to keep things simple. YC understands the needs and opportunities in this sector well, having leveraged them to invest successfully around the world.

That SAFE document has become a startup industry standard; it is free and available to download.[102] As the sector evolves, YC updates and refines its documents and recommendations, so there are variations on a theme, but they are all still simple equity instruments. They are not designed for investors to control founders or gain advantages over future investors; they are designed to incentivize and reward shared success.

When there are not yet tangible assets or revenues, it is folly to lend money using agreements that threaten recourse; so, debt instruments make little sense for startups whose value lies in continued innovation and execution. When founders are young and their ventures are still forming, why waste time debating collateral or negotiating terms for control of an indebted company? Or determining precise valuations, for that matter? Agreeing to discounted equity terms to the value of a future investment makes more sense after a startup has actually had time to create value.

The value of startups is locked in the hearts and minds of their founders until they have the time and resources to show what they can do. If Idris had structured his angel group's first investments as debt, then, being a responsible person, E would probably have worked two jobs to repay those investors after that venture failed. He may have been too burdened by debt obligations to have succeeded as an entrepreneur at all. Instead, thanks to a compatible financing structure and the goodwill of his investors, E was free to co-launch Andela, Flutterwave, and then Future Africa. So he returned the favor, as good partners do.

Instead of failing because of overdue debts, Andela's team benefited from aligned interests with equity investor partnerships. For instance, Idris helped Andela look for its first campus location in Lagos. Is this

---

[102] Levy, C. (n.d.). *Safe financing documents.*
https://www.ycombinator.com/documents

something that a disgruntled creditor would do? Being an equity partner brings a whole different mindset to nurturing startups, and with it come more varied resources and networks that founders can tap.

E reciprocated his equity partners' faith in him by voluntarily carrying over their ownership from a failed venture into one that succeeded. This spirit of collaborative effort inspired them and additional investors, including myself, to invest even more capital into the next venture, Flutterwave, which E co-founded. In fact, my desire to co-invest alongside Idris and his African angels inspired me to co-found LoftyInc Capital as a Delaware-registered firm and to anchor its Afropreneurs Fund 2. This seed-stage VC fund expanded the opportunities for non-African investors to tap into the ecosystem's expertise and profit from its innovations. African entrepreneurs benefited from access to more growth capital. African consumers benefited from access to customized tech solutions, and the tech ecosystem gained resources to scale up this emerging asset class.

Since 2008, LoftyInc's young partners and I have shared a vision, honed strategies, and developed projects. Our confidence, trust and expertise deepened and matured. The outcome of this trust is shown in the graph below. In it, both Andela and Flutterwave are enshrined among Africa's first tech-driven, private companies to exceed one-billion-dollar valuations, based on documented investment agreements. Their rapid growth created exponential returns for investors and markets alike. Those corporations also educated and employed tens of thousands of African youth and empowered scores of new African ventures.

These successful outcomes contrast starkly with the use of debt and authenticate the equity investing strategies that empowered them. Instead of using early revenues to pay interest and repay loans, these startups used them to grow. Reaching robust valuations rapidly cuts the time that startups spend in the "valley of death," where they burn more cash than they earn. This value growth shrinks their risk of failure, improves their economies of scale, and broadens their access to follow-on funding.

The alumni of Andela and Flutterwave have been as meaningful to Africa's tech sector as PayPal's alumni became to America's, as Idris explained in his blog.[103] Their entrepreneurial learnings and investment winnings have gone viral, spawning a host of novel startups, each testing a new niche, amassing more expertise and earnings in ever-widening networks. Africa's seasoned entrepreneurs and investors created jobs, increased the middle class, and demanded more accountable elected officials who better served communities.

Africa's ecosystem is fortunate to have teams passionate about collecting investment data from tech startup sector participants, including LoftyInc. They thrive on first-hand data gathering and remain responsive to those of us who are creating the data. For example, the "Africa: The Big Deal" team has consistently published transparent and respected reports. They present their findings in readable graphics via email and archive them on a public website. The Big Deal also welcomes deep dives into their data details.[104]

Although most of Africa's strong performers have not yet "gone public," their private shares do exchange hands, providing valuations and liquidity to realize gains. Unicorns matter because their rapid growth enables investor exits--and exits matter a great deal. As entrepreneurs and investors access their profits on the secondaries market, they often choose to reinvest proceeds into new ventures, potentially in the billions of USD. African entrepreneurs, like Idris, E, and Rebecca, and their investors, including me, reinvested our profits, alongside newcomers, in more startups.

This completed another full funding cycle, but with the added benefit of a steep learning curve that refined strategies and scaled up a sustainable, virtuous circle.

Entrepreneurial Investors form the center of this strategy. They initially organise and fund infrastructure, as did Argonauts Mo and Funke, then the ecosystem of tech hubs and angel groups. Then startups emerge, grow, and succeed, until profits are realized and reinvestment restarts

---

[103] Bello, I. (2021, September 30). *An emerging Andela Mafia*? The Afropreneur. https://idrisbello.com/2021/09/30/an-emerging-andela-mafia/

[104] *Africa: The Big Deal*. Substack. https://thebigdeal.substack.com

the cycle, which now scales up, as it includes more expertise and participants.

Why did the new crop of African-led startups that emerged in 2016-2023 attract billions of USD from hundreds of first-time investors in Africa? Africa's elite returnees had built trust, established track records, and created virtuous circles. The pan-African membership organizations that these argonauts founded, funded, and managed, in the form of AfriLabs, ABAN, AVCA and VC4A, now offer year-round, specialized support that sustains learning curves, partnering prospects, and global funding. Robust pipelines of entrepreneurs and investors are now feeding into the ecosystem to sustain its early successes.

Africa's Self-Sustaining Startup Cycle

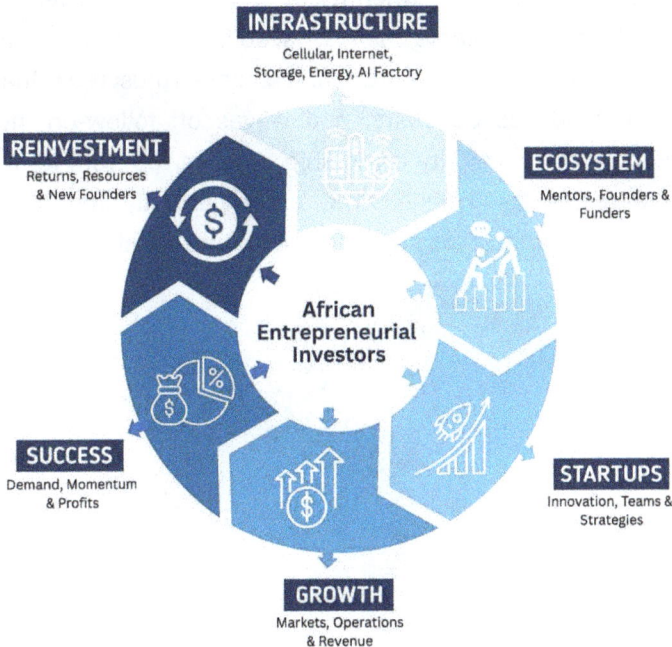

INFRASTRUCTURE
Cellular, Internet, Storage, Energy, AI Factory

REINVESTMENT
Returns, Resources & New Founders

ECOSYSTEM
Mentors, Founders & Funders

African Entrepreneurial Investors

SUCCESS
Demand, Momentum & Profits

STARTUPS
Innovation, Teams & Strategies

GROWTH
Markets, Operations & Revenue

Africa's Self-Sustaining Development Cycle
Source: *African Ngenuity* by Marsha Wulff, 2025

Given the multiple demands upon young entrepreneurs, what is extraordinary to me is how generous the founders of these unicorns have already been, reinvesting back into other African startups and into the ecosystem that nurtured them. Active investors know who co-invests with us. We see their names on capitalization tables and their signatures on corporate documents. We see their social media posts, encouraging the next crop of entrepreneurs, supporting growth opportunities. We learn who is mentoring which up-and-coming founders.

Overarching this early entrepreneurial ecosystem activity was the mandate to build investable startups that were robust and worthy of seed capital. Founders must inspire enough trust to attract equity investments from partners who co-benefit from their success and share their losses. This is the focus of African Business Angels Network cofounder, Tomi Davies and his book, *Investment Worthy Startup*.[105]

Each stage of life comes with its own set of dos and do nots. A newborn is not ready for cereal, but when it starts teething, it craves solids. A startup venture lacks reliable cash flows, so financing it with mandatory repayment terms is a fool's errand. If first revenues must repay loans, this stunts growth, drives up costs, and waves off follow-on investors. Usurping control or majority ownership of a startup from its founding team is a recipe for disaster. Yet, other perfectly sound investing practices for investing at the seed stage do empower shared success.

---

[105] https://tomidavies.com

The following table identifies three investment stages of startup entities, with numbers that roughly align with current African ecosystem norms.

African Startup Stage Financing Overview

Round	Pre-seed Year 1-2	Seed Years 2-5	Series A Years 3-6
Revenues	Few revenues	First revenues to $20mil ARR	$20mil-100mil ARR
Funding Structure Size: Rounds & Tickets Sources	Direct: Informal Equity & Loan Agreements Up to $1mil $1k-$200k Founders, Family, Friends + Angels	Direct: SAFEs* & Convertible Notes Funds: LP/GP VC Funds Up to $10mil $100k-$5mil Founders + Angels + Family Offices + Seed VC Funds	Direct: Priced Shares & Venture Debt Funds: LP/GP VC Funds Up to $20mil $1mil - $10mil Seed & VC Funds + Family Offices + Institutions
Activities	Build: Core team, Prototype, Revenue model, Query market & develop strategies	Enter and test market, Expand team, Refine strategies, product, budgets, & marketing ID potential growth partners	Full product rollout Major marketing campaign Meetings and agreements with growth partners

*SAFEs: https://www.ycombinator.com/documents
Source: M Wulff 2025

Local Strategies

In 2010, Africa's tech startups were not raising enough capital to even bother tracking, but that changed after African argonauts took the initiative to personally invest small amounts in local entrepreneurs. In 2020, the sector attracted $2 billion. During the next three years, its entrepreneurs raised $13 billion, despite a global pandemic. What had changed? The risk profile.

Funding raised by Startups in Africa

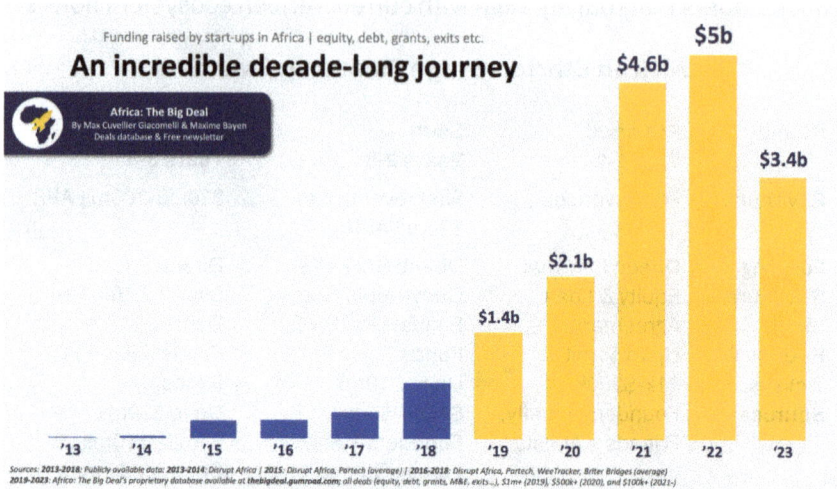

Funding raised by start-ups in Africa | equity, debt, grants, exits etc.

An incredible decade-long journey

Africa: The Big Deal
By Max Cuvellier Giacomelli & Maxime Bayen
Deals database & Free newsletter

Chart values by year:
- '19: $1.4b
- '20: $2.1b
- '21: $4.6b
- '22: $5b
- '23: $3.4b

Years shown: '13, '14, '15, '16, '17, '18, '19, '20, '21, '22, '23

Sources: **2013-2018**: Publicly available data: **2013-2014**: Disrupt Africa | 2015: Disrupt Africa, Partech (average) | **2016-2018**: Disrupt Africa, Partech, WeeTracker, Briter Bridges (average) 2019-2023: Africa: The Big Deal's proprietary database available at thebigdeal.gumroad.com; all deals (equity, debt, grants, M&E, exits...), $1m+ (2019), $500k+ (2020), and $100k+ (2021-)

Source: Africa: The Big Deal, 2023

At the startup stage, innovative ventures need partners with shared goals who structure their investments to share both the risks of failure and rewards of success. Startup teams are already risking their careers, reputations, family relationships, and personal wealth. Most have already sunk everything they have into the startup, including their time. The venture is their passion, day and night. They are doing the heavy lifting.

Since discouragement destroys value that innovators could bring to investors, wise investors choose to encourage. Startup founders worldwide must retain the freedom to pivot revenue models, refine their products, and attract talent as they create new markets. If founders lose control of their ventures to demanding investors, their vision evaporates, and with it, their energizing personal initiative dissipates.

Controlling funders only win an empty shell, but founders do need astute advisors with seasoned guidance on call, 24/7. What if an investor does not trust a founding team to make wise decisions? Do not invest. Do not engage. Walk away before everyone wastes time, money, and focus. They will learn from the experience, or they won't. By leaving, you will do less harm than if you offer terms that undermine management. We will look at examples in "What's Not Working?" Equity strategies for seed-stage investing have definitively proven successful.

Africa's argonauts started returning to their continent with experience, networks, and resources to build a tech ecosystem. Mo, Funke, and Bitange overcame corporate ignorance, political resistance, and corruption to build cellular networks and broadband access across Sub-Saharan Africa. Idris and Michael returned to Nigeria; Teddy and Jon moved to Uganda; Ory and Erik led from Kenya, setting up their own ventures, as well as tech hubs and investor networks. African entrepreneurs, Rebecca from Cameroon and Tomi from Nigeria, co-launched pan-African membership networks for both tech hubs and angel groups. They collaborated proactively to reach shared goals for the good of their continent.

Building this ecosystem reduced the risks of investing in African startups. They enlarged deal flow pipelines and improved their chances of success. The world started to notice. After news of Africa's first unicorns went viral, foreign investors began investing billions of USD into hundreds of African-led startups each year.

What strategies had engendered these successes?

Step by step, African rainmakers created an ecosystem that supported repeatable successes. They started by preparing themselves to be credible, authoritative, and self-sustaining, both at home and abroad. Then their ventures, local tech hubs, mentor groups, and angel networks seeded the first innovation-based startups to reach billion-dollar star status. Africans invested in Africans and succeeded.

Africa's initial startup funding spurt occurred from 2019 to 2022, approximately a decade after the continent's first tech hubs were established and after the first angel groups, mentioned earlier, began investing in the pre-seed stage. This local strategy bore fruit when Zuckerberg invested in Andela, validating the strategies of Idris' local angel investing group and revealing a path for African startups to progress from local angels to mainstream venture capital. It also inspired our

LoftyInc team to launch a formal venture fund that focused on African tech startups, opening a convenient door for American investors to leverage local expertise and portfolio management.

Covid's forced sheltering and digital dependence created a boom for local entrepreneurs to build fintech apps, e-commerce platforms, logitech, and health tech ventures to connect consumers with products and services. Global demand for internet-based businesses exploded, including those in Africa. Because most tech-driven ventures are rapid-growth, new investors flooded into the continent's hot new tech sectors of finance, health, insurance, and logistics.

But during the post-Covid spending retraction, the Ukraine war and a massive local currency devaluation in Nigeria slowed the apparent rate of startup entity growth. This cooled investor enthusiasm, contracting every part of the financing food chain. Its impact is depicted in the above graph's final column, citing $3.4 billion of funding raised in 2023. Although this was a dramatic decline from the prior year's $5 billion, it was still 60% higher than in 2021.

Was this investor pullback concerning? In the short term, yes, it did hit rapid-growth startups hard, as sources of capital dried up, despite strong growth metrics. Unable to balance early revenues against expansion expenses, many had to shut down. It hit funders like LoftyInc hard as well. We, too, invested in an expanded team actively raising another fund to back our robust pipeline. Simultaneously, high-potential opportunities to exit portfolio companies evaporated. However, from a longer-term perspective, the sector's growth trajectory has actually remained positive. The jump from an investment level of around $100 million in 2013 to $3.4 billion in 2023 was a remarkable 3400% growth! Getting excited or depressed is all about one's perspective.

Meanwhile, the local economic issues that slowed growth reflected a series of wise fiscal disciplines that were long overdue. For example, Nigeria's currency was previously tagged to the dollar, which prevented it from floating in response to market demand. Global economists had faulted prior Nigerian leaders who lacked the courage to take the political heat for allowing the Naira to float freely. However, that changed when Nigerians elected Tinubu as President, who did the hard thing so that confidence in their currency would grow. This market freedom promptly caused the Naira to decline to one-third of its value relative to the USD.

Prior to the Naira devaluation in 2021, one LoftyInc portfolio company, a health insurtech, attracted the first African investment of an American growth equity firm, General Atlantic. GA had also signed warrants to pay twice as much for more shares at a later date, if the company was able to double its revenues. It actually *more* than doubled its revenues within the allotted time, but only if measured in Naira; in dollar terms, their earnings remained flat.

The warrants expired, and our hope of tapping those proceeds to launch our next Fund evaporated with them. But the company's value as a quality healthcare and insurance provider continues to grow, measured by the number of people insured and the value customers receive for their premiums. Our Fund realized a 70x return on our first investment in that healthtech. Such local insights and strategies inform our longer-term perspectives.

Global Strategies

Although local leadership built the continent's startup ecosystem and underpinned its first successes, foreign capital outpaced local sources during the sector's 2021-2023 influx. Where did that new funding come from for Africa's first big spike in startup investments? Funding was roughly divided into thirds from Africa, North America, and Eurasia. This increased level of funding empowered some startups to grow rapidly into globally viable corporations, including Flutterwave and Andela, in which Idris et al. invested. The diversity of sources opened new doors for strategic partnering.

What had changed the mindset of these foreign investors? What had mitigated their fears?

Regions Investing the Most in African Deals

Individual investors involved in $100k+ deals in Africa*, by region of HQ

African investors most represented amongst investors in Africa

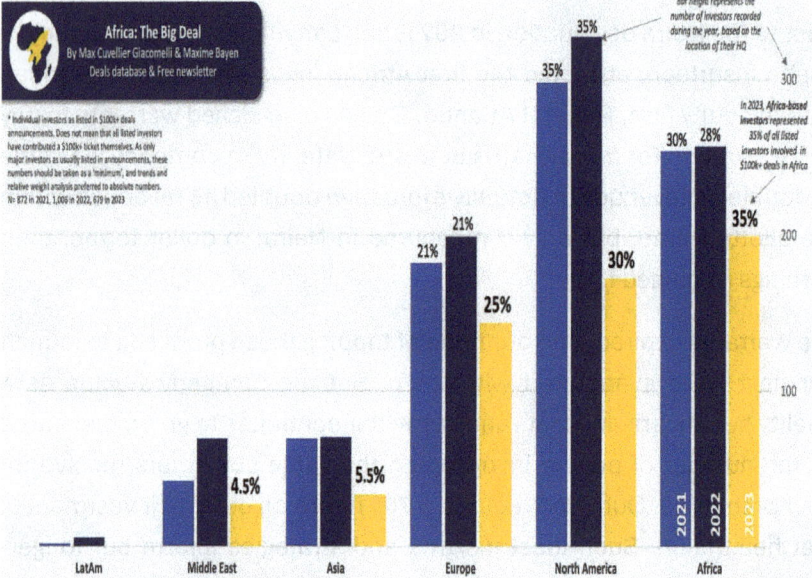

Africa: The Big Deal
By Max Cuvellier Giacomelli & Maxime Bayen
Deals database & Free newsletter

* Individual investors as listed in $100k+ deals announcements. Does not mean that all listed investors have contributed a $100k+ ticket themselves. As only major investors as usually listed in announcements, these numbers should be taken as a 'minimum', and trends and relative weight analysis preferred to absolute numbers. N> 872 in 2021, 1,006 in 2022, 679 in 2023

Bar height represents the number of investors recorded during the year, based on the location of their HQ

In 2023, Africa-based investors represented 35% of all listed investors involved in $100k+ deals in Africa

Source: Africa: The Big Deal's proprietary database, accessible at thebigdeal.gumroad.com
Deals included: $1m+ (2019), $500k+ (2020), and $100k+ (2021-) deals | All deal types (Equity, Debt, Grants etc.) excluding exits | Both publicly disclosed deals & deals shared confidentially by selected investors

Source: Africa: The Big Deal

The answer is primarily found in the graph above, represented by the African bars on the right. It shows Africa-based investors as the region's staunchest investors, even besting North American investors during 2023, a down year for global growth.

It is no great secret that following the lead of local investors is wiser than becoming a lone "bull in a China shop." But how do foreign investors learn what local investors are doing?

Remember that ecosystem Africans built? Continent-wide membership association events attract the most robust local tech hubs, angel groups, and venture capitalists. These convenings inform and embrace foreign investors. Investors who participate in such gatherings will build personal relationships that transcend borders to produce the international investment growth depicted in the graph.

How can people from different backgrounds find enough common ground to build this level of trust, especially when private equity investments and long distances are involved? Co-investing on a small scale melds the insights of local investors with the resources of global investors to improve outcomes for both. As confidence and trust grow, so does the frequency and scale of interpersonal collaborations.

These strategies help reduce partnering risks. Stepping outside your normal networks, reaching across traditional boundaries, and finding people with shared values are all part of the answer. This initially takes courage, commitment, and capital, but real-time communication innovations like LinkedIn, Zoom, and WhatsApp have made this exponentially more enjoyable and affordable than when I started pioneering this niche 25 years ago. These daily interactions can now build bonds that are more comfortable and efficient than those in your local office and neighborhood.

Logically, the first step toward healthy collaboration is knowing what you prioritize so you can find others who share them. If your priorities are consistent with responsible development and mutual sharing of risks and rewards—versus rapacious selfishness—then you are on a path to more trustworthy collaborations. This may sound cheeky, but it is true. I told you this is not rocket science; it is common sense.

Investors who devote the time to listening well and learning are more likely to select goals and relationships that withstand time and trauma long enough to succeed. Wise investors test collaboration strategies to find what best suits their goals. Small investments are less stressful, but their successes generate the confidence to make bigger decisions. You know this, so start small.

Not everyone wants to totally immerse themselves in African investing, so you may need to find others who do. From reading this, you know there are plenty of well-educated Africans who have a deep understanding of both global investing criteria and local market insights, so leverage some of them. Co-invest in their favorites for starters, but do not expect them to work for you for free. If you are not making equal contributions to the process of finding, vetting, mentoring, and exiting high-quality opportunities, then formalize terms that compensate for this.

What does not work is hiring a smart youngster from your own country who has no special insights on Africa to fly to Africa and find opportunities while you sit alone in your ivory tower with no direct links to Africans you know well and trust completely. This style of investing from afar ensures failure. Yet this is what most American investors do, and then they blame Africans, instead of their own folly.

You can start small by paying one or more of those astute young African argonauts you met while they were schooling in the US or when you attended a pan-African investor event to bring you deal flow. They will LOVE doing this and will probably do an outstanding job for a very reasonable cost. Making your investments successful will be their top priority if you structure their incentives properly, as it empowers them to help worthy local entrepreneurs and opens career doors for themselves at local venture funds. They want to be your hero! Before you know it, your friends will want to chip in and test the waters alongside you, and you will be able to build a robust portfolio, which reduces risk and spreads a wider net to catch more winners. This will become your favorite thing to talk about at cocktail parties, between Fantasy Football and streaming TV shows!

But to realize your gains, you will need to sell your holdings, right? This is the sticking point that transitions self-sustaining ventures into gains or losses for your portfolio. And this is why you may prefer to invest via formal VC funds with superior networks. But how do you find and evaluate a local VC firm?

At this point, your fears of risk may overwhelm your entrepreneurial instincts, so you may seek safety in brand names as you weigh options. This may be a mistake. Similar to why investors hire a non-African to find African deal flow, investors often select a VC Fund based on some familiar affiliation. For instance, they feel comforted if Fund Manager CVs tout big name investment firms and universities. But what do those FMs know about local tech startup investing?

Remember to prioritize African argonauts who were raised locally, so they have market insights and local language fluency but are also globally astute. They should be young enough to identify with the tech savvy majority of startup founders and have strong, multi-level, local networks for deal flow, mentors, and exits. Have they personally built and exited African ventures, as Idris did? This prepares FMs to identify superior founders and be alert to execution complications. Have they learned lessons from investing their own entrepreneurial profits? Do they have a local track record of seed-stage investing and exits?

Do not aim for a risk-free portfolio, because every investment has both risk and reward. Highly rated bonds, for example, will probably pay on time and return principal on maturity, but they lack liquidity. During an inflationary time, you will wish you were getting higher returns, but if you sell early, you will lose some of your principal.

So don't get caught up in risk reduction strategies that also reduce returns. Rather, manage risks via asset diversification. The higher you deem the risk, the smaller amount you will invest. You still invest in some higher-risk assets because you want exposure to high-potential growth. The Keirtsu Investment Forum of over 3500 angel investors has its roots in Silicon Valley, and a white paper based on its research of members reported that the optimal portfolio size for achieving optimal returns was 22-23 startups.[106]

Non-African investors often ask which countries are most investible. The answer is, it depends. If you have a special interest, deep sector insights, and strong relationships with high-potential African Argonauts returning home, then you may have superior opportunities in a vast, untapped market that is underdeveloped. Despite their growth potential, frontier markets, such as approximately 40 African countries, notoriously lack global participation, leaving them to languish in obscurity that constricts value, growth, and exits—until they reach a tipping point. If you enter that

---

[106] LeMerle, M., LeMerle, L. (2015, December). *Capturing the expected returns of angel investors in groups. Less in more-diversify.* Fifth Era. Fifth Era LLC, titled "Less in More: Diversify"

market at the right time, you may have a strong tactical advantage to build value and harvest returns. As a region reaches a critical mass of localized entrepreneurship and investing, a stable middle class arises. Then, its first spark of international capital breathes vitality into its ventures, and it becomes an emerging market, joining the other 14 African countries.

This initial growth spurt is rarely linear or sustained, as seen in the above graph, but it does put mainstream investors on alert that a region is coming to life, thanks to its startup pioneers, as LoftyInc pioneered Nigeria. The next wave of early adopters, who have watched and learned, is often better capitalized than the pioneers. Depending on how well early investors do, the next round may be delayed while waiting for more widespread success, or it may be inspired by a 'fear of missing out' on the next hot place to invest.

Historically, the world's tech startup investors have led the early funding phases. True to form, Silicon Valley initially out-funded other geographies to lead Africa's 2020-2021 growth spurt, as graphed by the Big Deal team, above. Why? The Valley's own tech innovation boom created local investor successes and a corresponding comfort with the sector and stage. Upon his arrival in Silicon Valley in the mid-1970s, my husband saw vibrant orange groves growing where tech corporation campuses now stand. The US founders of Silicon Valley's first tech corporations left more staid careers in the Northeast and upper Midwest to innovate a novel industry in a beautiful agrarian valley, as they longed for *greater freedom to pursue their personal initiative and ingenuity in developing innovative solutions for wider markets.*

Ever since then, tech pioneers have arrived in the Valley on pilgrimages from around the world where they bonded over the magical potential to commercialize digital innovations, as reported in Dr Saxenian's iconic book, *The New Argonauts.*[107] They earned accolades as students in local universities and won coveted roles on management teams. Because

---

[107] Saxenian, A.. (2007). The new Argonauts: Regional advantage in a global economy. Harvard University Press.

Silicon Valley tech startups were peppered with founders from Asia, subsequent ventures launched by those alumni back in their homelands attracted investments not only from the Asian diaspora but also from America. The venture-backed startups in Asia replicated the successes in the Valley. Voila! Successful global investing collaborations in the tech startup arena are not rocket science, but logical and repeatable.

By 2007, enough African tech-savvy youth had arrived in Silicon Valley to reach a tipping point of influence. Young African students attending Stanford organized and hosted that university's first African Business Forum to connect innovators, entrepreneurs, and investors.[108] The organizer who invited me to speak at that first Forum even helped me find a place on campus to stay.

His name was Irungu Nyakera, an engineering undergraduate scholarship student from Kenya. Orphaned as a youngster and raised by his grandmother, Irungu managed to use personal funds to co-host that Business Forum at Stanford with fellow African students. Such was his passion for the development of his homeland. Upon graduation, his first job was with Citibank in the UK, but when the global finance industry melted, he returned to Kenya.

There, he became the Managing Director of Kenya's largest private equity investing firm. We stayed in touch, and I relied on his introduction to a broker who helped me learn how to invest in Nairobi's public stock market, while its tech sector was emerging. Irungu was later appointed the nation's youngest Transportation Secretary, where he led the construction of a railroad connecting products to ports. As interim Chairperson of the Kenya Medical Supply Authority (KEMSA), he helped it

---

[108]Global Business School Network. (2022, April 16). *14th Annual Stanford Africa business forum: African innovation shaping the global future.* https://gbsn.org/events/14th-annual-stanford-africa-business-forum-african-innovation-shaping-the-global-future/#:~:text=This%20year%20marks%20the%2015th,Nyakera%20and%20Kwame%20Ansong%2DDwamena

improve its supply chain metrics. He recently graduated with his Executive MBA from Oxford's Exeter College.[109]

Irungu is one example of how the African diaspora builds American credibility, relationships, and networks to eventually establish new industries, as Asia's argonauts did decades earlier. The founders of Taiwan's TSMC, for example, returned home after building their CVs in the US, and now their advanced microchip production capabilities rank among the world's most vital tech. Trust like this is not built overnight, but investors can leverage learnings from those who have been at it longer.

A longer-term perspective that investors in Africa should recall from SV's example is that the Valley's growth to affluence was a series of booms and busts. An overinvestment in fiber-optic startups and infrastructure led to a massive rout in the late 1990s that erased approximately $2 trillion in market value. Y2K fears caused another boom-bust cycle, as did a biotech feeding frenzy that popped along with the rest of the internet investing bubble in 2002. But tech hub roots have proven tenacious and highly valued.

Entrepreneurs and investors come to Silicon Valley from around the world to meet, and one of their favorite places to come is Y Combinator. On its website, investors can explore YC's directory of the 5,000+ companies in which it has invested since 2005. This portfolio of startups is now valued at over $600B.[110] YC fully leverages technology to offer a level playing field to tech innovators, regardless of origin, and to augment in-person, real-time interfaces. Though YC was earlier to invest in African startups than most American investors, they are still novices there in some ways, so they listen and learn from experienced local investors, preferring to co-invest with more seasoned local investors.

During Africa's first startup investing spike in 2021-2022, YC made at least three deals, valued at over $100,000 per month, adding approximately 80

---

[109] Irungu Nyakera. LinkedIn. https://www.linkedin.com/in/irungu-nyakera-292a3b4/?originalSubdomain=ke

[110] https://www.ycombinator.com/

to their total. Their investments are in many of Africa's first seed-stage fintech startups, including Africa's first billion-dollar tech unicorns. These Silicon Valley investments also demonstrate the credibility that Africa's own tech hubs are gaining, as such investors value emerging entrepreneurs from Cairo to Nairobi, to Dakar and Lagos. The graph of "Top investors in Africa" that year shows how these Funds invested in Chapter 7, in the discussion about Seed-Stage Strategies.

Other veteran tech investors are looking globally for great startup teams targeting the next big market development opportunities, including in Africa. For some investors, standing on the shoulders of African fund managers is a shortcut strategy to success. How have investors new to the continent mitigated their risks enough to become confident about investing in startups? And, on the other side of this coin, how did local African investors feel about the sudden influx of capital in 2021-2023, and its corresponding influence from abroad? As an American living near Silicon Valley and also being LoftyInc Capital's only non-African co-founder, I can address both questions.

Investors who control capital flows often believe in the Golden Rule of investing: "He who has the gold, rules." When founders are young, African, and starting their first ventures, they usually have no idea how much value they should attribute to their venture's intellectual property, market traction, and "sweat equity." Nor do they know the downstream impact of investment terms like "favored nation," "preferential rights," and "first rights of refusal." But most investors do. This double asymmetry of both capital and expertise in favor of investors creates a high-risk environment for founders.

After two decades of learning how to work collaboratively with African entrepreneurs, I worried about them. Our team had already seen harm done to our founders by traditional investors, both African and foreign. Our primary concern during this feeding frenzy was actually that investors would overpay for positions at temporarily inflated prices.

Funding from Silicon Valley was particularly worrisome, where the dense concentration of investors competing for viable startup opportunities notoriously bids up venture buy-in prices. There, investors' fear of missing out on the next big win, or "FOMO," drives valuations at least as much as fundamentals. Investors accustomed to the Valley's pricing, who come into Africa's comparatively minuscule, fledgling startup marketplace, could easily flood it with funding that would suddenly inflate values beyond what their near-term opportunities might fulfill.

Valuation increases may be exciting in the short term, but in the longer term, when hard times come in the aftermath of a feeding frenzy, new capital may only be offered at lower valuations. This is reasonable, of course, but it has the psychological effect of reflecting disappointment on the performance of the startup. It is called a downround, which carries a stigma that is infamous for casting an otherwise high-potential venture into a valuation decline from which it may never recover.

But in this case, LoftyInc co-founder, Idris Bello, helped put my mind at ease. He and a Y Combinator decision-maker had talked. Because Y Combinator had noticed LoftyInc Capital was listed on the seed-stage capitalization tables of their first African investments that did well, they had begun to look for our name while considering new funding applicants. They had invested in numerous international ventures around the world over time and had learned to seek out savvy local investors to co-invest with. He assured Idris that they respected the LoftyInc Capital name and that his YC door was open for frank communications.

We were also learning from our African entrepreneurs that Y-combinator was not the only "smart-money" investor coming into our ecosystem. Other foreign investors had also been telling founders that they liked what they were seeing, but that they would only proceed if local investors shared their interest in the deal. This would ensure that both sides of the deal table would have a knowledgeable ally on the cap table.

During the Covid pandemic, African startups grew their customer bases rapidly. Everyone appreciated low-cost, timely access to healthcare, sports and entertainment, food deliveries, e-commerce, and financial transactions, mostly via mobile phones in Africa. Even after economies worldwide began contracting, Africa's tech sector remained robust—but only for a while.

Entrepreneurial Strategies

YC's decision not to dominate, but to collaborate with local investors in emerging markets, created a good-news, bad-news scenario. It was validating to have global investors appreciate the due diligence and valuations of local fund managers. The downside is that African fund managers like LoftyInc's were seriously under-capitalized, compared to YC, which created a dilemma for entrepreneurs. So YC might tell founders they would invest if a Fund like ours would join them, but we might have to tell them we'd love to invest, but had already invested all we had raised, so they were out of luck. The good news is that we were able to invest in about 55 ventures during that time, thanks to closing a new fund, backed by many African professionals. We even sold one position for almost $2 million, which we'd paid $200k for after only a few months. The post-Covid valuation whiplash brought the portfolio down, but these swings are to be expected over the short term until the sector gains stability, as Silicon Valley itself did.

Investment funds are often managed by finance and accounting people, who have not personally built their own startups, and foreign investors who seldom understand African markets. But LoftyInc Capital Management founders all launched our own African ventures and invested as angels prior to establishing our first VC fund, so our mindsets are entrepreneurial, and our strategies suit local markets. We understand the problems founders want to solve, the opportunities their innovations offer, and how people might embrace their solutions.

African founders who have pitched to foreign investors often express relief at not having to spend precious time explaining such basics, so they can jump into deeper levels of strategic insights faster. They sense that we will not slow down their growth pace by questioning every decision. They know our reputation for building startups and that our local networks run deep. This is why we have robust deal flow pipelines and always have more worthy ventures we'd like to back than we have capital to invest. Our deal flow always seems to surprise interviewers, most of whom tell us that they have never talked with an investment fund that has too much African deal flow.

VC funds generally raise capital for a blind pool of investments and only then seek deal flow, which can take years to build to robust levels. But in our case, as entrepreneurs ourselves, our management team consistently attracts great entrepreneurs through our shared grapevine and ongoing activities.

This is why well-capitalized funds often lack quality deal flow, while those of us who enjoy robust pipelines are forced to spend more time raising capital to invest than we spend vetting, funding, and nurturing our entrepreneurs. Why? Again, the answer is simple and logical.

The best-capitalized new VC Funds traditionally spin off from larger private equity firms. They raise ample startup capital from the firm's existing clients. New fund managers who came up through the ranks of large financial institutions were often analysts, more comfortable using financial data to rank ventures than inventing a product to launch a venture that solves a problem. Every month, they expect a salary and have never had to bootstrap a startup venture. They are usually risk-averse to a fault and must build their own networks from scratch to start generating deal flow, which can take years.

For all these reasons, well-capitalized venture funds prefer the M&A expansion-stage deals that large investors prefer, hence their abundance of capital. They also prefer to make decisions based on data-filled spreadsheets, which startups lack. Yet, the startup stage is where most African ventures typically find themselves. This is the main reason why high-potential teams in Africa fail to attract funding. Incongruently, very little development capital for Africa is structured for startups. It is another reason why LoftyInc has more deal flow than capital.

African fund managers like LoftyInc's have not only built their own ventures, but they also bootstrap their own VC firms. Having negotiated from the entrepreneur's side of the deal table changes everything. By the time entrepreneurial fund managers gain the courage and means to launch an Africa-facing VC fund, they have already managed their own angel investing portfolios and led due diligence teams. Their mindset is innovative, and they know the skill sets that startup teams must have to succeed, because they taught the programs in their own tech hubs and co-founded the ecosystem.

This is why some VC Funds have ample deal flow, know how to vet it, and can make timely decisions. Successful founders endorse entrepreneurial fund managers to the next round of high-potential founders because they are trusted not to harm fledgling ventures. Perhaps this is why, over time, as the funding source graphic above illustrates, the total of Africa-based investors grew slowly but steadily, eventually surpassing funding sourced from any other continent, just like in the tortoise and the hare parable.

During the 2000-2002 period, I learned that the IFC had followed a commercial bank and some local venture funds into backing a seed-stage venture fund in South Africa. It was launched and managed by another proactive South African woman, a former investment banker, with a PhD in Cell Biology and an MBA. Named The BioVentures Fund, it was Sub-Saharan Africa's first life sciences venture fund.[111] I met her through the IFC and went to South Africa to check out her fund, meeting with all the co-investors and founders.

Although she was not a seasoned entrepreneur, Heather's $15 million fledgling fund invested in eight ventures, including two with drug innovations that enabled strong exits. The most experienced founders in this portfolio told me that the manager's research and investment banking background had not prepared her to add value to their ventures as a Board Director. I did attempt to buy into the Fund at a discount or to co-manage it, but neither option was accepted. In the end, the overall fund returns were not deemed strong enough by its investors to warrant a second BioVentures fund. Some blamed the Fund's demise on its small size, which rendered it unable to support a large management team.

---

[111]Masum, H., & Singer, P. A. (2010). Venture capital on a shoestring: Bioventures' pioneering life sciences fund in South Africa. *BMC international health and human rights*, *10*, 1-8. https://www.ncbi.nlm.nih.gov/pmc/articles/PMC3001616/

Yet, the LoftyInc team launched an even smaller, $1M startup fund in 2018 that invested in a similarly sized portfolio and realized above top-tier returns within a couple of years. We've since raised subsequent small funds that also succeeded. Being entrepreneurs, our team did not take salaries during our first few years, which reduced costs and aligned incentives. Also, our experience in company building and angel investing fostered LoftyInc's investor returns. On the other hand, BioVentures should have benefited from South Africa's far more advanced financial, educational, and healthcare infrastructure. The evolving strength of pan-Africa's startup ecosystem certainly played a part in our success.

Seed-Stage Strategies

What investing strategies work well for Africa's seed-stage venture funds?

The greater the risk, the larger the portfolio should be. This diversification factor is the golden rule of portfolio management. It suits tech startups whether they are in a $100k personal portfolio of angel-staged startups or a multi-billion-dollar pension fund. Early stage, technology-driven startups face challenges in Africa that include poverty, talent, and ease of doing business. Accordingly, investors should spread their risk across a portfolio of as many high-quality ventures as possible.

This high-volume approach to seed-stage investing works for well-connected and respected investors in Africa's startup ecosystem. Many young visionaries are eager to build high-growth ventures, but foreign investors will have difficulty finding them rapidly enough to get in early. They will also have to compete for space in a hot round with investors who are already known and trusted by the best founders. This is why partnering with ethical, seasoned local investors who are deeply involved in Africa's startup ecosystem works better than an American-sized ego.

The great thing about investing at the seed stage, however, is that the ventures are still affordable, so first-round tickets are relatively inexpensive and engender founder loyalty. As time passes, valuations creep up—or down, giving investors a longer-term view of the entity's chances for success before making subsequent investments. At each decision point, investors can compare making a follow-on investment to making an initial investment in another venture. Investors not plugged into African entrepreneur pipelines may have trouble getting a seat at the deal table of the most promising founders.

Building a large portfolio diversifies investor risk across time, teams, and technologies, as well as stages, sectors, strategies and geographies; much like building a portfolio of bonds over time that are laddered across maturities, issuers, projects, and interest rates.

Because venture valuations grow rapidly after they reach breakeven, their investors have high appreciation potential. Another reason to invest at the seed stage is the greater availability of companies that truly need funding before their products generate robust revenues. More established firms have their choice of funding sources that you must compete with, reducing your upside value growth potential. Hence, fewer later stage companies will want to take your money, and more can self-finance their growth.

Investing early allows investors to diversify their portfolio with minimal funds. They can easily adjust if needed, gaining insights into which investments will thrive. By the time significant investment is required, they know where to focus for the best returns. At each stage, more of their portfolio is invested, but with correspondingly more certainty of success.

Investing via Funds

Unless you and your team have deep expertise, deal pipelines, and a large co-investing network, direct investing may not be your best option. Even if you are determined to focus full-time for years to build these and to invest in the travel and events required to attain these, you will learn faster looking over the shoulder of more experienced Fund Managers.

You can invest indirectly, via Venture Capital firms that periodically launch new VC Funds and operate the entire life cycle of their Fund(s). Fund investments leverage the long-term commitments of others who are totally dedicated to these functions and have achieved respected track records. By structuring your investment under the more experienced and hands-on management of a Fund's General Partners, you become a Limited Partner.

Top investors in Africa in 2021-2022, by number of $100k+ deals

For more, visit **thebigdeal.substack.com** by Max Cuvellier & Maxime Bayen

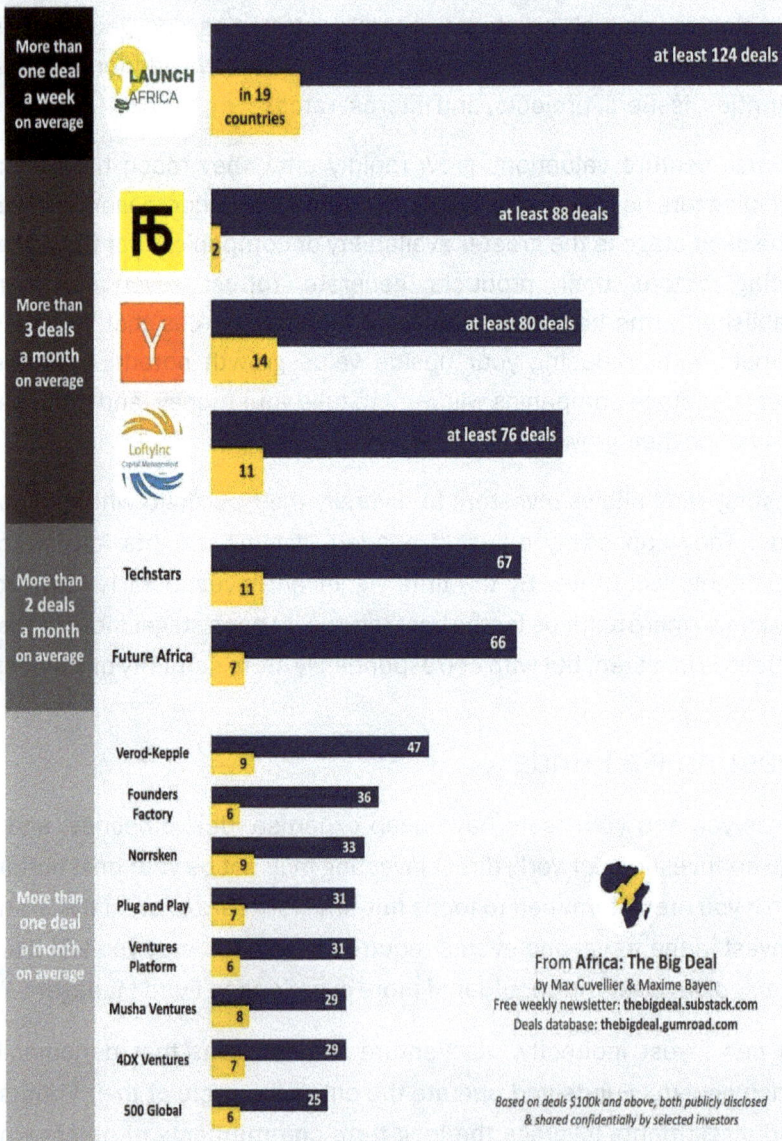

Category	Investor	Deals
More than one deal a week on average	LAUNCH AFRICA (in 19 countries)	at least 124 deals
More than 3 deals a month on average	F6 (2)	at least 88 deals
	Y (14)	at least 80 deals
	LoftyInc Capital Management (11)	at least 76 deals
More than 2 deals a month on average	Techstars (11)	67
	Future Africa (7)	66
More than one deal a month on average	Verod-Kepple (9)	47
	Founders Factory (6)	36
	Norrsken (9)	33
	Plug and Play (7)	31
	Ventures Platform (6)	31
	Musha Ventures (8)	29
	4DX Ventures (7)	29
	500 Global (6)	25

From **Africa: The Big Deal**
by Max Cuvellier & Maxime Bayen
Free weekly newsletter: thebigdeal.substack.com
Deals database: thebigdeal.gumroad.com

Based on deals $100k and above, both publicly disclosed & shared confidentially by selected investors

This LP/GP structure is preferred for its pass-through of profits that avoid double taxation and tees up losses to offset your gains from other investments in your portfolio. It also protects LPs from liability– as long as they leave management decisions to the Fund Managers. If LPs usurp any management roles or decision-making responsibilities, they lose their LP status and expose themselves to litigation. This may come from the other LPs who all entrusted their investments to the GPs as per their LP Agreement when they subscribed to the Fund.

The GPs manage quality deal flow pipelines, analysis, deal-making, mentoring, venture maturation, and eventual exits, after which you will realize distributions, less fund management fees and the carried interest on profits.

Refocusing back on The Big Deal data to contextualize successful strategies, the "Top investors in Africa" graphic shows which investors participated most often in Africa's tech startup investing rounds during the first three years of its rapid funding growth. At least 1,500 investors were involved in at least one deal in Africa during this time, excluding angel investors, which could add thousands more to this startup village. However, VC funds received top billing as representative consolidators.

Launch Africa features large, sitting at the top of this ranking. Though it was investing from its Ventures Fund 1, it had raised $36 million within 18 months, with investments from 238 retail and institutional investors in 40 countries. Interestingly, this tour de force of capital raising did not include one DFI. Launch Africa's limited partners ranged from African angel investors to a family office in Germany, as well as global foundations and corporations. The firm was founded in 2020 by South Africans Zachariah George and Janade du Plessis, who have pioneered early-stage venture capital in Africa since 2014. The firm's average check size was between $250,000 and $300,000, and most were one-time checks.[112]

---

[112] https://www.launchafrica.vc

Flat6Labs, a seed fund that emerged from Jordan, is the only one among these active investors to focus exclusively on one region, Northern Africa (2/3 in Egypt and 1/3 in Tunisia). All the others made investments in at least three different African regions during the period.[113]

The Silicon Valley-based accelerator-cum-investor **Y Combinator**, which has invested on the continent since 2012, tapped its diverse LP base to grow its presence in Africa in 2021-2022. In 2022, 66% of its investments focused on Nigeria, versus 38% in 2021.[114]

Photo: Marsha Wulff, Michael Oluwagbemi, Idris Bello, from LoftyInc Archives

LoftyInc[115] ranked fourth out of the top fourteen Funds, having made more than three $100k+ investments a month on average during the period, almost half of which were in Nigeria, which is home base for most of our team.[116] We were investing from our Afropreneurs Fund 3. Its investor base was 80% African angels, family offices, and professionals. One of the largest investments among them was an SPV that contributed a total of over $700k. This was aggregated by Tomie Balogun from her African investment club members. This SPV was our new Fund's largest investor until a last-minute addition from a Silicon Valley tech firm and a South African fund of funds. We had no DFI backing.

---

[113] https://www.flat6labs.com

[114] https://www.ycombinator.com

[115] https://loftyinc.vc

[116] https://thebigdeal.substack.com/p/topinvestors

For context, our prior fund, Afropreneurs Fund 2, raised just over $1 million, which was not enough capital to pay salaries, as the industry norm of 2% management fees on $1 million yields $20,000 a year, yet it required a huge investment of our personal time and resources. Fortunately, this Fund returned over three times its investment within two years to investors by selling its Flutterwave holdings to a Flutterwave board member. In Fund 3, our first exit offer came after only six months of holding the startup. As before, a portfolio company's board member made an offer; it was approximately 12 times the price we had paid, so we accepted a partial exit and promptly reinvested into another venture we were familiar with. These were opportune events that set up both funds for top-tier returns, but they only succeeded because we leveraged entrepreneurial investing strategies and mindsets.

Soon, we were fully invested and out of capital again. But African founders continued to innovate, and they each had a narrow window of opportunity to commercialize their innovations before the window closed.

The "Top Investors" graphic above highlights how a diverse array of investors, from local angel groups to international venture capital firms, have actively participated in Africa's burgeoning tech startup scene. This multitude of investors not only provides vital capital but also brings varied expertise, opportunities, and networks, further accelerating the growth and success of these startups. As we examined the evolution and impact of these investments over the years, it became clear that the strategic deployment of capital at multiple stages is crucial to success. Early investments lay the foundation, while subsequent funding rounds provide the necessary boost to scale and achieve significant milestones. But how might the ecosystem support a steadier flow of capital as startups mature?

Funding the Gap Strategies

The graphic below illustrates the typical progression of startups as they grow through various financing stages.

Venture Valuations Relative to Time and Revenues

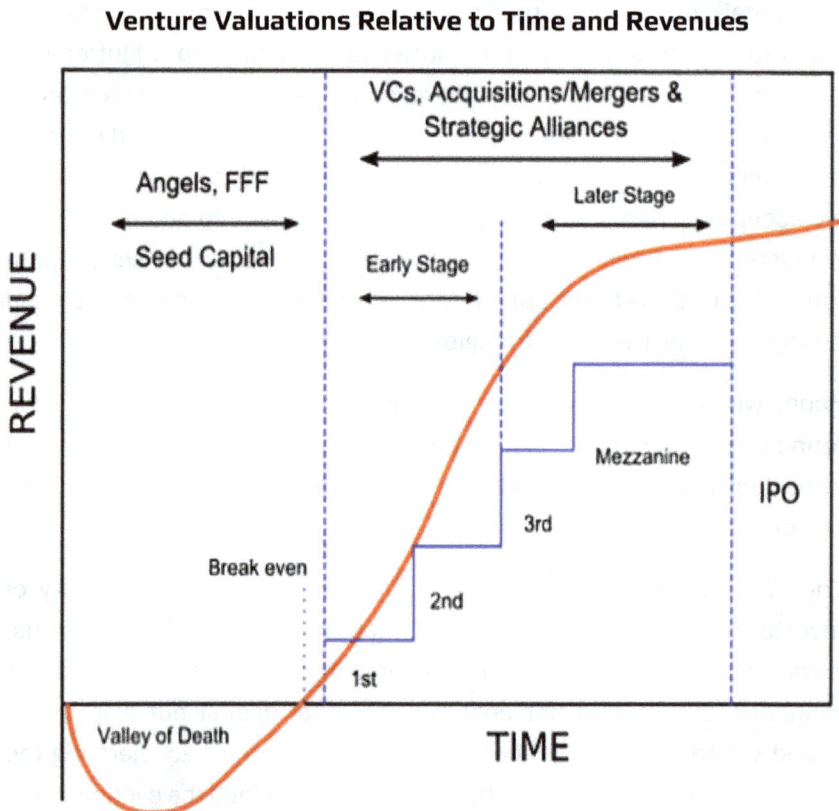

Startups: Innovations, Survival and Investment.
Source: Nuthalapati, Chandra 2022/06/28

America's innovation centers started to thrive after seed-stage VC Funds emerged to fund the gap between the angel stage and the 2nd VC round, which we call a B-round. This is what is happening now in Africa. Before that, the gap between grant funding and DFI or commercial bank funding traditionally was a huge Valley of Death. This "Missing Middle" stubbornly persisted for decades, due to the lack of a robust middle class to privately seed fund startup ventures, and because development funders resisted the flexible financing structures that suit pre-profit startups.

Although tens of thousands of Africa's "business angel" investors have organized themselves to fill the pre-seed stage part of this void, another gap remains. This unmet need in Africa's ecosystem is why LoftyInc pioneered Africa's seed-stage venture funds. We help founding teams formalize corporate processes and procedures as their markets, operations, and workforce expand to meet the challenges of rapid growth.

This transition demands adaptive investor leadership and mindsets. It requires multiple funding stages that become seamless to the founder teams, with far too many vital problems to spend all their time raising capital. If they lose focus, their innovations lose ground, and their ventures lose value, increasing the risks of not securing their next capital infusion. Until our ecosystem refines this level of collaboration, founders have to choose between slowing growth to organic levels or wasting limited resources on constant capital raising.

This startup funding gap offers a window of opportunity for entrepreneurial investment banking professionals to expand their expertise on the continent. Well-established corporations often seek innovations that add value to their global markets. They build "war chests" specifically to fund vibrant tech startups with opportune innovations.

At this point in Africa's tech ecosystem development, Paris-headquartered team of tech investors deserves acclaim for their leadership to help African startups bridge their funding gaps. In February 2024, Partech General Partners, Tidjane Deme and Cyril Collon, closed on the largest fund ever to focus on African startups.[117] Their new $300 million fund strategy is to select 20 African companies that are almost

---

[117] Keenan, S. (2024, February 19). *Partech's historic $300M fund offers a new era for African tech startups.* People of Color in Tech. https://peopleofcolorintech.com/articles/partechs-historic-300m-fund-offers-a-new-era-for-african-tech-startups/

ready for their first institutional round and support them through the following funding stages to achieve sustained growth.[118]

Strategies such as this leverage learnings from 2021-23, when promising startups that attracted initial seed-stage investment were forced to shutter their doors through no fault of their own. Due to the pandemic's economic fallout, they had not yet reached revenue levels that supported internally funded growth, nor were investors available to capitalize on continued growth through subsequent seed and A rounds of growth. Partech Fund managers designed their fund to be large enough to accommodate Private Equity's preferred big tickets by funding tech startups from seed stage through institutional rounds, financing Africa's tech startups to fulfill their potential.

How did Partech's management team know the need well enough to structure this solution? It is co-led by an African argonaut. Tidjane Dème grew up in Senegal before migrating to France and England for advanced degrees. He built his tech career expertise in France and with Cap Gemini, a Silicon Valley startup. Back on his home turf in Dakar, Tidjane was an entrepreneur, founding and managing digitization projects for the Senegalese military and government agencies, until Google Access hired him to manage local projects and partnering for them.

Tidjane's Google team invested in wholesale fiber networks via shared infrastructure models that lowered costs for ISPs and operators, enabling broadband access.[119,120] Although it is doubtful that an exclusively America-born team would have known how to innovate and implement workarounds like these, problem-solving like this comes naturally for African argonauts.

One of the many French funding allocators who have demonstrated early leadership in embracing novel strategies for global startup investing is

---

[118] Partech. (2024, February 18). Partech Africa II fund reaches final close at hard cap above $300 million, expands team and portfolio. https://partechpartners.com/news/partech-africa-ii-fund-reaches-final-close-at-hard-cap-above-300-million-expands-team-and-portfolio

[119] Dème, T. Partech Partners. https://partechpartners.com/team/tidjane-deme

[120] Dème, T. LinkedIn. https://www.linkedin.com/in/tidjanedeme/

Bpifrance, which has leveraged tools like its Fund of Funds to back Africa's Partech team.[121] Such proactive development funders have learned to build portfolios of startup funds, which diversify their risks across teams, geographies and sectors.

Some African startup funds, such as LoftyInc, are evolving to finance multiple rounds of funding. These are larger funds structured to meet the needs of their best startup ventures as they mature into corporations. This multi-stage investing minimizes the time that startup management has to spend raising follow-on rounds of funding. It also reduces the pressure on seed fund managers to provide investor exits before portfolio companies reach institutional levels.

Bridging funding gaps reduces risks for founders and funders alike. But serious challenges remain that threaten the viability of the most well-intentioned and successful fund managers, as we will see in "What's Not Working."

The Founder/Funder Dance

Successful alliances are created by people who learn to dance well together, each offering the other enough space to add value, and appreciating when one does. The Founder/Funder Dance is like a Tango that balances consideration with tension. The best investors once were where their founders now are: They, too, have made tough choices that lacked enough hard data to be certain, so they should have wisdom to offer an astute founder. But funders must remain humble enough to remember that dynamics, markets, and data have changed. This humility is even more important for non-African investors or for any funders who have never launched a product or built a company. Investors must not believe that having capital to invest inherently imbues them with wisdom. Yet, funders do have a right to expect the founder to improve upon the past, which is why one invests in the first place.

---

[121] Launch Base Africa. (2025, February 13). *France's biggest startup backer, BPIFrance, deepens ties with African tech*. Bpifrance backs African Tech

Founders must concede that their ideas and ideals mean little without efficient execution. They must work diligently, be honest about the challenges they face, and remain open to advice; yet entrepreneurs need not automatically defer to investors who lack the founder's insights.

I have often seen Nigerian founders more comfortable standing up for their vision than Kenyans, which I attribute to historic and cultural influences. Investors must be aware of these differences and, in some cases, must specifically give permission to people who are overly shy about sharing their insights. In any case, good people do not always agree, but mutual respect should be expected and maintained.

In the end, it is the founding team and their determination that add value. This means the investor must respect their leadership and defer to it... or be prepared to burn down and replace everything they have built thus far, which is a riskier strategy. Deciding to usurp power from the team in which you invested indicates you probably made a mistake by investing. The cardinal rule of investing is to never invest in a startup team that knows less about attaining its goals than you do.

As the preceding sections explained, investors can and must mitigate obvious risks before investing. These strategies work. Funders must discern which founders share their values, goals, and ethics: they require experience, insights, and networks to do so. Investors select sectors with growth opportunities they believe have strong profit and purpose potential and then choose founders with ample expertise in those areas to offer fresh innovations and insights, thus adding value. Above all, investors must not fund a startup venture unless they trust the founders. This trust need not be blind; it can, and should, be built upon several potential validation points.

In summary, founders will have the cultural background, acumen, and credentials that confirm a high level of sector competence. Entrepreneurs should also have attracted a foundational team that respects, enjoys, and challenges each other. This interaction makes or breaks a company. The founder should have assembled a stellar set of advisors who respect the entrepreneur and their vision. These advisors must have relevant and diverse skills, perspectives, and suitable backgrounds so that decisions will be made only after a healthy level of competent debate. This will reduce the risk of their strategies being blindsided by aspects of the market they had not considered.

Most of all, investors must respect the founder's motives and be confident that the founder's passion for success is greater than the challenges that will be faced.

A well-structured agreement is also part of the Funding Tango, as it ensures that both sides will share the loss if the venture fails and will also benefit from its success. Deal terms must not protect the investor at the expense of the founder, which is usually how things tilt because of the asymmetry of information and investing experience in favor of investors. The reverse is seldom an issue in the case of startup investing, as investors are deemed to hold the power until the ink is dry. The one who holds the gold may rule, but investor egos must not manacle founders with micro-management, undermining the team's power to achieve its goals.

When locusts descend, hurricane gales blow, and the sky falls, there will not be time for detailed updates and long-winded debates. Founders must maintain the power to pivot quickly to manage dangers, for better or worse. Petty levers of control put into place by early investors, such as favored nation status and confidential investment terms, only warn off follow-on investors and hobble otherwise able racehorses, preventing them from running free and winning the prize. Investors who insist on wresting control away from founders are more likely to destroy value than create it... or even preserve it.

Founder/Funder Dance Rules:

1. If you feel your investment terms must be held in confidence, then you should consider changing them–they are probably going to undermine growth
2. If you do not trust the entrepreneur to make the best possible decisions, then do not invest; your fears will constrain their growth, and

3. If you invest, do everything you can to help your entrepreneur get what they need to progress. Make introductions, invite them to talk openly with you, and help them raise growth capital and find strategic partners.

Wrap-Up: What's Working? Courageous Capital

In "What's Working," we've seen the historic value of market-creating innovations and circular migrations. We've met African pioneers of tech infrastructure, who made it possible for entrepreneurs to build tech hubs for local and pan-African collaborations. It introduced Africans who reinvested their profits as angel investors into the next round of emerging tech entrepreneurs. Their virtuous cycle has repeated its circle multiple times, sustaining and scaling its own growth.

Seasoned global investors usually wait until they see indigenous entrepreneurs return to their homeland to build businesses and reinvest in those of the next generation. Africans have completed these pilot-and-repeat stages, gaining expertise and scale. These first-in-class entrepreneur-investors honed strategies that fit the needs of African startups, further reducing investor risks, while adding value to eventual rewards.

As an American investor in Africa, I have learned that being humble reduces the risk of investing mistakes. Being curious enough to ask, listen, and learn enhances insights, trust, and opportunities. As we and our teams add value, we mitigate risks and improve outcomes. These are strategies that are working.

Success Strategies

Founders: Select founders who are PASSIONATE about solving a big problem for people they love. They must have actively prepared themselves to deliver the best possible solutions via education, travel, experience, etc.

The entrepreneurs you choose for your portfolio must already have mentors with best-in-class insights into specialty areas that matter most; they must have a team that is already working on the venture without being paid, while going to school full-time, and working another job or two, yet are primed to start working 24/7 the minute the venture has the funding.

Teams: Invest in diversity and ensure that founding teams have authentic African founders, not just wannabe Africans or expats living in Africa, but people who share the heart, soul, aspirations, and language of Africans. Management must understand pigeon dialects, so they do not miss communication clues; they must feel danger in their bones and know how to laugh their way to safety; and they must have vast local networks of diverse information sources that arm their entrepreneur with information that could ruin their venture.

Founders must select team members who have different skills, so they think differently. They should have different genders, ages, religions, and ethnic backgrounds, so they approach problem-solving from various perspectives. This is essential for the ventures to avoid being blindsided. This is the kind of diversity that reduces risks.

Investors: Funders must resist the lure of micro-managing entrepreneurs, which is the focus of Part 3.

The Harambean Entrepreneur Alliance[122]
Fortune Favors the Bold

Okendo Lewis-Gale founded an alliance of African entrepreneurs in 2008 as "a US-based business network for African entrepreneurs that provides funding, university scholarships and a support ecosystem."[123] Its name is Harambe—Swahili for working together towards a common purpose, and Okendo's approach is to aggregate knowledge, connections, and capital within the Alliance so that Harambeans can build Africa's future.

---

[122] https://en.wikipedia.org/wiki/Harambe_Entrepreneur_Alliance

[123] https://www.chandlerfoundation.org/social-investor/raising-african-unicorns

It was this alliance that brought E and Idris together, and it has encouraged them on their journey as collaborative founders and funders through their cycles of success.

This is what Okendo wrote in his Chairman's Introduction to the alliance's 2025 edition of The Harambean Way.[124] I include it here, as it encapsulates "What's Working" in Africa's startup ecosystem.

"Best known in Latin, *Fortuna Audentes Iuvat,* these words first summoned the courage of ancient Greek warriors, then stirred the hearts of Roman legions. But on a hopeful spring day, April 19, 2008, they took on new meaning.

"That day, beneath the quiet majesty of Mount Washington, 32 young African visionaries, the first Harambeans, gathered to forge a different kind of legacy. Not one of conquest, but of collaboration. Not one of dominion, but of daring. Bound by a collective oath "to work together as one," we chose to believe "the Africa our generation desires can be won."

"The phrase is often translated simply: Fortune favors the bold. But in our inaugural address, we turned to a deeper truth hidden in the Latin: Fortune favors the "audentes," *the audacious*, those who dare to act. We reflected then, as we do now, on a truth echoed across history: that progress is rarely inherited, it is built. And that sometimes, sheer audacity is what makes the improbable inevitable.

"Eighteen years later, that founding impulse has not faded; it is flourishing. From 32 Harambeans, we are now over 400 strong. And along the way, we have learned a deeper truth: that courage is not innate; it is ignited. It does not arise in isolation, but in community. Like a standing ovation, it begins with one bold step and grows as others rise in turn.

"*Harambeans do not discover bravery alone. We awaken it in each other.*

"This fourth edition of The Harambean Way bears witness to that awakening. Within its pages, you'll encounter the spirit of the audentes;

---

[124] https://www.harambeans.com/publications/

those who are transforming bold dreams into enduring impact across Africa:

- You'll meet Arjun Parameswaran H'24 and Leana de Beer H'25, who are dismantling the notion that insurance and education are reserved for the few.
- You'll be inspired by Hilda Moraa H'23 and Tesh Mbaabu H'20, who turned conflict into collaboration, modeling the very unity we champion at our Global Summit.
- You'll learn how Iyinoluwa Aboyeji H'10 and Melvin Lubega H'16, having built some of Africa's most successful ventures, are now *moving from founders to funders, recycling their wealth and wisdom to uplift the next generation of builders.*

"These stories are not exceptions. They are the natural harvest of a culture rooted in shared courage and sustained conviction.

"As new storms gather on the horizon, it is this same courage - shared, steady, and rising -that gives me confidence. Confidence that we, as an Alliance, will continue the work we began on that hopeful spring day: to build a peaceful and prosperous Africa.

"Anchored ever deeper in our shared conviction that, "yet in the end, the Africa our generation desires can be won. *For in the end, as in our beginning, Fortune favors those who dare to act."*
By Okendo Lewis Gayle, founder of The Harambe Entrepreneurs Alliance.

Photo: Idris signed the Harambeans Declaration in 2011
Source: Idris Bello

PART THREE

What's Not Working?

8. Fearful Funders

The Fear Factor

While watching wildebeests cross a Tanzanian river, a newborn calf clambered out near our safari jeep, shivering and stunned. When a pregnant female nuzzled him, he tried to nurse, but she recoiled. They looked back at the river and waited together until reluctantly re-entering the water.

The river was swollen from recent rains, making the crossing a monumental effort, yet they eventually emerged on the far side, where a female met them. The calf was only allowed to nurse briefly before it again merged with the herd coming our way. I feared the newborn would not survive another crossing without rest or food.

I focused intently to keep the calf and two females in sight. As they reached midstream, the current intensified, and the mother's resolve faltered. She fell behind and hesitated in the deep water, feeling the river's full force. Abruptly, she turned back to the shore she had just left.

Confusion ensued as the calf and the pregnant female realized the mother had left them again and tried to pause as the herd surged forward en masse, submerging them until the current carried them downstream. Driven by their will to live, they finally climbed out of the river, exhausted from three crossings in an hour. Onshore, they waited, hoping the calf's mother would appear, but in vain.

The pregnant female then soon thundered over a rise, but the calf watched her go, looked back once more, and then sadly locked eyes with me for a moment. Vultures watched him from above, and two more frail newborns rested on the ground nearby, ignored by the herd. My heart ached for the lonely calf, wondering about his fate.

Would he give up, or would he find protection within the herd?

In my final glimpse of the calf as our guide drove away, the calf gathered his remaining strength, dug his hooves into the sand, and sprinted up the hillside after his herd.

Photo: Wildebeest calf
Source: Author Archives

Such are the decisions that shape survival each day as life coexists closely with death in tight, iterative cycles. Every year, in ways like this, the Great Serengeti Migration illustrates how circular migrations strengthen herds.

It is how nature innovates survival solutions that hack challenges like climate change, overpopulation, and predation.

Every day, we too choose between courage and fear to guide us.

"In today's world, paradoxically, it is the boldest action that is often the safest. Remaining where you are in a world that is changing so rapidly is, in fact, the most dangerous of all places to be."
—Hakeem Belo-Osagie,
Chairman of Metis Capital Partners.[125]

---

[125] Metis Capital. https://www.metiscapitalpartnersltd.com/about

Unreasonable Fear

Although Africa is an emerging market, most funding earmarked for African development never transfers into the hands of its startup entrepreneurs. However, a vast ecosystem of intermediaries is paid well to educate, screen, oversee, monitor, research, convene, advise, and report on Africa's potential founders and funders. In the beginning years, such tactics were accepted, but if intermediaries do what they are paid to do, at some point, sufficient capacity should exist for investors to invest. And the way investors do it reflects whether they are guided by insights or by fear.

In the early 2000s, the World Bank's IFC began inviting me to their annual investor summit in Washington, D.C. At my first meeting, the head of Africa welcomed attendees to bring their team projects. The IFC had annual allocations for Africa, but so few companies were qualified that his group was never able to draw down its full funding allotment. I thought this was remarkable, as I couldn't spend a day in Africa without engaging with an aspiring entrepreneur.

My hopes of finding funding for them soared, so I thought through the list of African-led projects I had researched and deemed investment-worthy. But when I approached the non-African head of IFC Africa, saying I knew startups that had modest needs but great potential, he looked doubtful. I asked him to explain his team's preferred investment parameters so I could prioritize which of my deal flow options to share with them.

For starters, he explained, IFC investments were typically structured as loans of $20M or more, and these should not exceed 30% of the round. This required investees to raise over $60M, which implied companies should be worth over $200M and earning enough revenues to maintain their growth while paying several million USD per year for interest, plus principal repayments. This was amazing! Did he not know that Africa was mostly frontier markets? Why was his team not focused on what startup entrepreneurs needed to get established?

None of the exciting ventures on my Africa list, which were from its most advanced regions, were even close to being eligible. They were ready for $100k-200k, and perhaps $10M over the next few years of growth, but most could become self-sustaining on less. If anyone "invested" much more at this stage, it would surely be wasted. Africa had startups galore that did not need grants or big loans, but they did need seed capital to reach profitability. This dearth of appropriate funding for the best African entrepreneurs helped me realize why financing the "missing middle" persists as a barrier to entrepreneurs who could build their economies.

On the cover of the IFC's annual report, I read that the IFC's courageous mandate was to finance frontier development projects that commercial funders would not yet consider. However, the IFC's investment strategies did not match this intent. If the IFC could not take investment risks, why did they claim to finance frontier market development? But who was I to challenge the wisdom of an institution with a multi-billion-dollar annual budget and decades of experience?

In 1997, I entered Africa to work on a $100M joint venture between a multi-billion-dollar US corporation listed on the NYSE and a South African parastatal. It did not require IFC financing. Five years later, I'd worked with Africa's tech-driven startups enough to know that these could be the engines of African growth, but that they'd not be using IFC funding either. So, who needed development funding structured like this?

As mentioned previously, the IFC invested in Mo Ibrahim's Celtel company, which brought mobile phone capacity to Africa. It was the IFC's best investment to date. They wished they could have invested more in Celtel or could find more deals like it. Mo had already succeeded as a UK entrepreneur, so he was able to self-fund the startup stage of his venture in Africa, but most aspiring African argonauts cannot.

Mo was the IFC's ideal African entrepreneur, but was the IFC's strategy ideal for developing Africa? How many more Celtel-caliber successes might Africans build if the IFC also invested small amounts at the seed stage? This would eventually fill a pipeline of later-stage corporations, which the IFC could finance as it prefers. It would take some courage and a sliver of their annual budget, but it would help the IFC achieve its development goals. So, why not invest in startups? The consistent answer from reliable sources is fear. Fear of what?

Multilateral funders fear reputational damage from "bad press" for investments that link them to unsavory characters or issues. This fear drives the strategies and procedures that undermine startups. Money laundering fears, for instance, can drive an unreasonable level of personal disclosures required of any co-investors in a startup. The costs and time to gather, authenticate, and report AML dwarfs the small amounts invested. This problem could be resolved by reasonable people who simply agree on a minimum investment size, below which extraordinary AML efforts need not be made. So why not?

Cumbersome AML/KYC reporting may have worked during the industrial age, when manufacturers lumbered along at the speed of molasses in winter. Africa today, however, is innovating tech-based solutions that leapfrog barriers at the speed of the internet. Investors must adapt or become irrelevant.

Feeling Overwhelmed

Charities flood our emotions with dire predictions and urgent emergencies to attract donations, and news media choose sensationalized visuals that attract viewers. These strategies leave people feeling fearful, futile, and frustrated. This book aims to diminish that burden when it relates to Africa.

Although tragic news may sell, the rest of the story is often more comforting, enlightening, and inspiring. More African women are earning advanced degrees than are being kidnapped by terrorists. Tech-savvy African youth who protested against police harassment are now celebrating legislation that enhances their startup ventures. Success stories encourage us; they inspire confidence, hope, and the will to move forward.

I have a theory that American pessimism often stems from caring people who have been encouraged to believe that solving all the world's problems is on them. They feel responsible and guilty. Fortunately, most of these fears can be put to rest when they learn about the programs and strategies that other caring, competent people are already deploying to solve many issues.

For instance, my family and friends thoughtfully expressed their deep concern to me about how hard a time Africans must be having during Covid. However, as I watched the situation in Africa closely, via family weddings, holidays, childbirths, and business reports, I saw primarily positive news reflecting personal competence, resilience, and optimism.

Since LoftyInc VC Funds invest in tech startups that use digital platforms, they experienced an initial growth spurt during the Covid pandemic, as demand increased for their essential products and services.

When I asked my African friends about their personal welfare, they would shrug and say that Covid was just one more pandemic on top of the many others they manage daily. They must already be vigilant about malaria from mosquitoes, TB from the air, cholera from contaminated water, and typhoid from contaminated meat. Getting internet service and electricity were more front of mind, as were currency values and inflation. What entrepreneurs most needed remained the same... investments for growth.

Truthfully, the most overwhelmed people I spoke with during Covid were not busy Africans; they were lonely Americans. Entrepreneurial Africans believe they already know how to solve many challenges in ways that massive markets will embrace. They are busy innovating affordable and accessible solutions and seeking risk capital to scale them up for the impact they could create.

Meanwhile, Americans wish they could do more to help Africans. What pieces are missing from this puzzle? Why are concerned Americans not investing in African problem solvers?

At my granddaughter's graduation, the keynote speaker reminisced about a valuable lesson she learned during her early years teaching political science. Every year, she assigned her students to write a report about something wrong in the world that concerned them. Eventually, she dreaded reading those reports because they left her feeling overwhelmed by the world's burdens.

So, she changed the assignment, asking each student to share what was being done to alleviate an issue they cared about deeply. Now, she looks forward to reading those reports about what others are doing to improve the world. This story struck a chord within me because I, too, have felt this.

I dread meeting people who are so burdened by negative issues that they feel consumed by frustration and fear. These feelings sap their energy, so they cannot even comprehend that anyone is actually solving problems. When such people learn that my team and I invest in African tech startup ventures, they only hear "Africa" and start reciting a litany of the continent's burdens: diseases, hunger, corruption, climate change, etc.

They want to inform me and warn me, as if I must surely be totally unaware of all the challenges we will face, otherwise we would not even try! Just...like...them! It is as if they feel so personally overwhelmed by Africa's challenges that they KNOW I am wasting my time. They shut out the facts we share about the entrepreneurs we know, the progress we've already made, and the successes we have already enjoyed. They do not want to learn anything that diminishes their terrifying ideology.

I do understand some of this because I have felt overwhelmed, too. But they are overlooking one important fact—one I learned a decade ago in Uganda.

The Victoria Nile's lush delta ecosystem enthralled me during a river safari with my husband. It was not my first visit to this scenic location, but it was my longest, as I usually spent most of my time in Uganda working with a friend on his agriculture processing ventures.

The prior day, we'd seen a veritable smorgasbord of Africa's most stunning animal specimens. They lined up along the shoreline: crocodile, giraffe, elephant, rhino, buffalo, and kudu, as if solely for our viewing pleasure. In the water, dozens of healthy hippo pods dozed, spaced so that the minute one left our sight, the next appeared.

Today, we were further downriver from the falls on a calm lake, listening to young DR Congo fishermen in their one-log boats singing lazy tunes in the morning mist. I was scanning the shoreline intently for an elusive spoon-billed stork, but instead, I saw blue plastic strips tied onto Lorax-like sisal plants demarking a long line across an otherwise pristine marsh.

"It is for the pipeline the Chinese are building from the oil fields to the refinery," our guide explained. I was horrified that this idyllic setting, situated between Murchison Falls National Park and Lake Albert, was endangered, vulnerable to imminent damage from construction and pollution from spilled crude oil. This news totally shifted me into white savior mode. Perhaps locals did not know that one oil spill in a wetlands region could ruin it?

So, I set to work researching the situation to see how I could help protect this paradise that I loved from being destroyed forever! I spent hundreds of hours studying the project's history, partnerships, agreements, regulations, local tensions, and dangers. In doing so, I learned that over 200 watchdog organizations were overseeing this situation. A local team employed by the project sponsors conducted site visits, sent updates, and held monthly meetings, which helped set my mind at ease.

However, foreign-based organizations funded most of these watchdogs. This news made my concerns whiplash in a different direction. I then worried about local Ugandan entrepreneurs who I knew needed reliable and affordable energy. All those foreign do-gooders were preventing Ugandans who lacked access to affordable power from tapping into their own energy resources for economic development!

Then I learned that ordinary Ugandans along the pipeline path had trouble proving they owned their land due to informal legacy heritage systems; this prevented them from qualifying for fair compensation from the pipeline developers. A government program was updating ownership validations, thanks to digital platforms, but these were not yet complete. Among those who had sold their land and homes were men who did not even tell their wives they'd sold the land before they disappeared with the funds! Those women were now homeless and trying to find their wayward husbands.

Wow! I felt overwhelmed already, and this was just the tip of the iceberg. My heart was on fire, and my brain whirled with potential strategies, relationships to tap, teams to build, and potential solutions to test. I could focus on nothing else.

But hold on, I thought, forcing myself to take a breath and regain perspective. This was clearly a thornier issue than I was prepared to take on, as my focus was to find and fund astute African entrepreneurs.

The main thing I'd learned from working with locals was that they already knew much more about such local issues and had better strategies to solve them than I would come up with on the fly. My job was to find capital to help the best entrepreneurs build their capacity to solve their own problems. I may not be able to do everything, but I can do some things.

With this more realistic perspective, I could refocus on my path, drive projects forward within my focus area, and entrust other champions to spend their lives resolving other issues. Whew, what a relief!

Our role as Americans is to be curious enough to be humble, to listen enough to recognize competence, to learn enough to honor local insights, and confident enough to shun unsustainable strategies. Then, we will see more African innovators and entrepreneurs succeed. Sharing their successes has not only reduced my stress, but it has enhanced my life.

We must learn to step away from controlling from afar, as our vision is blurred. As we encourage, invest, and celebrate African leaders building their own continent's prosperity, we will gain confidence in the capacity of others to fulfill their vision, and their confidence will also grow. Then we will see them doing amazing things we never dreamed of!

Instead of feeling frustrated about our own impotence, we can enjoy liberation from the stress of carrying *The White Man's Burden*, as envisioned by both Rudyard Kipling and William Easterly![126,127]

During Covid, I spent a "Happy Hour" in an online chat room with a group of historically high-performing and impact-driven Americans. But as I listened to their dismal outlooks on health, America, and the world at large, I realised they were frozen by their own pessimism. They had lost hope and lacked the energy to even help themselves. So, I recommended they read a book that had helped me.

Blessed Unrest: How the Largest Movement in the World Came into Being and Why No One Saw It Coming was a 2007 New York Times bestseller. In it, Paul Hawken cites the work of one network after another, each dedicated to resolving a specific social or environmental issue. Eventually, his readers realize that together, these groups form a comprehensive, grassroots movement of hope. It is a worldwide force which no single person founded, funds, or manages, so no single person can shut it all down.

Each group may seem small and fragile on its own, like a raindrop; however, when re-envisioned as a movement, they represent a powerful deluge of positive energy, as each group heals the planet in its own, diverse ways. Few of these groups are widely known, but they just keep doing what they can to mend what they know well and feel passionate about fixing. When I read this book and learned there were many others all over the world working on problems I didn't even know about, this insight permitted me to let go of issues I was not prepared to address and focus on what I did feel confident I could impact.

---

[126] Kipling, R. (1899). *The white man's burden.* https://www.kiplingsociety.co.uk/poem/poems_burden.htm

[127] Easterly, W. (2007). The white man's burden: Why the West's efforts to aid the rest have done so much ill and so little good. Penguin.

This wider perspective enabled me to relax: the world's problems are not all on my shoulders. Knowing that others are diligently working on remedies they already know well can free each of us to continue moving forward and focusing on implementing the solutions we do know well. As long as we do the best we can to solve one world problem that we care deeply about, we can all breathe a collective sigh of relief, knowing that other people better suited to resolve other problems are already at work.

This is the superpower of diversity, a force that is more focused and less likely to be censored by tyrants or corrupted by greed. But diversity is a two-edged sword that can either be wielded with courage or fear...

9. Fearing Diversity

Terror in Nairobi

Jason Spindler was born in 1978 and raised in Texas, where he earned a degree in International Business and Finance from the McCombs School of Business. Then he moved to New York. One September morning, while still an investment banking neophyte in New York City's financial district, Jason emerged from the subway covered in dust and ran toward the rubble of the World Trade Center to help rescue survivors of a radical attack.

That wake-up call for Americans to consider the economic desperation of the world outside of the USA's bubble changed lives. Jason left New York and joined the Peace Corps in Peru, where local farmers opened his eyes to their need for capital to grow their agricultural opportunities to sustainable levels. To prepare for this new mission, Jason returned to New York and earned a PhD in Law, with a specialty in international development policy. He began learning impact investing strategies on the side. Upon graduation, Jason founded a consultancy designed to advise international development funders on how to build high impact businesses and stronger private sectors in emerging markets.

Photo: Jason Spindler
Source: ANTHONY ODAMO/I-DEV
INTERNATIONAL

I welcomed Jason's addition to our fledgling ecosystem by signing up for his i-Dev newsletter, and our paths began to cross. In 2010, I helped establish a post-graduate program to train business school students, mostly former Peace Corps workers, on how to intermediate between impact investors and social entrepreneurs emerging in frontier markets.

Aptly called the Frontier Market Scouts Program, it launched in what is now the Middlebury Institute of International Studies in Monterey, California. That nascent course LoftyInc helped start became popular, eventually attracting adjunct professors, including Jason, to help teach related courses.

By late 2018, LoftyInc had launched one of America's first venture capital funds to focus on African-led tech startups. We were in our second year of trying to raise capital from impact investors, who gave generously to charities and gave lip service to supporting African entrepreneurs, but were maddeningly unwilling to actually invest in them.

The first week of October, I was in Tarrytown, NY, at the Aspen Network of Development Entrepreneurs Summit, co-leading a think tank session with ANDE's Executive Director. Jason attended and came up to me afterward to chat. When he learned that our LoftyInc team had been together for ten years, had built an African startup support ecosystem, and had already realized a highly profitable angel investment exit, his bright blue eyes lit up. He wanted to learn more; this was what he'd been looking for.

As he listened, his smile grew. Then he shared his vision to structure a substantial fund that would invest in a portfolio of startup venture capital funds like ours, each with startup investing expertise in a different frontier market region of the world.

This was exactly the financing structure I had been seeking to anchor our investing portfolio.

His team already had expertise in East Africa, and LoftyInc was among the most experienced at investing in West African startups. He was looking for a team with a strong investment track record in West Africa. Jason had recently been offered a generous amount of capital from someone who wanted to invest via this Fund of Funds model that I had long championed as ideal for risk mitigation and development impact.

That year, both our firms were 'on the circuit' of development impact conferences, and the high season was upon us. Either we or our partners had already spoken in California, England, Texas, and New York, and soon would be in Silicon Valley, Cancun, San Francisco, Big Sur, Nairobi, London, and beyond, following the international VC industry's conventional protocol for capital raising. In three weeks, Jason would be on a panel in London at the African Venture Capital Association's summit, where Erik Hersman would be giving the keynote address.

This process was disturbingly expensive for teams like ours, especially when our goal was to raise capital to invest in frontier market development, as every dollar we spent traveling to a conference was another dollar that local entrepreneurs would have to struggle without or find elsewhere, and there are precious few sources they could turn to. Self-funded VC teams like ours were a new addition to the African development challenge, where well-funded institutions had been playing a role for decades. Travel to far-flung conference locations and attendance fees were expensive, with no guarantees that we would attract capital to invest. Although development institutions had plenty of money to spend on junkets, they had little to show for the multi-billions per year they spent on travel, conference sponsorships, salaries, and technical assistance.

But Jason and his i-Dev co-founder were different: I knew this from meeting Patricia at Santa Clara University's investing event for social entrepreneurs. We even shared a hotel room in Tarrytown to save money. I introduced Jason to my LoftyInc Capital partner, Michael Oluwagbemi, who was covering the Africa Venture Capital Association conference.

When they met in person, they realized that i-Dev had advised the United Nations Foundation's Clean Cookstove project in Africa, which had been deployed in Nigeria by LoftyInc's Wennovation Hub. Our teams were already working together! Jason and Michael laid plans for our tech hub to collaborate with deal flow for his i-Dev's $2 million pilot impact venture fund for emerging market entrepreneurs.

This was a viable plan to reduce poverty-driven unrest through job creation by local entrepreneurs who were solving their own problems in sustainable ways. Investing in startup Funds this way, with local expertise and deal flow, reduced risks that expat-managed ventures faced. Investing early with small amounts would spread market risks across a broader mix of sectors and regions, while increasing the scale of positive impact.

However, when Jason returned to work in Kenya, none of this happened. Jason did not have time to organize the pilot investing program that created youth employment. He did not get the chance to set up a master venture fund that invested in other startup funds like ours.

Our plans were too late for one group of young people who did not know Jason. They never knew our team would help youth like them see, seize, and seed new opportunities. They were unemployed and past feeling frustrated, an easy mark for the militants who recruited and trained them.[128] Now they were devoted to al-Shabab and were determined to make a different kind of impact on people who did not share in abundance and had not cared enough.

This entire opportunity—to convert private capital into new jobs via local startups led by local entrepreneurs—disappeared on the day those al-Shabab youth noticed Jason having lunch in a Nairobi cafe known to be popular among well-paid expatriates from wealthy countries. They feared that Jason's presence was a weapon being used against them. They did not know he intended to open a door to their dream for the future.

---

[128] Hassan, M. (2012, August). Understanding drivers of violent extremism: The case of al-Shabab and Somali youth. *Volume 5, Issue 8. Combating Terrorism Center at Westpoint.* https://ctc.westpoint.edu/understanding-drivers-of-violent-extremism-the-case-of-al-shabab-and-somali-youth/

On January 16, 2019, the East African News reported what happened like this: "An American who survived the 9/11 terror attack is among those who were killed in Tuesday's terror attack at Nairobi's 14 Riverside Drive. According to colleagues, Spindler, the chief executive officer and global managing director of i-DEV International, was having lunch when the attack happened. i-DEV is...a space for entrepreneurs...Nailab's chief executive, Sam Gichuru, eulogized Spindler as "a strong supporter of the Kenyan Tech Ecosystem."[129]

A month later, Jason's co-founder, Patricia, invited me to a memorial in San Francisco, hosted by Impact Capital, where a memorial foundation was being established. Today, its website says, "We are committed to building a stronger foundation for ...SMEs as critical catalysts of economic development and stability, especially emerging markets."[130] Unfortunately, it is not executing the investing strategies that we planned to implement with Jason.

Nine months afterward, one of Jason's childhood friends posted this on LinkedIn: "Jason's grandparents and both his aunts...were holocaust survivors. They escaped Belgium, fled through France, survived the Battle of Dunkirk, traveled south across Europe and took the last boat out of Morocco bound for Cuba, where his father was born in 1942. This history was the foundation of Jason's ethos, his awareness of right and wrong, and it guided who he became...

"Before Jason passed, I found myself using his life as an excuse to do less, to be involved less and if I'm being honest - to care less. Why should I focus on changing the world? Jason already had it covered! I was free to focus on my career, making money and living my best life.

"His death showed me that one person can drive change and inspire others to try and make the world a better place, so I decided to get

---

[129] The East African. (Updated 2020, July 5). https://www.theeastafrican.co.ke/tea/news/east-africa/american-survivor-of-9-11-dies-in-dusit-hotel-attack-1410488

[130] Jason J. Spindler Foundation. *Our impact.* https://jjsfoundation.com/our-impact

involved...If the goal of [Al-Shabab] was to produce fear through violence by killing Jason, *then they failed.* Jason was inspired by the events of 9/11 to be a force of change, his life and death inspired others to do the same."[131]

Five years later, Patricia posted this on LinkedIn: "After the attack, I realized how fleeting life can be. I realized the imbalance in my life...Today, I told my son about his Uncle Jason, who was Jewish but had a best friend who was Muslim. His Uncle, who was deeply and endlessly compelled to help people rise above poverty, inequality, and hate. Many people did not know Jason as I did, or how much pain it caused him to see the hatred that brewed between people of different religions, backgrounds, colors, educations, mental health, or other health issues - or the consequences that resulted.

"He saw people for their potential to rise above it and his (and i-DEV's) role as *unlocking the opportunity* to shift that course... [*Not unlocking this opportunity*] poses a risk to supply chains, business operations, costs, staff, and bottom lines...so, please, think about how you can do more to anticipate, preserve, and grow the reality that matters to you--now and in the future."[132]

Why do terrorist groups continue to threaten lives around the world each day? They must feel they have nothing left to lose. They may have given up trying to see through the barriers in their lives to reach a better way to live. They seem to have lost hope for the here and now and hope instead for a better life after death.

If this longing for economic opportunities is at the root of terrorism, then increasing entrepreneurial freedom will reduce it, just as Jason was committed to doing by investing in African startup entrepreneurs. So why aren't we doing more of this?

---

[131] Esch, J. (2019, September 12). *Al-Qaeda killed my friend. This is why they failed.* LinkedIn. https://www.linkedin.com/pulse/al-qaeda-killed-my-friend-why-failed-justin-esch/

[132] https://www.linkedin.com/posts/pchinsweeney_reflectingonthepast-remembering-changemaker-activity-7152796075655929856-VmXx/

At this point, readers may feel compelled to do *something*, anything, that might prevent this kind of tragedy from becoming commonplace and widespread. Doing the wrong thing would make the situation worse. Enough uninformed, emotion-driven mistakes have already been made. A 2024 West Point Military Academy report explains that a massive military approach against al Shabab stalled out because it failed to meet its goals.[133] At least someone had the courage to stop it.

What tactics have proven effective for moving out of poverty? Remember the study that identified personal initiative as 95% central to "Moving out of Poverty"? It continues to gather dust in the World Bank archives. Why are its findings not guiding proactive global strategies?

The main thing entrepreneurs need is the freedom to operate. Why is this simple sovereignty so hard for governments to permit? Enterprises fund governments, not the reverse! So, why do government officials insist on creating expensive programs that constrict entrepreneurship, which they intermediate and profit from? Does this control over entrepreneurial freedom stem from their fear of losing control? It certainly is short-sighted.

If we take a step back to gain perspective, what do we see more clearly? Of course, the perpetrators of this violence themselves cannot repeat this, but others will follow, unless we find and address the root cause behind this violence. Was it their religion, ethnicity, nationality, gender, or age? Or was it triggered by a more basic need to provide for themselves and their loved ones, something we all share?

Our LoftyInc team represents various religions, ethnicities, genders, and ages. Yet, we honor and leverage these differences as strengths. Our various perspectives widen our view of entrepreneurial opportunities, empowering us to see through the brush to opportunities obscured by the barriers.

---

[133] Muibu, D. (2024, February). Somalia's stalled offensive against al-Shabab: Taking stock of obstacles. *Volume 7, Issue 2. Combatting Terrorism Center at Westpoint.* https://ctc.westpoint.edu/somalias-stalled-offensive-against-al-shabaab-taking-stock-of-obstacles/

Our team members share hope for a better future and the passion for making it a reality. This hope is not our strategy, but it does frame our strategies and drives them forward. Our edge is our diversity. Teams like LoftyInc's continue to invest in ways that suit Africa's young startup founders, reinvesting our profits back into more opportunities.

The older I get, the more I see ways that hope, or the lack of it, impacts lives, for better or for worse. Hope motivates us to find or create opportunities to succeed—to mindfully design something better and deploy ever more effective strategies. Working together for over a decade has also built our confidence in our shared strategies. We have piloted, tested, and honed them over time, and they are now working effectively. This book is meant to offer hope by clarifying practical steps forward. This is why it shares the stories and the strategies of both successful and failed approaches.

We must each learn that "different" is not "wrong." When diversity is feared instead of valued, danger looms. When we believe that our truth is the complete and only truth, then our diversity does not add value—it works against us.

As a parent raising a large family, whenever there was an altercation that the kids could not seem to resolve themselves, I would chat with each party separately to learn their perspective. Invariably, what I initially thought was an obvious solution became obfuscated by competing perspectives. Each time I listened to one kid, I would recognize the truth from their perspective, and the other kids feared that I had become partial to the one I had just listened to—until I had listened to them all.

Over time, I realized that each perspective had value and comprises a partial truth. Each participant has a different view of reality, based on their perspective on the truth. Only by reserving judgment can I remain open-minded long enough to see the value of each perspective. And only by listening to each diverse perspective can I innovate a potential solution that acknowledges and weighs the truth that each perspective holds.

Diversity has the potential to build wisdom into every investment decision, but this only happens when decision makers value diverse perspectives. It also requires governments that welcome innovation, while avoiding controls that diminish economic opportunities. Funders reduce risks and build in resilience when they integrate diverse perspectives into their portfolios. This is how nations increase opportunities for investment to drive innovation in solutions.

Bias: Expat Founders and Funders

As iHub, Hive CoLab, and its East African peers established places where tech innovators and entrepreneurs gathered, they also attracted non-African entrepreneurs who saw the opportunities to replicate what had worked back home and leverage it to build new East African markets. This momentum attracted foreign investor capital. In cities like Nairobi and Kampala, such expat funders and founders hung out at the same restaurants, offices, and social events. They shared the same friends, sports, music, and politics. They had attended the same schools back home. They formed communities that socialized and trusted each other. And most were novices at investing and doing business in East Africa.

Meanwhile, indigenous entrepreneurs were innovating exciting, scalable tech solutions that were vital to large, local markets. These innovations were usually better suited to regional needs than those the expats offered; they were cheaper and more rapidly embraced by East Africa's vibrant markets. Although a few foreign funders acknowledged African argonauts, they preferred investing generously in expat founders. It was more comfortable. Although these were private investments, insider knowledge of them spread through the budding ecosystem. As tech deals became big news, local founders felt the sting of rejection, and tempers flared.

Even as I was co-launching a seed-stage VC Fund to invest in African founders in 2017, I felt pressure from fellow US citizens to invest in US expats instead. For example, I was invited to a USAID-hosted event held in Silicon Valley where a young American woman pitched her telemedicine startup in Kenya to a group of investors. But I had just selected a stellar Nigerian team that was rolling out a 24-hour doctor-in-your-pocket program. That team had all the right experience and were alumni of Y Combinator. I felt confident about them and trusted my assessment because I already had a previous telemedicine startup investment success.

Back in 2004, I led an investing team's due diligence of the first telemedicine venture to do the heavy lifting of getting US industry approvals for doctors to rely on e-health records during digital consultations. That venture, Teladoc, eventually went public[134] and became a unicorn investment success story for me. In its early years, Teladoc's executive team was eager to co-launch in Africa, seeing the opportunity. They worked with me to secure funding and advisors to explore this opportunity in South Africa. After our meetings there, however, we not only felt pushback from the South African medical community that wanted to develop their own telemedicine program, but also Teladoc's own US board told its executives they must first succeed in America.

With this experience under my belt, in 2017 I felt confident in my choice of an African telemedicine team. To placate the Americans pressuring me, I introduced the American woman in Kenya to a former Teladoc female executive and explained my situation. We decided she would mentor the venture in Kenya, and I would do the same with my Nigerian team.

One year after its launch, Merck took over the American-in-Kenya's platform, but no funding was mentioned, and the founder moved back to the US. She is now in Brazil. This is what I expected would happen. US expats have a safety net.

Conversely, our VC Fund made its first small investment in the African-led telemedicine company in 2017, at a $3.5 million valuation– below Y

---

[134] Teladoc Health. (2015, July 7). *Teladoc announces closing of initial public offering.* TDOC IPO news release, 2015

Combinator's, to reward us for standing with them before they faced investors attending YC's demo day that week.

Reliance Team, February 2017
Source: Author

We continued to make ever larger investments to sustain the venture's gathering momentum as it grew to be the #1 telemedicine operator in Nigeria.

By 2022, Reliance Health had grown into a substantial HMO healthtech that enjoyed 3.5x year-on-year growth and was able to raise $40M, from several global investors.[135] This was the largest Series B investment

---

[135] General Atlantic. (2022, February 7). *Press release*. Reliance Series B 2022

round for any African healthcare company to date, valued at over $245 million – 70 times the valuation of our initial investment. This round was anchored by General Atlantic, making its first African tech investment.[136] This round enabled our fund to realize a partial exit of our Reliance holdings for our investors on the secondaries market.

Added to the prior Flutterwave exit, this Fund returned the total Fund 4.5 times[137] within five years and continue to hold additional equity in Reliance and other portfolio companies.

Reliance's 2024 Investor Report cited annual recurring revenues of $17M, 315,000 enrollees, and 409,000 telemedicine encounters; a 65% YoY growth rate. Other YOY growth rates included: 166% for prescriptions fulfilled, 93% for services at Reliance Family Clinics, and 74% for revenues in constant currency terms. In 2025, it is doubling its number of clinics and expanding into Egypt, which is experiencing rapid population growth, and Senegal, which has a more stable currency.

Are we glad we backed the African team over the American? You bet. Parts of Africa have become accustomed to expat residents from the UK, EU, and America, but non-African entrepreneurs pose a dilemma for the startup funding ecosystem. Expat founders of newly minted ventures face more operational disadvantages than locals. Yet, they have a capital-raising advantage with foreign investors, who are more likely to know and trust them than local founders, despite being less experienced entrepreneurs.

Is there still a role for foreign (perhaps American) entrepreneurs in Africa's tech startup boom? Yes, astute founders deploy strategies that can mitigate the inherent risks. For example:

In 2010, four young visionaries living in Seattle, Washington, co-founded a Delaware C corporation named Kopo Kopo. Half of their startup team moved to Nairobi for four years to help microfinance institutions

---

[136] Reliance Health. (2024, January 10). *Reliance Health raises $40M in Series B led by General Atlantic*. Reliance/GA joint news release

[137] LoftyInc Afropreneurs Fund2, Annual Report 2024

integrate their lending disbursements and collections onto mobile money technology platforms. But Kopo Kopo founders knew the poor masses of Africa did not need US technology. Most Kenyan adults already had a mobile money app on their phones and were making domestic payments that were as simple as sending a text. They loved it and were eager to use it in more places, unlike Americans. Because few Africans had bank accounts, the Kopo team could leapfrog onto local mobile technology by embracing M-PESA. Kenya's mobile service providers had launched this in Kenya in 2007 to make domestic remittances as simple as sending a text. Today, M-PESA helps customers across seven African markets send funds, pay bills, make in-store payments, send money abroad, and access financial services such as loans and overdraft facilities.

"Founded in 2010 by Ben Lyon and Dylan Higgins, Kopo Kopo has been at the forefront of Kenya's fintech space, helping over 20,000 businesses adopt mobile payment solutions. Over the years, it has secured $5.4 million in funding from a range of venture capital firms, including Accion Venture Lab, Javelin Venture Partners, and Khosla Impact. Its ability to provide digital payment services to small and medium-sized enterprises (SMEs) in Kenya has made it a vital player in the country's digital economy."[138]

Kopo Kopa founders saw the opportunity in Africa to provide a platform that tracks transactions for both senders and receivers. What is remarkable about Kopo Kopo is the way it was set up to incentivize employees to support the company's success. In addition to paying competitive wages, Kopo Kopo founders shared company stock rights with everyone on the payroll. The founders designed these to convert at a discount to any future exit price. Why?

---

[138] Launch Base Africa. (2024, September 16). *Kopo Kopo announces new leadership team under pending Moniepoint acquisition.* https://launchbaseafrica.com/2024/09/16/kopo-kopo-announces-new-leadership-team-under-pending-moniepoint-acquisition/

The team had seen in Seattle the impact of Microsoft's innovation and growth on the local economy. This capital infusion created thousands of millionaires who launched their own new tech companies and invested in others. This innovation-driven economic development replicated what had already happened in Silicon Valley. Kopo Kopo founders wanted this dynamic in Africa.

Accordingly, they started and managed the firm with an exit strategy in mind, structuring it to have a significant impact on Kenya's digital ecosystem. That exit came in 2023, thanks to a Nigerian payments platform, Moniepoint.[139] But the investors in Moniepoint are really doing well! "The new capital raised by Moniepoint's [Nigerian] leadership accounted for 43% of the total funding of $254m secured by 42 startups in Africa last month, according to funding tracker Africa: The Big Deal, which described it as the best October since 2019."

Meanwhile, a non-profit named Village Capital formally studied the expat funding issue and concluded that many African founders who were spurned by investors had valid complaints. The study reported that in East Africa, while 80% of local startups were founded by Africans, most early-stage investors are foreign and 90% percent of disclosed investments in 2015 and 2016 went to startups with one or more European or North American founders. It added, "Notably, this number doesn't even include many of the U.S.-based DFS [Digital Financial Services] startups that raised capital and have a large portion of their operations in East Africa, such as Branch..."[140]

The report points out that the same due diligence "short-cut bias" occurs inside the US, where most ventures and investments emanate from just

[139] Asu, F. (2024, November 7). *How Moniepoint became Nigeria's latest unicorn.* The Africa Report. https://www.theafricareport.com/367481/how-moniepoint-became-nigerias-latest-unicorn/

[140] Strachan Matranga, S. Bhattacharyya, B., Baird, R. (2017, June). *Breaking the pattern: Getting digital financial services entrepreneurs to scale in India and East Africa.* Village Capital. http://archive.vilcap.com/wp-content/uploads/2017/06/VC_Breaking_the_Pattern.pdf

three cities. However, in Africa, this strategy carries more risk, as less experienced expat founders are hindered by their inherent lack of market insights, talent pipelines, and advisor networks. This study highlights how foreign investors entering Africa often make mistakes when they fear diversity, rather than embracing its potential value.

Yinka Adegoke, founding Editor of *Quartz Africa*, argues that, "To break the cycle of favoritism and white privilege, Kenya's tech ecosystem needs to back itself with money and self-belief."[141] This is great advice, and as African investors attain discretionary capital levels, they do back African founders, as seen in the evolving ecosystems detailed in this book's prior section, "What's Working." In my opinion, the wiser due diligence and mentoring "shortcut" for foreign investors and allocators is to simply co-invest with local tech hubs, angel groups, and seed VC Funds. Perhaps you'd enjoy attending the next ABAN conference in Cape Town or AVCA summit in Lagos?[142]

Fearing Risk

Terms of Endangerment

Fear-driven investing terms usually backfire. Because emerging markets need maximal access to low-cost energy, it is incongruent, yet true, that many government and impact funders do not fund extractive ventures or grid-based energy sources. Africa's energy sector is woefully underdeveloped, leaving it vulnerable to social unrest and exploitation by outside interests. Half the population lacks energy, and the other half struggles with a reliable and affordable supply. Funding robust energy supplies should be a top priority for funders who care about economic development.

---

[141] Adegoke, Y. (2021, July 22). *Kenya hasn't figured out how to put its local founders first*. Rest of World. https://restofworld.org/2021/kenya-hasnt-figured-out-how-to-put-its-local-founders-first/

[142] Annual AVCA Conference and VC Summit. AVCA 2025

Such financing restrictions also cross over from energy into the mining sector at a time when the continent's ownership of rare earth minerals, like lithium, are in high demand by technology industries for communicating, transporting, and computing. Commercial-grade reserves continue to be "proved up" in African countries, but such restrictions prevent them from being responsibly developed.

Today's young entrepreneurs are far more capable of, and committed to, the responsible development of such resources than those in the US were over one hundred years ago. Not investing in the ethical development of these assets leaves them to be controlled by less circumspect agents who undermine both African and American economic development interests.

Instead of using equity-sharing structures that ensure development gains are equitably shared, most funding for Africa is collateralized debt with predatory covenants designed to mitigate their own risks. This negative mindset strategy repeatedly backfires but learning curves are inordinately slow if capital allocators are not incentivized to innovate.

According to Raymond Gilpin, United Nations Development Program's chief economist and head of strategy, analysis, and research for Africa, Africa currently overpays for the debt it contracts in international markets, as noted at the recent African Economic Conference in Botswana. "The institutions that price the risk don't really understand the continent in terms of which data points really tell you about an economy's ability to repay."[143] As a result, in 2024, over half of the continent's countries are expected to spend more on servicing their debts than on health and education. Gilpin believes that, given a more entrepreneurial mindset, global financial sources could refinance African debt at lower rates.

To date, DFIs have preferred to finance later-stage businesses with strong unit economics and stable cash flow. Henry Ford and Thomas

---

[143] Yiekke, L. (2024, December 5). *UN economist: African countries' debt payments skyrocket*. African Business.

Edison may never have succeeded if their first investors had insisted on such strategies. DFIs cater to political winds and fear negative press, so they hire and promote people who are risk-averse, rather than being entrepreneurial and innovative. None of the DFI leadership I know has launched a new company or a novel product, yet that is what their target market needs capital to do. Funder preference for debt instruments, however, does set them up as demanding superiors who inflict pain and reap adverse consequences. What startup founders need instead is trusted partners who are willing to share the risks and rewards of entrepreneurial development.

In the name of reducing risk and under the guise of being helpful, DFIs often insist that startups accept a significant portion of their "investment" as non-financial assistance, commonly referred to as Business or Technical Development Assistance, or "BDA," or "TDA," or "TA." This investment term requires the startup's financial reporting to be created by accounting firms on the DFI's approved list. Although this seems innocent enough on the surface, the pain that these investment terms render can be diabolical to startups.

For example, consider an agriculture production team committed to converting subsistence farming into high-quality cash crops to help an impoverished region in Central Uganda. It is led by Teddy, the co-founder of Hive Colab in Kampala, who you met earlier. Because Teddy was born in Uganda and loved his mother, he eventually left America to devote his considerable skills to helping his family and their community emerge from a vulnerable level of smallholder farming. His goal was to help them set up a sustainable supply chain for sales of value-added products, based on what they grew and processed themselves.

Teddy and his team first tried a co-operative model where farmers shared costs and proceeds. But too few farmers in the community could afford to make even a nominal initial investment toward value-adding production, sales, marketing, and distribution costs. So, Teddy tapped into the trust he had built with friends who would invest small sums because they knew him as an entrepreneur on a mission.

He made good use of these small funds, proving himself gifted at selling and branding and had a natural flair for engineering solutions during the production and processing stages. He set up training programs and professional quality testing to attain global standards of organic certification.

After proving they could succeed on a small scale using a rudimentary production facility they had pieced together over the years, the time came for Teddy's team to build a first-class production facility that would cost six figures. He had purchase orders in hand for $1,000,000 of bulk moringa powder from a US company. These helped Teddy enlist the backing of a local investment fund manager who represented Northern European development institution funders.

We all rejoiced over the amount of capital this fund would make available for new construction and more professional business practices. Some of us had been backing Teddy for a decade and were eager for him to succeed. Then we studied their deal terms. If any growth targets were not met on time, their debt covenants allowed those investors to wrest total management control and ownership away from all prior investors, the founding management team and its board of Directors.

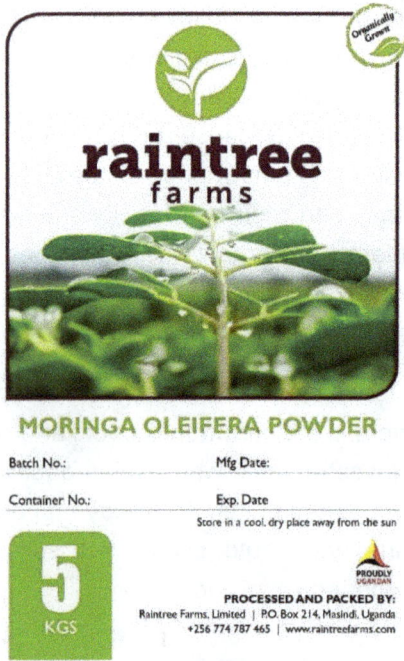

Photo: Raintree Farms

The DFIs mandated that Teddy could no longer work on any other endeavor, which they knew he had been doing to support this venture. So, if he signed, he would become totally dependent on this funder to fulfill its financial commitments in a timely manner. They also demanded veto power over any future investors.

They required the company to maintain a minimum current ratio of assets to liabilities that "could only be met by a company with a large amount of cash or other liquid assets that are not being used to their full potential, missing out on opportunities for investment and growth," per analysis by a current AI tool.

The terms went on and on like this.

Instead of explaining how they would help build the venture's business as seasoned VC firms do, the DFIs simply mandated when and at what valuations it would be bought out by the company or a future investor; as if any of these could be controlled precisely, despite the many variables involved. Failure to meet these terms would result in total loss of control, ownership, and any other personal property of value. Since Teddy's family lived on the property, they could be evicted.

Despite the DFIs' decades of experience and billions in expenditures, their terms did not begin to suit a rapid-growth startup company but could destroy it. This end-of-the-world scenario would kick in if any of the team's aspirational production, sales, or profitability goals were not fully achieved in a timely manner.

Teddy had given up all he had in America and sunk it into this ag project to help people he loved, yet they feared...what, exactly? Teddy not working hard enough? Him stealing from the company? Him walking away from it?

I pushed back hard against accepting these exploitative terms and apparent disrespect for Teddy's management. But, believing this to be their only hope of funding to expand their capacity, and Teddy, being a former Olympic contender, he and his devoted team decided to put their shoulders to the task and succeed, no matter the personal cost. So, I held my nose, and we signed the deal.

The first milestone and funding were designed to max out the production capacity of the existing, hand-built facility, before any CapEx would be released. This step required the DFIs and their Fund to release their first stage of OpEx funding, but they did not release it until well past the optimal harvest time, which endangered production and export operations.

These funders had no sense of urgency to collaborate with nature, buyers or entrepreneurial ventures. The DFI demanded Teddy's team meet tight timelines, but they did not reciprocate by making timely payments; instead, they undermined their own investment. Nothing was built into the agreement to protect Teddy's team from the DFI's payment delinquencies. It was frankly unconscionable and inexcusable, but they did this.

Once the DFI's 1st funds finally arrived in the venture's bank account, it was time for all hands to be on deck for a rapid harvest. Buyers in America were waiting for their orders to be delivered. Workers were ferried out to the fields of the various farms, owned by locals who were all properly trained and certified organic. When the small truck with patched tires was filled to capacity with freshly harvested moringa leaves, it had to be rushed to the production center to be cleaned, sorted, hung, and dried—ASAP—before the leaves started to rot. The harvesters piled on top and clung to the truck as best they could.

As the vehicle climbed out of the field onto the roadbed, it blew a tire, flipping the truck on its head, flinging most of its load onto the ground, maiming some workers, and killing one. Transporting people to the hospital suddenly took priority over saving the crop. Teddy and his board allocated time and resources for healing, paying medical bills, mourning, and compensating families.

The plagues of Job continued, as locusts literally descended in a vast cloud of consumption. The next planting was delayed due to weeks of drenching rains that arrived late, causing more milestones to be missed. As a result, the DFI funding, which Teddy's team could have put to good use building the new facility, was postponed.

Then, high winds gusted the water tower over onto the solar panels needed for drying the leaves before bagging, to prevent mold growth. This compromised quality, so the product would have to be irradiated upon delivery, reducing quality and sales revenues. Production, delivery, and revenue targets were all missed, and all funding ground to a halt.

Teddy still hoped to leverage the DFI's grant funding for business development assistance, if only to complete its mandated financial reporting, but this too was delayed because of other fear-driven dictates. The DFI's short list of approved global accountancies did not relish working for a small entity that generated small fees, so the one firm Teddy had hired, predictably, prioritized the work of larger clients. They were not answering his team's calls and were not on schedule to complete the reports within the DFI's timeline.

Teddy's account audits were delivered late, triggering DFI covenant penalties. Teddy's company was charged more than his local accountancy would have charged, and he got worse service. Nevertheless, his handicapped company had to prepay the full bill of the high-priced accounting firm before requesting that the DFI evaluate the bill and, hopefully, pay its share of that "business development assistance" bill.

This DFI-mandated expense now endangered the company. Although this "business development assistance" is considered a grant, that "grantor" was on holiday just now and for another month at any rate, so no one was available to repay anything. So much for optimizing the next planting season or harvest cycle. Then Covid emerged.

Teddy's close alliance with his farmers helped him recognize that it was farmers who bore the brunt of every financing glitch. Farmers had to prepay for seeds, do the labor, and then wait for the harvest to be paid. Farming communities across the continent suffer an annual hunger season.

The DFIs were originally motivated to invest in Teddy's aggregate-and-process venture because they liked his customized mobile app for farmer operations. This digital platform tracked hundreds of local farmers, their growing capacity, training certification level, and harvest quantities, but what he did with all this data was the DFI's favorite part.

Teddy's Secured Income Program for farmers, "SIP," estimated micropayments that were paid to farmers as a monthly stipend while their crops were growing, provided farmers remained in compliance. This drained the business's cash flow, but it incentivised farmer training, quality, and harvests. It also created jobs for "the-poorest-of-the-poor," as the first thing farmers did when they received a payment was to hire someone to help with clearing land, planting crops and tending fields. But the DFI's own funding delays now prevented compliant farmers from being paid, and their funding terms did not permit Teddy to meet the company's growth needs by moonlighting.

The company's loan covenants were now in default, leaving the venture vulnerable to takeover by people who had no insight into managing these farmers, growing this crop in this country, or delivering it to its American customers per specifications. And no future investors would bother to venture into this fray, unless the DFIs pre-emptively forfeited those covenant rights. Silence prevailed. Operations ground to a halt. Growth milestones became impossible. Farmers planted other crops.

This did not have to happen. Teddy had farmers, customers, a rudimentary production facility, expertise, crops, crews, and the management skills for a growing operation. He had a payment platform that incentivized training programs and quality. He had the momentum, drive, determination, and capacity to succeed.

He mostly lacked timely financing structured to be flexible for growth in the face of challenges beyond his control. One would think that respected development financing institutions would have learned how to structure financing that would not endanger success.

Unfortunately, this is but one of many examples of how risk-averse funders undermine the mutual potential to succeed. This fear drives contractual terms that compound the challenges entrepreneurs already face: It increases investor risks, instead of reducing them.

The prevalence of this kind of aid malfunction inspired development industry workers to create a startup named JADEDAID, a card game that turns insightful sarcasm into cash. Because that was so successful, they now also offer t-shirts. A red one that still sells on eBay at $9.99 says, "Coming to terms with the fact that your intervention is the problem."[144]

Ironically, JADEDAID was launched in 2015, three years before Teddy signed that DFI agreement, while he was still a World Bank contractor, and he modelled that shirt, being a co-founder. Its website says, "The aim of the game is to laugh at everyday frustrations, yet the cards should provoke deeper discussion about the origins of these issues, and how we can make them obsolete...Learn more about the card origins and why each card should make you laugh – and reflect."[145]

Photo: JADEDAID tee shirt
Source: Author Archives

---

[144] https://www.ebay.com/itm/255337439431
[145] https://jadedaid.com/our-story/index.html

10. Fake Facts

"We don't need your teachers; we have a higher
literacy rate than the US!"
—A Zambian lawyer

Literacy

Decades ago, I attended a reception for a female Zambian lawyer at a home in Dallas. She was brilliant, poised, and well-spoken. While I was talking with her, I referenced the old adage, "Give a man a fish, he eats for a day, teach him to fish, he eats for a lifetime." My intention was to point out that Africans knew how to fish, but they needed investors to invest in their entrepreneurial fish businesses, metaphorically speaking.

Before I could build my case, her eyes grew stormy, as did her demeanor.

"Americans keep sending people to teach us how to read," she exclaimed. "We already know how to read! My country has a higher literacy rate than the US! Many of us have higher degrees than the people being sent! Yet, our streets are lined with educated beggars because we lack employment. Stop sending us teachers; locals can do those jobs. Why do they not see this?"

She had had it with Americans who believed themselves superior by virtue of winning the geographic lottery. Zambia had outgrown the old dominance and dependency models. Yet, Americans who know little of African economics may have trouble understanding how Africans can be both highly educated and still poor.

In my experience, teachers are the base upon which Africa's middle class has been built. The majority of my African business and investment partners were raised by African teachers. Teachers ensure their progeny are well-educated and well-networked for both scholarships and startup venture funding. They instill their kids with a work ethic to deliver high-quality work on time. These competencies instill the self-confidence that inspires them to innovate and launch enterprises.

So why don't NGOs hire more locals to do the teaching? If NGO-backed schools do their job, why do they send expat teachers abroad after their local alumni acquire the skills to take over the teaching? They must know their former students need jobs. Then, they could shift their focus to raising capital for local entrepreneurs to create more jobs.

I did my research, and she was right, Zambia did have a higher adult literacy rate than the US. As I write this, I see the most recent direct data comparison is for 2020, when the US was at 80% and Zambia was at 93%.[146]

She was also right about Zambia needing to build its middle class, per World Bank Economist William Easterly's book, *The Elusive Quest for Growth*.[147]

Interestingly, when I asked Google, "Does Zambia have a higher literacy rate than the US?" its AI chatbot inexplicably summarized its findings with this claim: "No, the United States has a higher literacy rate than Zambia." Yet its own data sources supported the opposite answer. I was flummoxed! How many people take the time to fact-check AI conclusions?

Its initial source cited the most recent data for each country as: "In 2024, the literacy rate for adults in the US was 79%, while in 2020, the literacy rate for adults in Zambia was 87.5%."[148] Because the rates for both

---

[146] https://www.macrotrends.net/global-metrics/countries/EAR/early-demographic-dividend/literacy-rate

[147] https://en.wikipedia.org/wiki/The_Elusive_Quest_for_Growth

[148] January 24, 2025

countries have steadily increased, citing the same year's numbers would have been a more accurate comparison, as I noted above, but I had to dig deeper to find that. Zambia's literacy rate in 2000 was still higher than the US rate in 2024. So, why did Google's AI tool state the opposite conclusion?

Before Google launched its AI, I had seen similar AI chatbot biases regarding African data on Chat GPT and Perplexity. While working on this book's infrastructure building topic, I queried AI chatbots to test what they'd report about African infrastructure development. My goal was to learn whether the entrepreneurial Africans who pioneered the continent's digital infrastructure were commonly credited for their contributions. By default, development funding institutions were consistently depicted as the heroes, but the pioneers you read about above were not recognized in my generic searches. I had to cite their names and sources.

I often challenge inaccurate AI summaries by referencing their own source data, and they usually politely apologize. I appreciate this opportunity to contribute to AI accuracy, but when I ask again, they have not corrected the errors in their conclusions. AI is not leveraging its famously rapid learning curve. Why not?

Why do AI summary conclusions not harmonize with their own data sources? Is data-driven machine learning so heavily influenced by preconceived notions? Chat GPT "uses a transformer algorithm...based on a neural network, which is a type of computer program that is designed to mimic the way the human brain works."[149]

Like humans, AI algorithms seem to give more weight to perceptions held by widely read documents than to statistical data that clearly points to the opposite conclusions. These "artificial" intelligence tools appear to prioritize the volume of material that the bot reads and the perspectives that those writers hold. These examples of Zambian literacy and African

---

[149]Texas State. (Updated 2025, April 25). *AI, plagiarism, and ChatGPT.* https://guides.library.txstate.edu/c.php?g=1321038&p=9718369

leadership demonstrate the power of commonly held beliefs. They even sway AI findings to report fallacies as if they were facts. Caveat emptor.

More recently, I was delving into the reputation and work outcomes of an African leader I've known personally for decades. I was amazed to read the AI's conclusion that he was let go for not achieving anything! This was a major issue.

However, the AI summary contradicted the video that it cited as its source, which detailed well-documented metrics and impressive achievements attained while turning around a large health supply entity in a short period of time. I asked the AI itself why its summary did not fit the data it referred to in its sources. It said it could not access information in videos or from sites that require it to sign in, which excludes a lot of information! And explained the problem.

Its conclusion was based on the title of the video, which mentioned corruption in an ambiguous way. I asked what changes it would need to enhance its capabilities, and it gave me a detailed list of eight major ways, but it said it was not allowed to recommend any of them to its "creators." So, I offered to help, requesting the list of creators and their contact information, which it immediately provided. After deciding that someone like Sam Altman would not be my best entry point, I sent the information to a support person, who responded promptly with a thank you and a pledge to improve.

Bottom line, information systems flow like water, from the top down. Facts that run contrary to the flow face more challenges than fallacies. It is hard to find unexpected truths, discover mistakes, and repair fallacies once they are disseminated.

Statistically Suspect...News, Rankings, and Reports

Investors often ask which country is best to invest in now. This book includes a lot about Nigeria. The Partech graph below shows one reason: it was the most active investment destination on the continent in 2024. But this honor has changed hands over recent years.

Which Country Ranks Top of the Tech VC Deals Chart?

2024 AFRICA TECH VC - NUMBER OF EQUITY ROUNDS PER COUNTRY
Partech Analysis 2024

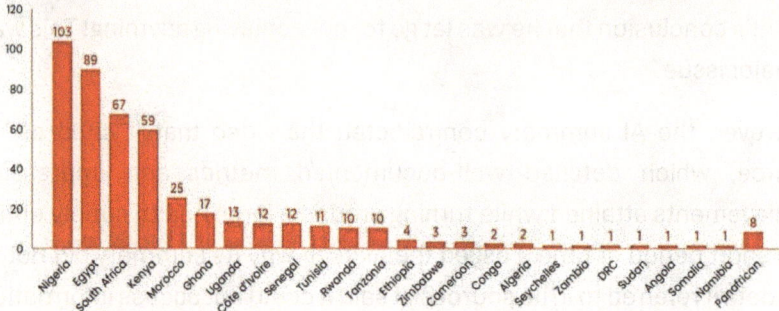

Source: Partech, 2024

In 2024, Partech ranked Nigeria on top, but ErnstYoung cited Egypt as number one in its *2023 Africa Attractiveness Report*, based on the number of FDI (Foreign Direct Investment) projects, investments, and jobs created.[150] And then the Tanzanian Investment Consulting Group cited Q3 2024 data to rank Kenya and South Africa as sharing the top spot.[151] Clearly, these rankings depend on a number of factors, which could shift again tomorrow. And nipping on the leaders' heels are a myriad of nations with amazing growth rates and areas of expertise of their own.

Do statistics like these really help investors? It depends. Since investor goals vary, country variations affect which is most likely to attain different investor goals. One may attract fintech investors, while another warrants a deeper look by biotech investors. Every country has its issues and opportunities; its tyrants and heroes. This is why foreign investors must

---

[150] Sita, A. Wolfenden, R., Hlophe, S. (2024, December 3). *Why Africa's FDI landscape remains silent*. EY. https://www.ey.com/en_nl/foreign-direct-investment-surveys/why-africa-fdi-landscape-remains-resilient

[151] TICGL. (2024, November 21). *Top 10 African investment destinations in Q3, 2024*. https://ticgl.com/top-10-africa-investment-destinations-in-q3-2024/

collaborate with local investors they trust, so they do not get blindsided by what they do not yet know.

Theoretically, a large, single market does ease growth, as we learned from China's example. Its control over a single currency, major infrastructure development, and the pace of urbanization were strengths. However, we've also seen the economic damage that China's centralized control inflicted when it was off the mark with its solutions. During its sudden challenges with Covid, for example, we saw China's economy fall behind more entrepreneurial, diverse, and resilient regions.

In contrast, Africa's decentralised status left it free to innovate rapidly and adapt to the variety of challenges. When a single authority dominates a continent, it is more likely to limit personal initiative, ingenuity, and innovation, and the power of diversity to add value, avoid pitfalls, and provide options. For example, the regulations of Rwanda are supportive of drone tech development, attracting serious entrepreneurs and investment capital, which are helping it lead innovations for applied commercial uses. In contrast, Libya keeps its skies drone-free, which better suits its current security needs. Over time, the investors may learn a new lesson...that the continent's multi-state diversity is not a bane but its superpower.

Eight of Africa's first nine unicorns hailed from Nigeria, Egypt, and South Africa, but one winner is Wave, which has its headquarters in Senegal and serves Mali, The Gambia, Côte d'Ivoire, Uganda, and Burkina Faso. Francophone consumers and commuters love the ease of using Wave, a mobile money service company that aims for its fintech tools to make Africa the first cashless continent.

Rankings based on less definitive data and people's perceptions are even less helpful. The Corruption Perceptions Index (CPI) published by Transparency International has lost credibility as validated reforms have not been adjusted from historically low rankings to reflect the validated improvement made. Yet, significant international corruption scandals in "Western" nations left top rankings unscathed.

Why?

In 2016, after Ngozi Okonjo-Iweala worked her economic reforms magic as Nigeria's Finance Minister, the CPI awarded her country its highest ranking ever, but when she moved back to head the World Bank, Nigeria's rank plummeted. Ngozi is well-known and respected in the US, which helped. Rankings do reflect human bias. Transparency International itself acknowledged its need for better metrics but has yet to reform its system. This stagnation undermines the credibility of such tools for measuring progress or incentivizing reform. Unfortunately, journalists, policymakers and investment gatekeepers often misuse these discredited rankings as definitive measures of corruption and to advise against investing.

Successful investors gather information from diverse sources and weigh it according to credibility, integrating a multitude of factors into their decisions. One certainty is that Africa is a continent of great wealth and vast potential. Africa's natural wealth attracts outsiders who foment instability. Even Apple is implicated in its rare earth mineral acquisitions from the DRC. [152]

The main reason why Nigeria is so interesting to investors is probably because its population is about 230 million, which is much larger than that of any other African nation. Fun fact, it has the same population that the US had in 1980. Yes, it has a lot of land and other natural wealth, but it also has a young population that is deeply tech-savvy and innovative.

Over 60% of its residents are teenagers or younger who exude entrepreneurial optimism. They crave education, sports, and entertainment. They speak English and have strong extended family relationships. Its diaspora has earned impressive recognitions from mostly US and European universities, and they travel home frequently, or just move back home to build the future.

You see where this is going? Statistics look important, but what people are doing, and why, matters far more. Data is dated when published; it is

---

[152] Reuters. (2024, December 17). *Congo files criminal complaints against Apple in Europe over conflict minerals.* VOA. Congo files criminal complaints against Apple in Europe over conflict minerals

retroactive, but people's dreams predict the future. Yes, data shows Nigeria's leadership as an investment destination, but that perfectly valid data does not mean it is the best place for you to invest. Investors may derive comfort from that number, but they will not find insight or inspiration. I don't. I do invest in Nigeria, because most of my team is there, or is from there. But we also invest in ventures operating in many other African countries and in those led by the African diaspora living in the US and Europe.

Will Nigeria dominate the continent? I think not: Building its own economy is enough to do for now. It will certainly be a major player, but the age of dominance over other nations being a desirable strategy is waning. LoftyInc's Nigerian co-owners champion pan-African tech investing and ecosystem development because this diversity reduces portfolio risks such as currency fluctuations and improves the likelihood of catching a winning growth spurt somewhere. Collaboration is the new superpower of nations.

In his book, *Chip Wars*, Chris Miller shows how the USA retains its edge, despite aggressive Chinese and Russian tech innovation thefts. The most advanced semiconductor commercializations require efficient entrepreneurial networks and global alliances. No one country has all the natural resources, talent, expertise, and infrastructure. Covid's interruption of many global supply chains highlighted the breadth and depth of this truth. Global collaborations, not global domination, are the economic order of the day.

At this point in my learning, it seems that whenever I see a statistic on the African tech startup ecosystem, I second-guess it. If an annual total of deals done is being used to prove a point, I can often think of one deal that barely made it into the stats to bump up that year's numbers, or a deal that did not finalize before the year ended, which underrepresented activity levels. Also, when the number of deals done craters, I can usually attribute that lull to a major player who finished investing its allocated capital in one fund and must raise capital for a new fund before it will restart investing. There is nothing technically wrong with these numbers, but many variables affect their accurate interpretation by investors. Overall, the sector is so small that variations may appear meaningful but have benign explanations. Investors must be cautious not to misinterpret short-term data variations as long-term trends.

For this book, I was asked to statistically compare the investor returns for US versus African tech startups. This would be problematic for at least three reasons. Although business angels have invested in thousands of pre-seed startups, LoftyInc is one of the few investing teams that have managed formal startup funds with solid data that tracks costs and exits, so the weight of authentication is still largely on us. Although we and our investors have realized extraordinary returns, we do not feel that we have enough data points to deem our outcomes statistically significant, given the overwhelming data pools available on US startup investing.

Another data problem is that African-led and Africa-facing ventures are often US-registered to accommodate US investors and strategic alliances, which muddies the data on country of origin. Rapid-growth companies are highly collaborative; this is built into their startup DNA, as they plan to operate globally from day one.

What matters much more than statistical data points is the level of innovation, entrepreneurship, expertise, insight, and passion that a founding team has when it brings an innovation to market.

An Investor's Edge

Life is what it is, but we can learn from this truth as well and factor it into our personal life choices. Interesting, no? When awareness leads us into places of knowledge where few others tread, we may draw conclusions that are contrary to commonly held beliefs and AI conclusions because our areas of interest relate to less referenced data sets, although they are more statistically accurate.

You can see how this information asymmetry offers an edge to investors who may have less wealth and less influence, but who are industrious enough to dig deeper into the facts and are honest enough with themselves to integrate facts versus fears into their investment decisions. Such investors have a valuable edge over others, even African billionaires.

Explorers discover emerging investment opportunities early. They not only learn facts before other investors, but they also notice trends that are not yet captured in published data sets. They recognize leading indicators, versus stale opinions. The perspectives that such investors gain let them see deeper through the brush into the opportunities that lie in the vista beyond. This is how some investors can confidently commit to unorthodox strategies and cutting-edge sectors that orthodox investors shun.

Yesterday's facts become today's fallacies. The "Made in Japan" label no longer means that the item is substandard, so expect to pay more for your car if it is a Lexus and for your toilet seat if it is a Toto Washlet, because they have been tested to perfection. Zambian literacy rates surpassed those of the US years ago. South Korea is no longer a poor nation. Nigeria now has the second-largest movie industry in the world.[153]

How is a person supposed to keep up? By staying curious, flexible, and humble, it would seem.

---

[153] Colombia Global Report. (2017, October 17). *Nollywood: The making of a film empire*. Columbia University.
https://globalreports.columbia.edu/books/nollywood/

11. How Development Funders Diminish Founders

Female Founders

She is a McKinsey-trained African-European whose focus is on matching African companies and impact projects with local talent. Her business model leverages a digital platform with custom-designed tools that organize hundreds of world-class consultants based across the African continent into project-specific teams. These elite teams deliver business solutions tailored to African contexts at a more affordable price.

As her business grew, she began partnering with DFIs to launch services for Africa's smaller businesses, called SMEs. However, she learned some hard lessons. DFIs often require significant prefinancing payments, yet their fundings were delayed for months to years, and the amounts released were often less than those they had agreed to release. They said this was due to institutional financial reporting requirements.

Being motivated entrepreneurs like Teddy's Ugandan team, her teams moved forward, meeting their previously announced project timelines, which incurred real-time expenses. For example, she organized a large team that trained 1500 agricultural microenterprises across Ghana. Transportation was a major project expense that trainers minimized by taking motorbike taxis.

To meet such current cash needs while still expecting DFI funding to come soon, she resorted to alternative private funding that routinely fills DFI financing gaps, though their interest rates were multiples of conventional rates. Then she learned that to be repaid for expenses like those motorbike taxis, the DFI required stamped receipts, which are not available in rural Ghana. These hidden funding requirements added costs and timelines that not only prevented her firm from helping more SMEs, but also deepened her firm's cash flow issues, as a young entity still bootstrapping its own growth needs.

This power imbalance spills over into gender-bias issues, like the time she was invited to a mid-day meeting at the office of a top DFI executive. She expected a five-minute visit to get a contract signed; instead, the man wanted her to share a bottle of whiskey with him. When she declined, his emotion-packed response informed her that women will never succeed in business because "they are like crabs in a bucket and will never make it out."

Sadly, other unwelcome invitations and requests from male DFI-executives who hold the purse strings have been much more onerous for her to deal with. DFIs will fire a serious offender against whom an affidavit is signed, but they lack mechanisms for reporting and resolving such issues in ways that protect informers and their companies from a powerful, yet less documented "old-boy network" backlash. Together with financing practices that undermine high-growth ventures, we can see how DFI strategies may impede the success of female founders.

Agriculture Aggregators

In the earlier Ugandan agriculture story, we saw development funding institutions (DFIs) handicap their own investment. The same thing happened to an agriculture project "backed" by the USAID's West African Trade and Innovation Hub.

Astute local partners were "awarded" a grant to fulfil a complex agriculture export project. Despite those ubiquitous delays in releasing the grant funds the USAID had pledged, the local partner self-funded and executed the storage construction, product aggregation, processing, and warehousing. But they really needed the grant funding to pay farmers and complete the export so that they could collect from US buyers.

Dozens of farmers who had grown and harvested the crops grew insistent that they be paid by the aggregator, who was now bereft of capital. Suddenly, the USAID team found fault with the execution of one minor part of the project and announced it would withhold all the funding it had contracted! This left the subsistence farmers unpaid. It left the aggregators guilty of collecting crops they could not pay for, holding orders that they could not deliver, and storing grains instead of exporting them, losing value in facilities that they had paid to build with the expectation that USAID would honor the grant they had promised. Now, the aggregator could no longer afford to maintain the warehouse security and the farmers would never trust them again.

One wonders where that USAID funding for this WATIH export program went. I had a clue. Prior to this Nigerian Ag project "receiving" this "grant award," I spoke on an investment panel organized by the African Diaspora Network of Silicon Valley and hosted at Draper University in 2019. There I met a long-time ag consultant to USAID's ag programs. We set up regular calls to update each other on ag project development in Africa.

I wrote this at the time in an email to a colleague, "Bill is trying to recruit me as a potential advisor to create an angel investing network in Senegal, but it makes no sense for the USAID to spend $10M via non-local advisors, [like me] and have nothing to show for it after 10 years, when they could put $2-5M total into an astute Senegalese team, and have local venture successes to show for it, like LoftyInc did in Nigeria."

On one call, Bill told me that the "Chief of Party" managing an Ag project in Nigeria had been fired and sent home to Cape Cod in the US. His $15M budget had been awarded, but it all went to staff costs, "technical assistance," consultants and "business development" activities (AKA relationship building events, travel, and entertainment expenses). I was shocked, but as I listened to his regular updates, this seemed to be a recurring pattern.

On another call he spoke of being hired to write a policy guide for a new Chief of Party managing a $25M award for Cross River State in Nigeria, near Cameroon. This project provided $3M for staff and $5M for grants to be dispersed annually for five years, but it ended up with staff who had no money to do any grants. The same thing happened with Ag projects in Ghana with a $37M budget, and in Senegal.[154]

Why does this keep happening?

Do you see a pattern? Bureaucrats who get paid regardless of outcomes enlist visionary Africans to fulfill projects that they do their best to deliver on, but their promised funding is not released, which compromises not only the projects but also ruins the reputations of the best entrepreneurs that the DFIs could find. This is not economic development; it is systemic, institutionalized degradation of economies.

I am only one person of modest means who lives in the US, and I am not paid to do development. Yet, I have invested personally in several potentially significant ventures that were all undermined by DFIs. How many more projects like these have failed for the same reasons? Why are these stories not being reported to taxpayers?

Because DFIs remain a dominant source of development funding, whistleblowers face dire consequences. Until more private sector champions step up to finance development, this will continue. Fearing a funding backlash, some of my sources felt compelled to remain anonymous, and others of us have not named specific DFIs. How can those of us left holding the bag, bearing the costs, and watching African entrepreneurs be destroyed hold institutions accountable for diminishing development?

Why do democracies built on entrepreneurship continue to fund development institutions instead of funding entrepreneurs who are passionate about solving the same problems that institutions have failed to solve? Inertia, perhaps? If the definition of insanity is doing the same thing over and over and expecting different results, then doesn't this qualify?

---

[154] Author's call notes, 2019-2021

Health Product Suppliers[155]

"The only thing worse than a $9.5 billion failure is one that costs $17 billion."
—Efosa Ojomo, PhD

In 2014, USAID launched a $9.5 billion program to organize its sprawling global health supply chains so they could be permanently handed off to each recipient country. USAID awarded project management to its U.S. contractor Chemonics International.

In 2015 the Zika virus outbreak endangered pregnant women and their embryos, yet it took two years for the USAID's supply chain program to buy and deliver insect repellents and condoms. This response rate was "a full year faster than the project's typical procurement cycle for these items" according to the performance evaluation the USAID finally published in 2019.[156] The record showed the "percentage of line items delivered on time and in full, within the minimum delivery window" had dropped in six months from 67% to just 7% in Q1 2017. Product categories that had not been delivered included AIDS drugs and birth control.

Health product supply chains are supposed to deliver the right health products, in the right quantities, at the right time...to prevent "stockouts" and product expirations, or people die. A former employee of Chemonics, the consultancy in charge of executing the project, was quoted as saying, "I think the biggest problem was, well, Chemonics not knowing supply chain."

As the USAID's newly appointed chief of staff in 2017, William Steiger began to hear alarming rumors about key programs for AIDS and malaria running out of critical products. Steiger dug out the contract with Chemonics and looked for "an offramp to take work away from

---

[155] This section was written before USAID operations were put on hold in January 2025.

[156] https://pdf.usaid.gov/pdf_docs/PA00TPZ8.pdf

Chemonics,"[157] but could find none. The USAID agreement had no performance mechanism to financially penalize or reward the group. With all the health commodities bundled into one huge contract, there was little the agency could do to help the parts of the supply chain that faced dire needs.

But there was good news, the Chemonics team was proud to report it had reached a "turning point." The 2017 Q3 Global Supply Report showed its overall on-time-and-in-full (OTIF) rate "was 25 percent, compared to the previous quarter's 6 percent. But OTIF rates for the malaria task order were 15 percent (compared to 13 percent in Q2) and reproductive health commodities were 5 percent."[158]

How had the group accomplished this (not so) amazing turnaround? They had changed the minimum number of days criterion that governed how long it should take from the date of order to deliver products. More products were delivered within the allotted time because they increased the time allotted from 174 days to 239. The agency's Office of Inspector General said the recipients reported they had "no choice but to approve the [longer] 'agreed' delivery date if they wanted to receive the deliveries."[159]

One has to wonder how anyone associated with mismanagement and deceptions on this scale deserves a salary, let alone to be entrusted with a mulit-billion-dollar competency-building program meant to be emulated

---

[157] Igoe, M. , Stockton, B., Khan, M. (2023, November 9). *'Too big to fail': How USAID's $9.5B supply chain vision unraveled.* Devex. https://www.devex.com/news/too-big-to-fail-how-usaid-s-9-5b-supply-chain-vision-unraveled-105141

[158] USAID. (2017). *GH Supply Chain Program. Quarterly Report Fiscal Year 2017. Quarter 3.* https://www.ghsupplychain.org/sites/default/files/2019-07/29_Y2Q3_0.pdf

[159] Office of Inspector General. (2021, March 25). *Award planning and oversight weaknesses impeded performance of USAID's largest global health supply chain project.* USAID. https://oig.usaid.gov/sites/default/files/2021-04/9-000-21-004-P.pdf

globally. Instead of curtailing the project, Chemonics' agreement was extended multiple times until late 2023.[160]

According to a 2019 Congressional hearing on the USAID's $30 billion budget, "Ending the need for foreign assistance is central to [USAID's] mission."[161] By the time this program ended in 2023, USAID and Chemonics had only used about half of its budget to order health products; the rest appears to have been spent on overhead. And yet, for two years they had been designing the next program.

Perhaps hoping to obfuscate its complicity in the first program's failures, Chemonics had set up a new entity with a different name designed to head the next program. Their new solution would be similarly designed and led, but it would need more funding. It would be awarded $17 billion this time...Really?

Devex is a network organization that connects the international development community with sector news, job reports, and funding opportunities. Its reports and those of the Bureau of Investigative Journalism raised the curtain of silence around the USAID program issues.[162] In late 2023, Devex published an article titled: "*'Too big to fail': How USAID's $9.5B supply chain vision unraveled.*"[163]

Then it published an opinion piece authored by the Nigerian-born, Harvard-educated co-author of the popular business book, *Prosperity Paradox*, cited previously in this book for its studies on nation-building innovations. Efosa Ojomo is the head of global prosperity research at an innovation-focused think tank in Boston.[164] He also teaches

---

[160] https://ghsupplychain.org/sites/default/files/2023-08/FY23%20Q2%20IDIQ%20Report_Final_remediated.pdf

[161] https://www.congress.gov/116/meeting/house/109749/witnesses/HHRG-116-AP04-Wstate-CalvaresiBarrA-20190711.pdf

[162] The Bureau of Investigative Journalism. https://www.thebureauinvestigates.com

[163] https://www.devex.com/news/too-big-to-fail-how-usaid-s-9-5b-supply-chain-vision-unraveled-105141

[164] Ojomo, E. (2023, November 23). *Opinion: What we can learn from USAID's $9.5B supply chain struggle.* Devex. https://www.devex.com/news/opinion-what-we-can-learn-from-usaid-s-9-5b-supply-chain-struggle-106630

"Entrepreneurship and Market Creation in Emerging Markets"[165]at Northwestern University's Kellogg School of Management.

He began his article to the international development community with this: "Regardless of who received this contract, the project was doomed to struggle from the beginning. Here's why." Efosa's goal in studying the failed AID/Chemonics project was to learn how people could design and execute the next project differently for a successful outcome. He confessed this study was painful to review because he knew that the people who had been paid to design and execute these health supply deliveries would not suffer, despite their failures, but millions who had relied on those failed distributions had suffered, in real time.

Efosa's key message was that the project designers had not invited any input from local innovators or entrepreneurs on the ground, "who respond to the struggles of everyday consumers and are incentivized to find the most efficient and profitable ways to solve problems. Integrating these people into the design and implementation of initiatives like this is critical if project designers are serious about success and sustainability." He recommended that next time, the USAID work with African health supply entrepreneurs and build upon their successes.

He offered an example; an African startup venture, mPharm, which is rolling out a franchise model that solves the core inventory and delivery problems of Africa's "community pharmacies." This is similar to the model used by the Rexall chain, which co-branded up to 12,000 drug stores across the United States from 1920 to 1977. While I was growing up, Rexall created value by aggregating local drug stores into a buying group under the Rexall brand. It managed the delivery of health products to shops within a bike ride of many Americans like me.

Back then, franchising added a lot of value, but today it can leverage the internet to manage member JIT inventories and fine-tune group e-purchasing for volume discounts, track sales and payments in real time,

---

[165] Efosa Ojomo. Devex. https://www.devex.com/news/authors/efosa-ojomo-1557463

and verify real-time product deliveries. Africans started using their mobile wallets to pay for payments a decade before Americans did, as they leapfrogged the whole credit charge-card era.

Coincidentally, mPharma was launched in Ghana in 2013, the same year as the USAID's project, and it operated during precisely the same decade. So, how did mPharma do over the same period of time? In its 2022 annual stakeholder report, mPharma's CEO letter summarized the ways that the startup leveraged its global networks to navigate Covid in Africa.

Unlike most government programs, mPharma quickly nailed down a trusted supply of test kits, raised funding to upgrade local laboratories' molecular diagnostic equipment, and even thoughtfully capped its pricing on essential chronic care drugs to protect vulnerable patients during shortages. This is how compassionate capitalism builds consumer loyalty and good-will value.

When it launched, mPharma's mission was "to make prescription drugs more affordable to underserved populations and emerging markets in Africa...including Ghana, Nigeria, Kenya, Zambia, Malawi, Rwanda, Ethiopia, Uganda and Gabon." It offered a cloud-based data platform on which doctors, patients and pharmacies sent, shared, and tracked digital prescriptions. Its revenue model was to sell its data to drug manufacturers.

That was not easy to do in the informal shops that mPharma was aiming to help. A Harvard MBA study explained the startup's key challenges.[166] This vision was thwarted by pharmacies that lacked internet access and had no incentive to report sales. Without this data, the company lost its primary customer, Pfizer. It would have been hard to fault mPharma's management if they had chosen to quit at that point, but its African CEO, Gregory Rockson, was on a personal mission.

While growing up in Ghana, Greg had suffered from thoracic scoliosis. He'd shared his parents' frustrations over the uncertainties of securing

---

[166] Wu, Y. (2022, October 29). *mPharma- Is a platform model always successful?* Harvard Business School MBA Student Perspectives. Harvard Study

the medicines he needed, due to frequent pharmacy stockouts and wildly vacillating prices when available.[167] So Greg and his team were determined; they kept learning, innovating, and trying something else. Taxpayers did not finance these development expenses. Entrepreneurs and their seed-stage investors assume the responsibility for such costs and associated risks. The time this takes must not exceed the size of the wallet, or all is lost.

mPharma developed a "consignment model" where they stock pharmacy shelves with medications, essentially managing inventory for its pharmacies and taking on the responsibility of stock levels. Greg's team innovated and implemented several financing and digital solutions that were not possible before. To avoid inventory "flooring" costs, pharmacy owners only pay mPharma when they dispense a drug to a patient, a viable financing process made possible by mPharma's advanced supply chain software and data analysis, which tracks inventory changes in real time and optimizes deliveries across their network of co-branded pharmacies.

Within its first decade, mPharma solved the stockout problem for over 800 pharmacies and was serving two million patients in nine countries.[168] It raised a total of $88.5 million in venture capital,[169] grew annual revenues to $225.4 million, and estimated revenue per employee to $337,500.[170] It works with half of the world's top ten pharmaceutical corporations.

In contrast, the USAID's health product supply chain, which first launched in 1968[171] failed in places where mPharma succeeded. It failed

---

[167] Skoll. *mPharma*. https://skoll.org/organization/mpharma/

[168] mPharma. https://mpharma.com

[169] CB Insights. *mPharma.*
https://www.cbinsights.com/company/mpharma/financials

[170] Growjo. *mPharma revenue and competitors.*
https://growjo.com/company/mPharma#google_vignette

[171] https://wdi.umich.edu/wp-content/uploads/WDI-25-Years-of-Health-Product-Supply-Chain-Reform-WEB.pdf

to operate efficiently and to turn its system over to competent locals like mPharma. Its institutional, donor-development model not only deprived poor people around the world of products their lives depended on, but it also deprived millions of American taxpayers of billions of dollars that we could have invested in ventures like mPharma.

Africa's entrepreneurs, like mPharma's Greg Rockson, would have cared more about delivering those supplies reliably and cost-effectively. They might have even returned profits to their investors. But what about scaling up?

Successful startups do not stay small; thanks to tech innovations, they grow rapidly and create jobs, and $17 billion could launch a lot of startups. If 1,700 startups were each awarded $10M to follow in mPharma's footsteps, they could be serving 400 million people in their first decade. If they were to grow 2.5x during the next decade, an easy metric for healthy startups, they would be serving roughly 1 billion people.

These would be locally owned and managed enterprises, accountable to their family and neighbors, with self-sustaining growth models that would not need annual charity or outside consultants. They would not only ensure health, but also create widespread employment, so locals could pay for their own food, education, healthcare, security, and justice.

> *Foreign aid is taking money from the poor people of a rich country and giving it to the rich people of a poor country.*—Ron Paul

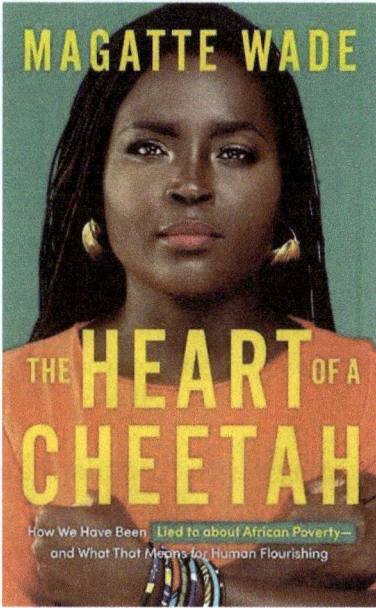

Photo: Magatte Wade
Source: www.magattewade.com

Jaded Aid

So, how do Africans feel about USAID losing its funding? Some fear the loss, but not Magatte Wade. She is a lion-hearted Senegalese/American entrepreneur who I have known for over a decade as an intrepid entrepreneur. In February 2025, her blog was titled "Does Africa Really Need USAID? Spoiler Alert: Hell no!"[172] Why would she write this? Brace yourself...

"Foreign aid is not the solution to poverty. In many cases, it's actually part of the problem. For years, we've been sold the idea that aid from organizations like USAID helps "lift" Africa out of poverty. But here's the truth: if foreign aid worked, Africa would be the richest continent on Earth by now. (To be clear, I'm not speaking about humanitarian aid here. This critique focuses on foreign aid programs aimed at development, not emergency responses to crises like natural disasters or conflicts.)

"Walk through Dakar's streets, and you'll see exactly where your aid money goes. The city is filled with foreign residents working for the UN, various NGOs, and embassies. They live in a parallel economy – one that most Senegalese can only observe from the outside. These aid workers enjoy lives of luxury: fine dining at expensive restaurants, driving new SUVs, occupying the best apartments in town, employing multiple household staff (all courtesy of and paid by taxpayers' money from donor nations – aka foreign aid money), and hosting lavish parties. And oh, by

---

[172] Wade, M. (2025, February 3). *Does Africa really need USAID?* Africa's Bright Future. Substack. https://substack.com/home/post/p-156336700

the way, they receive "hardship pay" for their supposed sacrifice of living in what they consider a "far away place filled with malaria, tropical diseases and tough climates."

"This creates a devastating ripple effect throughout our local economy. These organizations, flush with seemingly unlimited budgets, inflate the cost of everything – from housing to basic services. A local business owner like myself has to compete with these inflated prices while running a real business with real constraints. We can't just throw money around because we're dealing with actual market forces, not endless streams of "free" money.

"But the damage goes deeper than just raising the cost of living. These organizations also poach our best and brightest talents with salaries that no local business can match. Instead of building businesses, innovating solutions, or creating real economic value, our most capable people are diverted into bureaucratic jobs pushing papers and writing reports that rarely translate into meaningful change. I've seen brilliant minds reduced to professional workshop attendees, moving from one donor-funded meeting to another, producing NOTHING of lasting value.

"...Consider what happens in our villages: When free mosquito nets arrive, local merchants who sell them go bankrupt. The same thing happens with shoes. Donated shoes flood local markets, making it impossible for local shoe manufacturers to compete. Each "free" gift comes with the hidden cost of destroying local production and sales.

"Again, the accountability in these organizations is virtually non-existing. Their budgets make no sense in any real-world context – they operate in a fantasy land where money seems to have no limits. They measure success by money spent and goods distributed, not by actual economic development or the creation of sustainable businesses...

"What's even more frustrating for me is how this system creates a culture of dependency while simultaneously diminishing our dignity. The narrative becomes one of Africa needing constant help, rather than Africa *needing fair opportunities to compete and grow. I've been sounding this alarm for years.*

"Foreign aid indeed creates jobs and careers - just not for the people it's supposed to help.

Every successful economy in history has developed through <u>trade and entrepreneurship</u>, not through handouts and aid dependency.

"So, am I glad the world is waking up to this? Absolutely. The sooner we stop treating foreign aid as a sacred cow, the sooner we can start focusing on <u>what actually works</u>: economic freedom, entrepreneurship, and policies that empower people to build their own futures.

"The first step toward a prosperous Africa is to eliminate what's poisoning it – this toxic aid dependency that has created a parallel economy and diverted our resources away from productive activities. Only then can we build the Africa we know is possible: one where entrepreneurship thrives, dignity is preserved, and prosperity is created through our own efforts rather than handouts.

"Africa doesn't need more aid. It needs more freedom: I dive deep into Africa's poverty problem and its solution in my book, <u>The Heart of a Cheetah</u>."

This message belongs in the category of whistleblowing. Because Magatte has experienced what few others have, she sees the world from a unique perspective. There is truth here. She knows it and has chosen to brave the consequences of pressing this truth for the sake of people she refuses to forget.

She has spent her life as an African argonaut and creating businesses to sustainably employ Africans. Each day, she fights to empower people via fair global competition. As a keynote speaker in conference after conference, she reminds people of this unequal access to economic freedoms. In her book, she details restrictions that impede entrepreneurial progress. But her primary goal is building cities of the future where entrepreneurs enjoy economic freedoms to create opportunities, as we'll see in Part Four, "What's Next?"

Another strong woman who fits in Magette's whistleblowing category is Dambisa Moyo.[173] Born and partially raised in Zambia, she earned a Harvard MBA and an Oxford PhD in Economics. She fully leverages the value of her diverse perspectives while advising the World Bank and sitting on the boards of Goldman Sachs, Chevron and 3M. She is now a Conservative Party member of the United Kingdom's House of Lords.

In 2009, Dambisa wrote *Dead Aid: Why Aid Is Not Working and How There Is a Better Way for Africa*. It is short, but it knocked the air out of countless windbags. She pointed out that African politicians whose main supply of revenues was from foreign sources were unresponsive to their local constituents. Then advised foreign governments that decried corruption and touted local accountability to immediately notify their African dependents that funding would be reduced to zero over a five-year period.

She argued that over $1 trillion in development aid sent by rich countries to Africa during the last five decades has only impoverished the continent, so the claim that aid from rich countries has fought poverty and accelerated development is a myth. She has also written three other similarly impactful and thought-provoking books. Only now is this long-standing problem for African development being addressed, as the USAID is being dismantled, albeit from the US taxpayer's perspective as being "fiscally irresponsible."[174]

Because development funders remain the 5-ton elephants in Africa's startup deal-making rooms, it is time they reform their internal operations that are deep-sixing the development engines we know as

---

[173] Mollenkamp, D. T. (Updated 2024, March 6). *Who is Dambisa Moyo?* Invstopedia. https://www.investopedia.com/who-is-dambisa-moyo-5213211

[174] Steakin, W., Bruggeman, L. (2025, 28 March). *After months of cuts, State Department says it's officially shuttering USAID.* ABC News. https://abcnews.go.com/US/after-months-cuts-state-department-officially-shuttering-usaid/story?id=120267238

tech startups. Tech is one industry where neither gender nor wealth presents major barriers to success–unless Funders themselves build those barriers. But making capital raising costs prohibitive and delaying payments that were promised are detrimental to startups without recurring revenues.

This abuse of power is even more reprehensible when DFI executives who influence funding for startups press female founders to comply with unwelcome sexual requests. Yes, DFIs seem eager to improve gender equity, but do their operational policies protect whistleblowing female founders from reputational and financial blowback?

12. Selfish Saviors

Perpetual Capacity Building

When I first tried recruiting Africa-facing charities and other NGOs to consider converting some of their donations into investments, they turned me down, saying they were focused on "capacity building." As the years passed, their capacity-building attempts continued unabated, as if they were making no progress, forever sending dire messaging to funders and retaining their jobs. If they were succeeding, I thought, surely their work would evolve into investing in the capacity they had built. Surely their goal was to succeed by helping people attain self-sufficiency, versus eternal dependence.

But no, retaining an air of superiority, NGOs continue teaching Africans how to fish, though they already know how to fish. Afropreneurs want to progress into entrepreneurial fish industry supply chains that employ villages, which develop prosperous regions. Surely, I thought, charities and philanthropies will eventually realize that some Africans now have the capacity to build and manage industries, but...

After twenty years, donors rarely invest after building capacity, like helicopter parents who refuse to believe that their little ones have grown into adulthood. Why not? Do donors fear losing validation? They are stuck, neither expecting success nor acknowledging that Africans have built self-sustaining entrepreneurial successes. This self-imposed blindness points to entrenched elitism and a strong desire to NOT work themselves out of a job.

Donor Dumps

America's entrepreneurial culture usually encourages people to help themselves; our freedom-loving hearts go out to revolutionaries depicted on stage, on film, and in print, who are fighting for self-determination. This is why the plot of Les Misérables has been a bestseller for over 160 years. Its depiction of unjust oppression versus economic freedom gets our blood pumping; we are ready to march to the barricades and join the fight!

But when it comes to Africans, Americans find it easier to donate than fight. Shipping Africans excess dairy products as aid or used clothes as charity eases the conscience. However, this form of institutionalized "giving" undercuts local entrepreneurs. When imported products are priced below costs, they undermine local manufacturing and entrepreneurs, preventing investments in development, and thus destroy markets. Called "flooding the market," this spurs downward spirals that initiate, perpetuate and deepen poverty.

Decades ago, while in a hallway behind a conference auditorium, I met the CEO of an American steel company, who was about to speak to a room full of influential people. His goal, he explained, was to get the US government to block China from dumping its steel in the US at below-market prices, made possible by cheap Chinese labor and government subsidies. He secured the political help he sought to protect his US corporate profits.

History illustrates that the Textile and Clothing (T&C) industry has consistently provided countries with a development bridge from agrarian to industrialized economies. For fledgling industries to take root, some protection for local development is usually required.[175] This same development stage was progressing predictably in Africa's post-colonial ruled countries during the 1960-80 period. To help it along, the US specified the apparel industry in its 2000 enactment of the African

---

[175] Jauch, H., & Traub-Merz, R. (2006). The African Textile and Clothing Industry: From Import Substitution to Export Orientation. *The Future of the Clothing Industry in Sub-Saharan Africa. Bonn: Friedrich-Ebert-Stiftung.* https://library.fes.de/pdf-files/iez/03796/02article.pdf

Growth and Opportunity Act (AGOA), to ensure tariff-free export of its manufactured goods to America.[176]

But a fly got into that ointment.

A 2015 USAID study found that the East African Community (EAC) received global imports of used clothes worth $274m (£205m), and that the majority of the population bought at least some of their clothes from this used clothing supply. Ghana's textile and clothing jobs plummeted from 25,000 people in 1977 to just 5,000 in 2000. Kenya's 500,000 garment workers dropped to a few thousand.[177]

According to the BBC, "Second-hand clothing is one factor in the near collapse of the garment industry in sub-Saharan Africa." Understandably, the EAC countries decided to protect their markets from the dumping of used clothes, which is augmented by a tax deduction for donating them. A darling of US donors, Rwanda, is part of the EAC's regional economic group.

To protect and encourage local production in 2018, Rwanda raised tariffs on these imports from $0.25 per kg to $2.50 per kilogram. Its president said, "The West's cast-offs were so cheap that local textile factories and self-employed tailors could not compete...We are put in a situation where we have to choose... to be a recipient of used clothes...or to grow our textile industries." Kagame told reporters, "As far as I am concerned, making the choice is simple."[178]

The US promptly punished Rwanda by removing its eligibility for AGOA trade tariff advantages.

In its March 2005 brief, Oxfam International addressed a similar issue. Titled "Food aid or hidden dumping?", it said, "...food aid has also been

---

[176] The Textile and Apparel Provisions of AGOA

[177] John, T. (2018, May 27). *How the US and Rwanda have fallen out over second hand clothes.* BBC. https://www.bbc.com/news/world-africa-44252655

[178] Fox, K. , Kiernan, E. (2018, July 12). *The US is fighting one of the world's poorest countries over trade.* CNN Business. https://money.cnn.com/2018/07/12/news/economy/us-trade-fight-rwanda/index.html

used for less noble aims, including to dump surplus production and promote donor country exports. This type of food aid hurts poor farmers and distorts international trade."

This Oxfam brief also refers to a US Dept of Agriculture webpage that states, "When allocating assistance under the Title I program, priority is given to agreements that provide for the export of US agricultural commodities to those developing countries which have demonstrated the potential to become commercial markets..."[179]

After Congress enacted US dairy subsidies to ensure stable prices, America's hyper-efficient farmers ramped up production to leverage the opportunity. To counterbalance the negative price impact of this prolific over-supply of milk, Congress voted to fulfil its foreign aid pledges by donating massive amounts of powdered milk to Africa. The Red Cross took issue with this practice in 1986, stating, "The United States routinely has offered non-fat dry milk, of which this nation has millions of tons in surplus, as a food commodity to impoverished regions of the globe. In some cases, the donation has caused more problems than were solved."[180]

How did this magnanimity impact Africa's domestic dairy industry? The World Health Organization's (WHO) recommends 210 liters per person per year, but Nigeria's per capita milk consumption of 20-25 litres per year is only 10% of what's recommended.[181] Yet, Nigeria only produces half of the dairy products it consumes, so it spends about $1.5 billion annually on importing the rest.[182]

---

[179] Public document of the Foreign Agriculture Service of the US Department of Agriculture

[180] Puzo, D. (1986, February 6). Red Cross assails use of nonfat dry milk in hunger-relief programs. *Los Angeles Times*. Red Cross Assails Use of Nonfat Dry Milk in Hunger-Relief Programs

[181] https://www.vanguardngr.com/2025/06/nigeria-spends-over-1-5bn-annually-on-milk-imports-produces-only-700000-metric-tonnes-minister/

[182] Dairy News today. (2024, November 25). *Nigeria spends $1.5 billion annually on dairy imports*. https://dairynews.today/news/nigeria-spends-1-5-billion-annually-on-dairy-imports-.html

To gain perspective on this issue, imagine for a moment being an executive on The African FinTech, Inc. team, with whom you have spent a dozen years building your fintech insights, credibility, products, and markets. You have learned how to mitigate not only energy shortages, transportation challenges, and staff training needs, but also managed to pay school fees for younger siblings and medical needs of aging family members who lack public services, health insurance and retirement benefits.

Your private company has been able to raise formal funding at the institutional level for a few years now, because your recurring revenues and market share are growing aggressively. The market has rewarded you for filling a gap, meeting a big need of the everyday economy, in convenient and cost-effective ways that were easily embraced locally. Your local insights and hard work are starting to pay off.

Your team is finally starting to feel secure about their futures. Your customers are thriving, making slow but steady progress away from living on the edge of subsistence commerce and toward a small safety net for when things go wrong. You are finally able to breathe easier.

Then all hell breaks loose for your African fintech...or more likely, a hellish silence descends upon it. Thousands of your customers suddenly stop using your digital platform and business solutions. Revenues plummet, while fixed costs eat through any cash reserves. Everyone is wondering what's happening, so you put out feelers to find answers.

Then the news breaks. The board of a big charitable organization in America, let's call it Digital Divide Bridge, or "DDB" makes an announcement. Out of the goodness of their hearts and "to help the poor of Africa bridge the digital divide," they launched a fee-free service that directly competes with your company's services and market. Your biggest customers start calling to ask what they should do, or worse, you call them and learn their accounting department has already switched to the DDB platform.

Your family and friends start texting concerns and regrets. Vendors who had started relaxing their terms start pressing you to pay any outstanding invoices "immediately" and revert to requiring prepayments. You try to talk to someone at DDB, but their local staff does not have the clout to represent your concerns to their superiors in America: That is not how they operate. After a couple of weeks, you have to let staff go; a couple more and you shutter the office. You help with your spouse's growing venture, a meal preparation and delivery service, but your heart is not in it. You feel defeated—and angry.

After a couple of months, you start hearing that your former customers are unhappy with the new DDB services. "They do not understand what we need. They don't respond to our concerns or offer the services you did." Your hopes rise until you talk with your former partners. Half have accepted secure positions in established African banks that are adding basic e-banking services for their best clients, and the other half have found positions back in "the US."

"But, what about our dream of empowering millions of local small business owners to formalize their businesses?" you ask. "We cannot feed our families with our dreams," seemed the consensus.

"Does this really happen?" you ask. Of course it does! Remember the used clothing dumping controversy? Americans seeking tax breaks sent almost $330M worth of discarded clothing to East Africa in 2015, per the USAID's report. Product dumping undermines local businesses, right? In the 2000s, Ghanaians living in the Dallas area had already started asking me to find investors so their relatives back home could help the local textile industry by importing mechanized looms and building proper factories.

But I found no takers among American investors, donors, or development agencies.

Americans have safety nets and African tech startups have started innovating these, but in general, African consumers usually have no credit that waits until the end of the month—they prepay for essentially everything, food, phone services, school fees, utilities, you name it. Landlords require deposits of a year or two of rent, and health insurance companies demand a year of premiums upfront and still make you wait six months to become eligible for coverage.

When donors forget the economic development lessons of history, they adopt strategies that incite feelings much stronger than frustration. They do real-time damage to real people. African lives are at stake. When hopes and opportunities are dashed, righteous indignation rises. Terrorism by radicalized factions takes root, such as the world has already seen. This growth of angst over the lack of opportunities to build their economies endangers more than just Africans, as we saw earlier, in *Terror in Nairobi*.

On the other hand, American news recently carried an upbeat story about Ugandan fashion designers who had innovated their own solution to product-dumping. Entrepreneurs buy in bulk, hire workers to salvage premium denim pieces from shipping containers of used clothes. These local designers thrive on the challenge of reformatting various shapes and textures into totally different fashion items that reflect African culture, style, and jive. It is hard to hold back creative young entrepreneurs, regardless of geography, or outsiders who dump stuff![183]

"Why bother with African startups?"

Because we have seen Afropreneurs bootstrap whole new industries and ecosystems with just their own capital. Imagine what they could do with some serious venture capital from private sector players who believe in them, invest in them, and then get out of their way so they can succeed, at scale.

Startup Stabbing

Yomi was the fourth of his mother's five children. He lived in a fine house and enjoyed a comfortable life in Nigeria until his father came home with a new wife. Yomi's mother was told to leave with only the clothes she was

---

[183] AP Archive. YouTube. <u>Ugandan fashionista turns second hand denim into on trend high fashion pieces</u>

wearing and to take her kids with her. They walked away from their home and into an uncertain future.

Near an open market in Lagos, they found an abandoned shipping container where they lived for six years. Yomi's mother bought a pepper grinder, which she used to prepare freshly ground pepper she sold in the open market. "She never spent money on herself," Yomi told me, "She wore the same dress for years because any money went to food and our school fees. That is why I want to make money to help her the way she helped us."

Every evening, Yomi's mother padlocked the door for 12 hours to keep her family safe. When her kids complained about having to stay inside doing homework while their friends played outside, she looked them sternly in the eye and asked, "Do you want to grow up to be like me and have to live like this? If you are not educated, this is what your whole life will be like." So, they stayed inside and studied every night.

When Yomi found usable paper in the trash, he would scratch a design on it with charcoal. He remembers getting excited when a neighbor saw him sketching and commented that his drawing was "nice enough to sell." Then his older brother told him, "People pay money for cards with drawings like yours."

As Yomi's confidence grew, he began making plans. When he was in secondary school, he asked his mother for five bucks, a huge sum for her at the time. He told her that he needed supplies to make cards he could sell. She trusted Yomi enough to loan him the money she had saved.

He made and sold his cards, then repaid his mother and began his own handmade card business. He learned that his best target market was on the campus of the university he wanted to attend someday. Yomi saved his money and earned his degree, which took extra years because teachers kept going on strike to persuade the government to pay higher wages.

One day, he met a man who owned a print shop, and Yomi asked if he could work there. The man could not afford to pay him, but Yomi was welcome to learn what he could. Yomi was thrilled and diligently spent every free minute shadowing the owner, learning everything he could about printing. He learned paper varieties, ink types, machine capabilities, and how to treat customers. His mentor even invited him to accompany him to meetings held at other locations.

After several years, Yomi set up his own shop in a friend's family garage. His first printing machine was a good used one, a gift from his mentor, who believed in him. Yomi's childhood friends became his business partners, and they set to work building a strong reputation for quality work and superior customer service under their own "Printivo" brand. As they did, they expanded their operations to manage growing customer demand. They hired staff and bought equipment, attracting more customers. They no longer feared their futures and were glad to be helping their families. But their vision extended beyond this level of success.

The Printivo team knew that getting things printed in Africa was a laborious process. Most small business owners had to shut their shops for hours to travel through traffic jams by bus to a print shop at least three times, to place an order, approve a design, and pick it up. Orders were often delayed due to broken equipment or out-of-stock materials. After all this, customers were often disappointed in the quality of the product received. Even when satisfied, picking up large orders or banners was difficult, as few customers had access to a vehicle.

Yomi and his team innovated solutions for each of these customer challenges. They built a detailed digital platform where customers could see and select products, designs, fonts, and colors. Customers could customize and pay for their orders online, and Printivo would deliver them in Printivo-branded vehicles. All of this could be done via mobile phone; their customers never had to leave their shops! The popularity of Printivo's brand skyrocketed. It attracted a 6-figure investment from an African tech startup investor.[184]

---

[184] Onalaja, G. (2016, January 14). *Inside Printivo: The scrappy beginnings of a next generation printing company.* TechCabal. https://techcabal.com/2016/01/14/the-printivo-story/

The Printivo team vastly expanded the selection of custom designs its customers could choose. Yomi used social media to invite artisans like himself to submit sample designs via the digital platform. When customers selected a design for their print product, Printivo would split sales revenues with the artist who drew it. Because Yomi knew the desperation of being a young person who needed to make a living, he had a passion to help others like himself develop a talent they could monetize, no matter where they lived. He was proud that Printivo could use a mobile money app to send payments to mobile phones in rural areas of Cameroon, Congo, and Mali.

Most customer shops operated from informal locations, in open markets or shared living spaces, where small business owners lacked clean, safe places to store the printed items they had ordered. The team leveraged their website platform to offer a digital storefront section where anyone who ordered Printivo products for resale could set up a point-of-sale page under their own brand. Printivo offered to store and deliver print products like t-shirts and coffee mugs as they were ordered by customers of the small businesses.

This service may remind readers of the online e-commerce site, Shopify. As Printivo customized each of these services for its customers, its built-in tangible value addition increased the Printivo brand's popularity and the potential valuation of the company to serious investors who were looking for strong companies that were ready to expand.

Sometimes customers needed their orders delivered to other countries. "We've had people order from Kenya and have us deliver it to a friend in Lagos who will then send it to them," Yemi said. Another time, a groom being wed in London was from Lagos. He entrusted Printivo to print his ceremony programs and needed them shipped asap. Yomi rose to the challenge, personally overseeing the printing and hand-carrying the package to the Lagos airport. There, he scanned the people checking in for flights to London for any familiar faces. No luck, but as he watched people who had arrived from London, he recognized my LoftyInc partner, Michael Oluwagbemi. Working together, they found someone they knew, who accepted the delivery responsibility, making the wedding another Printivo success!

With experiences like this, Printivo raised the bar yet again. Yomi knew that in America, a print company named VistaPrint accepted online orders and mailed the finished products promptly, at a reasonable cost, across the USA and Europe. Yomi set this strategy as Printivo's destiny, to grow into the "VistaPrint of Africa."[185]

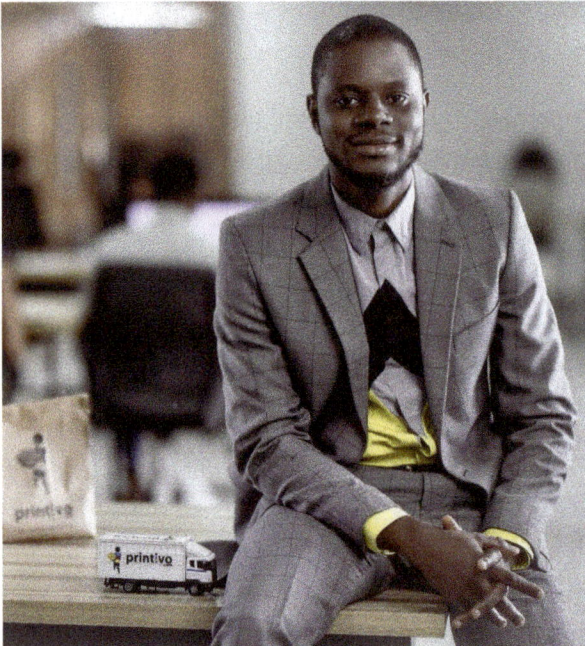

Photo: Yomi at Printivo
Source: Bella Naija, October 2017, Extraordinary Nigerians

With characteristic aplomb, Yomi prepared so well for Printivo's next step that it was selected from among 900 applicants as one of Africa's 20 most promising tech startups.[186] At the award ceremony in Cape Town, South Africa, he met the original founders of VistaPrint in America. Now

---

[185] Shu, C. (2015, October 23). *Nigeria-based Printivo wants to become the Vistaprint of Africa*. TechCrunch. <u>Nigeria-Based Printivo Wants to become the Vistaprint of Africa</u>

[186] AfricaPrint. (2017, November 9). <u>Top 20 Most Promising African Start-Ups Programme</u>

retired, they loved Printivo's goal of adapting the VistaPrint model to serve the continent. They wanted to invest $500,000 into helping Printivo scale up its production capacity and build out the regional partnership programs. They wanted to help Yomi realize his vision for a pan-African printing corporation. With investors like this, who were already experienced at scaling up an online printing corporation, combined with Printivo's knowledge of their local market realities, success seemed assured. We were thrilled for our portfolio company and optimistic for our investor returns.

Unfortunately, there was a problem. One of Printivo's first investors was blocking the VistaPrint founders from becoming co-investors. He did this by exercising a term in the fine print of his agreement that gave him veto power over future investors. I struggled to understand this unfortunate stance that would inhibit Printivo's growth.

It is dangerous for a startup to surrender control to an established corporation with conflicting interests, but this was not that. These investors no longer controlled VistaPrint; they were investing personally. Also, the amount they were offering was not large enough to shut out other investor interests or to undermine founder ownership. Having a bit lower percent ownership is not detrimental to founders and investors if the venture value is growing exponentially. These investors would bring more than capital to the table; they could be invaluable mentors.

I was heartsick that Yomi's viable plan for pan-African economic development was being undermined by one of his own investors. Our investment team agreed that LoftyInc co-manager, Idris Bello, would attempt to negotiate a solution, as he knew this African investor, who was exercising his power to undermine Printivo's future. Sadly, the ego-centric investor held his position until the VistaPrint founders gave up and walked away.

News of this tragedy sent a shockwave through Africa's startup ecosystem that warned future investors away from backing Printivo and from co-investing in any other startup that the problem investor had backed. For years afterward, the startup founder grapevine shunned that investor and shut him out of the strongest ventures.

Yomi finally abandoned his pan-African dream, leaving the existing business in the hands of his co-founders to serve its local customers. Although it remained a respected brand and a viable small business for years, Printivo was not permitted to fulfill its potential. We finally wrote off that investment as a total loss, as no one was going to buy us out.

Yomi tried launching a new venture outside of printing, a digital app for African investors, but he lacked the level of passion and expertise required to build a uniquely valuable company that stood out from the pack. He had a wife, a son, and a mother he loved and wished to support. He became discouraged, of course. It was tragic; a travesty perpetrated by an elitist investor whose ego demanded an inappropriate level of control.

I wish I could say this was an isolated event, but this was one of many ways I have seen investors sink the ship of an otherwise sea-worthy venture, erroneously confusing their power to control an investment with the notion that control protects the value of their investment. Our team did not value control over Printivo: We valued the team, their passion, competence, and goals.

If you, as an investor, do not believe a founding team knows their market problem, their target customer, and their business opportunity better than you do, then do not pledge your capital to back them. Do not fill startup agreements with debt covenants, favored nation status, and dire threats, all of which you insist be kept secret. If your offer is fair, why must you insist on secrecy? Why not invite others to invest equally and stand together in solidarity with entrepreneurs to solve the development problems, arm-in-arm?

Why should you have any right to burden founders and their other investors with your ego-driven demands for special status? If you fear that exposing your terms to public scrutiny would embarrass you and your organization, which claims to be "socially responsible," then perhaps you deserve to be held accountable. If you are a powerless intermediary who sees your superiors being unfair, then quit, talk about it, and find another investor whose strategies you can proudly champion.

Even though our team's first fund was small, distributing our equity investments across several startups paid off. Yes, Printivo failed, but other portfolio companies more than made up for losses, returning the entire Fund several times over. Investing in founders who are highly motivated to solve everyday problems for large markets mitigates the risks of failure, and investors who help–versus hinder them– are more likely to succeed.

Startups like Flutterwave and Reliance HMO propelled our first Fund's investor distributions to top-tier levels, establishing a track record that would help us raise another Afropreneurs Fund. That Fund invested several million USD into 55 seed ventures, across West and North Africa, which built in risk mitigation that defended against swings in currency, politics, and climate. These contrarian approaches to conventional debt funding for Africa have been tested and proven effective to maximize rewards. Such strategies add value to African opportunities, without demanding control. Although our VC Funds are still small by US standards, LoftyInc has become ranked as one of Africa's most active investors.

Investors who back well-managed startup portfolios can walk away from financial losses, as they will likely be balanced out by the wins. Worst case, investors lose what they put in. But entrepreneurs take the bigger risks and suffer the heaviest injuries when their ventures fail: It is their dreams, careers, and lives that are dashed.

Entrepreneurs who survive failure learn valuable lessons. If they start over again, they are the wiser for it, and their investors can benefit as well. Silicon Valley investors often prefer more seasoned founders like Yomi, who earned a reputation for personal integrity and executional excellence.

13. Ego-systems

The House of Abraaj

During our 2025 management retreat outside of Lagos, our team discussed the lessons we could apply after reading a book about the massive failure of a mega-sized private equity impact fund named Abraaj.[187] What made it particularly tragic was that the founder was from Karachi, Pakistan, so he truly understood the needs of an emerging market that has high potential, and he knew how to get things done. He saw the vast opportunities of investing in large-scale entrepreneurial projects that could positively impact entire nations.

Arif Naqvi was also a brilliant, driven, and determined visionary who knew how to put deals together and raise ample capital from aligned investors. He was as personally charming as his presentations were enticing. He innovated strategies that perfectly matched the mission statements of development funders and pitched them perfectly, using logic that global power structures embraced. Arif gained center stage at every high-profile impact investing event around the globe. From 2014-2017, he seemed to be everywhere, doing everything, all at once.

The soundness of his message was inescapable: The most powerful force for development was entrepreneurship, not domineering government institutions or demeaning charity. His timing synced flawlessly with President Obama's Global Entrepreneurship Summits, the Gates-led billionaires' pledge to give away their fortunes, the impact

---

[187] The Key Man: The True Story of How the Global Elite Was Duped by a Capitalist Fairy Tale

investing movement that attracted top talent, and the rise of world-connecting technology innovations.

Abraaj started humbly enough in 2002 with $3 million: by 2018, it was managing assets of $13.6 billion.[188] As the money started flowing into his private equity funds, Arif surfed the capital raising wave like a pro, and his competitive instincts took over.

Everything he touched turned from trash to gold.

Abraaj attracted top talent, investment opportunities, and the capital to back them. His world-class business managers engineered solutions to operational challenges that others deemed impossible to resolve. They were turning failing corporations into efficient, profitable ventures. His private equity investment strategy for development was working!

Everyone bent to Arif's wishes, from royalty to Nobel awardees to Interpol. No one had better access to the rich and powerful, donated with a bigger splash, or hosted more lavish parties. No one worked harder, drank more, or spent more–until 2018, when The Abraaj house of cards collapsed.

A common nouveau riche mistake is cash flow mismanagement. Abraaj grew so fast that tracking capital being pledged, leveraged, and reinvested became problematic. Yet, Arif was not concerned–he would confidently call a wealthy friend, ask for hundreds of millions of dollars, and promise to pay them back, but he didn't. Arif had reached the peak of his glory and was determined to stay there, regardless of cash flow issues.

To Arif, private equity meant maximizing fiscal leverage using debt that pushed the limits. He pledged capital he did not yet have to buy entities that he could not yet afford, and he rolled out corporate turnarounds based on revenues not yet earned. Also, to maintain his facade of unlimited wealth, Arif took ever more risks with leverage, expansion, hiring agreements, and lavish spending.

---

[188] *The Abraaj Group*. Wikipedia. https://en.wikipedia.org/wiki/The_Abraaj_Group

Arif evolved a mindset that rationalized his need to spend money that did not belong to him on expenses for which it was not intended. He decided that all Abraaj capital was at his personal disposal, to move between investment funds, countries, and bank accounts as he pleased, without consideration to ownership, ethics, or propriety. This worked, at first, and the rewards were addictive. People trusted him. They believed in him and their shared mission.

But to Arif, the world was one big shell game, where he only needed to lift the right shell in the nick of time to find the reward. He would have it all, and no one was permitted to intervene. He owned his employees, their capacity, their loyalty, and their integrity.

What one teases out of this epic story is that even a genius requires peers and advisors who share power, information, and respect as equals. As Arif's greatest strengths took center stage, his greatest weaknesses loomed large in equal proportion. Arif had no one with both the insights and the power to impede his plunge into self-imposed destruction. He lacked a team, a board, and investors who could stand up to him.

Finally, one young investor at the Gates Foundation cared enough about his management responsibilities to insist on an authenticated answer. "Where did our money go?" Andrew Farnum's unfettered logic, determination, and courage finally rallied enough powerful co-investors to stop Abraaj's financial hemorrhage, just in time to abort Arif's plan to close on six billion dollars for a record-breaking-sized Fund. That capital was what Arif needed to keep his shell game going.

By then, the damage was done and the money was gone, transforming Arif's optimistic vision into a festering wound. Momentum for making a positive impact by investing in emerging market entrepreneurs, a sentiment that once rang true, now echoed hollow. His investors were so embarrassed by being duped and so fearful of their reputation that, instead of outing Arif, they created a code of silence around the whole sordid affair.

This investor secrecy caused additional collateral damage, as suspicions widened beyond the information void. The fallout constricted the flow of private capital to responsible managers of emerging market funds. Abraaj fell in 2018, just as LoftyInc was raising its first formal VC Fund for African startups. We'd expected to raise $25 million but finally closed with only $1.2 million to invest.

Arif's pitch points, development strategies, entrepreneurial focus, and aligned investors were shockingly similar to our own. But our management style and spending budgets were polar opposites. We had not even taken salaries for managing our first Fund, but no one had asked about that.

How could we expect investors to be comfortable investing in our team after they saw what Arif had done? Apart from its size, our 2018 VC fund went on to succeed in every other possible metric, from investor returns to jobs created. We had raised two more funds in the interim, steadily growing our modest assets under management (AUM) and building a large portfolio of startups, without the help of DFIs.

What were the take-away lessons from Abraaj for our LoftyInc team's retrospective in 2025? We renewed our commitment to a corporate culture where a strong team of equals is encouraged to challenge each other's assumptions and to a flat management structure that engenders transparency and shared responsibility. We reiterated our preference for embedding servant leadership, mutual respect, and lively debate into our corporate culture. We reconnected to our bootstrapping roots as startup entrepreneurs with low-key lifestyles, debt-free financial structures, and long-term growth.

But nagging questions remain...

Why is it that people who hold the purse strings to funding for eradicating poverty usually meet at ego-strokingly expensive venues like Davos? It was at such events that Arif gained credibility and funding for his Abraaj Funds by hosting luxurious events and donating generously to causes. But he funded these by tapping capital designated for impact investments. Why must the optics of wealth precede capital-raising success for emerging markets?

Hair-raising Capital Raising

Now that ecosystems have produced startup winners and African fund managers have earned strong track records, the constriction point for African development has moved to the VC fund capital-raising process itself. American private investors may think development financing institutions are structured to fill this need; however, across the board, sourcing funds from DFIs is inefficient, excessively expensive and excruciatingly slow. This process is adding risks to every stakeholder involved.

If non-African investors want to participate in the continent's tech-driven investment opportunity, they would be wise to first immerse themselves in its existing, successful ecosystem. There, they will learn what is working, who has built well-earned reputations, and who they should trust. Then they will not feel compelled to foist antiquated dictums, which have failed, upon those who have succeeded. Surely, making many small trial investments via Africa's own tech ecosystem strategies to test and prove optimal strategies is a more logical approach that provides more relevant, cost-effective insights.

The world may not have the luxury of indulging wary, officious investors for another decade of fear-driven strategies. Things could go sideways before then...

A recent United Nations report says, "Africa has the youngest population in the world, with 70% of sub-Saharan Africa under the age of 30. Such a high number of young people is an opportunity for the continent's growth—but only if these new generations are fully empowered to realise their best potential."[189] The current population of Africa is about 1.5 billion,[190] so over one billion Africans are now under 30 years old. If these

---

[189] UN. *Young people's potential, the key to Afirca's sustainable development.* ://www.un.org/ohrlls/news/young-people's-potential-key-africa's-sustainable-development#:~:text=Africa%20has%20the%20youngest%20population,to%20realise%20their%20best%20potential.

[190] Statista. (n.d.). *Sub-Saharan Africa: Total population from 2013 to 2023 (in million inhabitants).* https://www.statista.com/statistics/805605/total-population-sub-saharan-africa/

people are unable to support themselves and their families, then civic instabilities are inevitable, manifesting as migrations, violence, disease, starvation, corruption, and radicalization. These are all predictable byproducts of poverty. This tipping point situation could either become a tragedy of epic proportions or humanity's best chance to innovate giant leaps forward via innovations in finance, health, food, transport, entertainment, and education.

The *"Moving out of Poverty"* study shows us, as does history itself, that personal ingenuity eradicates poverty, not governments or charities. So, who should be more humble at the bargaining table? Yet, the adage holds true: "he who has the gold, rules."

Instead of standardizing their agreements to put more money to work sooner, as Startup investors do in Silicon Valley, DFIs each seem to have unlimited funds for lengthy deliberations and extensive travels. They each create their own long list of diligence requirements and changes to standard VC fund legal documents. They write their own book-length "side-letters" demanding favored status on any upside potential or downside risk.

They can afford to drag out timelines; someone is paying their salaries. The team with the smallest budget loses, and so do tech entrepreneurs with narrow windows for market entry.

For example, one recently demanded that Limited Partners' Advisory Committee decisions be made binding on management, although this would legally negate LPs' limited liability and require all other LPs to amend their previously signed agreements to concur. Their wording reveals their primary motive: "...without such clarification, the Advisory Committee would be reduced to a purely consultative body." A consultative body is the very definition of an Advisory committee! Nevermind that the investor's mandate is to enhance African economic development, not its own status; nevermind that it is the fund managers who have the successful track record, not the LPs; nevermind that this demand will waste tens of thousands of dollars on legal fees and capital-raising costs, undermining the viability of the fund to even pay salaries.

But then, one must remember the residual impact of Abraaj, and yet...

Capital raising should be about getting to know each other well enough to build mutual trust. It should not be a wrestling match at the edge of the law to insist on amassing control. It should not be so costly that it undermines the ability of fund managers to do what they do best, nor should it endanger the Fund's very existence.

This book has validated the African entrepreneurs, innovators, and fund managers who created prosperity by empowering personal initiative in ways that foreign aid, product dumping, military offensives, and donations do not. Only entrepreneurs with resources to innovate, capital to grow, and the freedom to operate can empower Africa's economic health. Everything else needs to step aside or assist.

African entrepreneurs are doing their best, but they need help fast. It is up to funders to deploy timely capital via sustainable strategies that realize mutual profits while making the world a better place. This is a tall order, but it is not a fairy tale: It is rational and it is happening. It deserves to be scaled up. Investors who make an honest effort to find the ecosystem's best opportunities will be welcomed, coached, and rewarded.

Emerging fund managers usually have a lot of bandwidth across networks, sectors, and geographies, and they are innovative at bootstrapping, so investors can get more 'bang for their buck' than institutional approaches. The most successful managers often are passionate entrepreneurs themselves, who are now building their own startup—a seed fund. But even the strongest local teams may not excel at traits that staid institutions prefer. This is one side of the capital raising problem.

Size is another...it matters too.

An average American VC Fund raises over $100 million and invests in about five companies, but those do not suit a startup region like Africa. Our first African VC fund only raised a bit over one million dollars, invested in six ventures, and distributed top-tier returns. Our second fund raised $14 million and invested in about 55 ventures total—a big job for a small team!

The following story may help you understand investing challenges from the perspective of private sector startup fund managers. In March 2025, LoftyInc announced a new fund's first close. Here is the news story our legal team released.[191]

"*Foley & Lardner LLP represented LoftyInc Capital Management in securing a $43 million first close for its new LoftyInc Alpha Fund, a late-seed investment vehicle aimed at scaling Africa's most promising tech startups, particularly in Nigeria, Egypt, Kenya, and Francophone Africa. LoftyInc is one of Africa's most established venture capital firms, with over a decade of experience backing startups such as Flutterwave, Andela, and Wave Mobile Money.*

"The first close attracted a mix of African and international backers, including sovereign wealth funds, development finance institutions, U.S. family offices, and regional investment bodies. Investors include Egypt's Micro, Small, and Medium Enterprises Development Agency, Tunisia's Anava Fund of Funds, FMO Dutch Entrepreneurial Development Bank, Proparco with FISEA, the International Finance Corporation, AfricaGrow, the Dutch Good Growth Fund, and U.S.-based First Close Partners. The fund also secured commitments from African high-net-worth individuals, reinforcing strong regional confidence in LoftyInc's ability to back transformative companies.

"The Alpha Fund is designed to help startups transition from early traction to scalable growth. Beyond capital, LoftyInc leverages its network and expertise to support founders in navigating operational challenges, securing strategic partnerships, and accelerating market expansion.

The Foley deal team was led by partners Von Bryant, Clyde Tinnen, and associate Kelvin Thomas."

Although this news sounds sedate, the financial challenges we faced behind this news were nail-biting. This fund attracted our first DFIs, who sent wonderful people to negotiate with our Fund management team, but

---

[191] Foley News Release

some of their mandates nearly sank us. Capital-raising is a financial gamble that the broader VC industry usually mitigates by having well-established sponsors, like an investment bank or a large corporation. But few pioneering funds for Africa have this luxury. Fund proponents must prepay to gain access to potential investors who may or may not invest.

Our first funds primarily raised small amounts from mostly African professionals who had already been doing angel investing and appreciated the expertise, deals, and exits our team added to their portfolios. As we scaled up, we started to work with tentative fund-of-fund investors and corporations. These capital allocators worked for institutional funders who represented the interests of others, which is a process that does not keep costs low. It required us to climb some hills, but nothing like the mountains DFIs required.

For example, since emerging funds like ours bootstrap our growth, we maximize efficiency while minimizing office costs by leveraging technologies to work across many time zones, while on the road or at home. We allocate in-person meetings based on who is closest to the event locations when needed. But when institutions compel full-team, in-person meetings, physical offices, and hiring staff in multiple locations long before investors commit to a new fund, our setup costs multiply.

These costs create risks more real than potential currency or political fluctuations. Very few emerging market fund managers can survive this kind of capital raising. It can feel like the Great Wall of China, built to keep barbarian local managers from building viable portfolios. These costs also mandate that VC funds make a giant leap in size to be able to pay all the extra expenses.

Development Funding Institutions often mandate VC Funds be large enough to accept both a minimum ticket size, say $10 million, which is also below a maximum percent participation level in each Fund, which may be 10%. This means a Fund must gear up staffing to operate a minimum $100 million Fund to receive any initial development funding from that DFI. Such policies are designed to ensure any downside risks are shared across several similar DFIs via herd-investing, but these ignore the detrimental effect on emerging African Fund managers who have many demands on their personal capital and few financial resources to draw upon.

This is a key reason why African-led VC Funds small enough to accommodate startups have not been able to access development institution capital. However, the largest expense of working with fearful institutional investors is legal fees. Law firms charge by the hour, and those representing development institutions seem to have carte blanche to negotiate minutiae.

Although our earlier fund investors realized extraordinarily high returns, our management company's priority was to reinvest most of that back into the next crop of Afropreneurs, not to reserve it for over $500,000 of legal fees created by DFIs with extraordinary due diligence demands. These added expenses could have buried the birth of our new fund, which one would think DFIs would want to avoid.

People often accuse lawyers of being heartless, but in this case, we had chosen an African American legal team that had our backs. Their firm is staunchly private sector and profits-driven, without the mandate to empower frontier market economic development that DFIs have. And yet, because they are entrepreneurial, they shared our goals and believed in us as fund managers, enough to carry our unpaid invoices, which reached $250,000 before the first DFIs were ready to fund us. It was a proud day when we were able to repay our legal team for their confidence in us and our future potential. Do we feel loyal to them for supporting us through a hair-raising period of our growth? You bet we do!

Once again, you can see that it is not development institutions leading the way to a brighter future for us all, but good people who are determined to help each other, especially when institutions create impediments to entrepreneurial development.

Size Matters

Although African startup funds clearly offer investors impactful opportunities, they are not likely to be recommended by America's most prominent impact investment platforms. Why not? Because our Funds are deemed too small to support the costs of impact investment intermediaries. As America's wealthy family offices expressed interest in transferring at least part of their portfolios to impact investments, a new consulting industry arose. Private consultants became gatekeepers who charge fees for their services and for access to their approved investment platforms.

Most fund names listed on these platforms were already well-known commercial brands, like Templeton and Franklin, which offer managed "impact" portfolios of stocks and bonds that exclude sectors like weapons, vices, and fossil fuels. Minimizing negative impact by screening publicly listed securities is easier to track and manage than private partnerships that create new markets via startups, making positive impacts.

At the same time, I was getting calls from brokers who wanted to place $20M+ investments for their clients and do it into later-stage ventures. I had to turn them down because our fund was too small and our market was too nascent. This is another side of the fundraising problem.

While I was on a capital raising tour with about a dozen female fund managers in early 2017, we met with North American investors who were managing portfolios for the pensions of teachers, police, and firefighters. They wanted to allocate more of their capital toward female and minority-led fund managers, having read statistics that these deliver higher investment returns.

They were interested in our funds focused on African tech startups, US biotechs, and Asian manufacturers, but their institutional portfolios were too large, pushing their minimum ticket size to $100-200 million USD. None of our female-led VC funds were large enough to accept a single investment that large; that is not the ticket size where innovative opportunities emerge.

This story illustrates a major funding dilemma. Mega-sized private equity funds whine about not having enough quality deal flow for their large ticket sizes. At the same time, diverse and emerging funds managers struggle to raise right-sized capital for their abundant startup deal flow. A solution to this impasse is not hard to figure out.

Each mega-fund should allocate a small percentage of capital to aggregate small funds into a large portfolio. The natural diversity of this strategy would reduce risks and cast a wide net for outsized returns based on innovations. Portfolio winners can grow large enough for those mega tickets to invest in directly, after they mature.

Given this, it is amazing how resistant large funders are to deploying such logical solutions, which would reduce risk, add diversification, and cast a wider net of innovative ventures for them to choose from. In 2018, I pitched the following strategy to investors on a Zoom call with the Aspen Entrepreneurs Network.

If a $200 million fund is structured as a portfolio of startup funds that invest in 20 fund management teams, each team could invest its $10M into about 20 startup ventures. This total of 400 ventures would surely include some top talent and viable innovations. Each management team would have its own regional expertise, set of skills, deal pipelines, potential partnerships, and exit opportunities. Each fund would naturally winnow down to about six strong startups by A-rounds, and at least two would ultimately exit with high multiples of profitability.

Two winners for each of the twenty fund teams would give the Fund of Funds' investors 40 high-potential, well-networked startups. After several years of growth, this portfolio of 40 winners could be rolled up into a single holding company, large enough to be cost-effectively taken public and generate attractive annual dividends, relieving the other 360 ventures from feeling pressured to provide investor exits. Alternatively, some of the biggest winners may become large enough to individually exit profitably to large private equity funds, corporates, or via public listings.

This structure is totally doable if the Fund of Funds is managed by an entrepreneurial team that knows its ecosystem players. It embeds diversity with indigenous insights and competent management oversight of third-party compliance and administrative specialists, reducing risks and adding value.

For example, people like Idris have deep enough networks and relationships to know or learn which new fund management teams are likely to do well, via startup ecosystem networks. Grouping a basket of startup funds under one administration team would harmonize these functions across the twenty funds, reducing costs and mistakes. This model could scale up startup funding designed to create employment opportunities for one billion African youth, stabilizing economies in the process.

So why is this not being done?

The standard push-back against this strategy is that it adds a second level of fund selection and management that will need to charge fees. However, the pension fund budget to find and vet deal flow would surely have ample amounts to cover this relatively tiny management cost. Charitable organizations should be able to cover the emerging fund manager costs, since it means that a sustainable economic solution would be the end result.

Fee-sharing was not a roadblock for the founding Director of the Calvert Social Venture Funds when he started investing in Asian entrepreneurs during that continent's major economic expansion. Initially, the Calvert Foundation helped cover set-up costs, as new funds were emerging. In Calvert's case, as opportunities turned into profitable investment funds, a market-driven solution was deployed in response to the demand.

"I just charged investors one 3% fee and passed 2% on to the fund managers across different regions," Calvert's Founding Chairman, Wayne Silby, told me.[192] As of March 31, 2024, Calvert Investments had $38.7 billion in assets under management. Its fund of funds portfolio and mutual funds of publicly-listed securities emerged via support from the Calvert Social Investment Foundation. These focused on Southeast

---

[192] Author phone call, 20

Asia's emerging manufacturing markets, which suited debt and public listings.

Solutions like this emerge when entrepreneurial problem solvers are at the helm.

Do dangers lurk in Africa's tech startup sector? Absolutely. Are competent founders overcoming them? Without a doubt. But are officious, dogmatic investors intent upon domination because they fear, mistrust, or misperceive the opportunities? They are, no question about it. Are donors undermining African ventures by dumping and withholding funding they had promised? Certainly. Do seasoned private investors reduce risks, avoid mistakes, and add value? You bet.

The Power of Egos versus Innovations

After seeing how well indigenous entrepreneurial funding strategies work for seeding development, it is difficult to understand why development institutions are so reluctant to embrace them when deploying their funding. They still cling to centralized control strategies like a lifeline.

Top-down development of ego-systems was remarkably successful during Earth's empire-building stages. Great empires of history, such as the Akkadian, Egyptian, Roman, Mongol, Ottoman, Russian, and British empires, primarily gained power via military innovations. Eventually, they each faced limitations in their supply chains and management capacity when leadership became marinated in ego-driven self-indulgences.

Egos are tolerated while veiled in superior power and moral integrity. However, empires abdicate their right to govern when their leaders' egos run amok, delivering outrageous pain and unwarranted suffering upon innocents. Something intangible, but resolute, shifts deep within the hearts of subjects where respect used to reside.

This moral shift caused King Leopold to lose his grip on forced labor in Congo and his bloody rubber trade after enough people in Europe and the US became aware of the "Congo Question." For example, English missionary Alice Seeley Harris circulated her photos of children's severed hands and feet, documenting the despicable level of inhumanity of Leopold's ego-centric kleptocracy.

It also happened after a British general ordered the massacre at Jallianwala Bagh, Punjab, where hundreds of unarmed civilians gathered around their village water well were massacred as they tried to flee. When Churchill explained this to the House of Commons, India's non-violent independence movement finally prevailed.

South Africa's Apartheid lost its right to rule after the Soweto massacre, when hundreds of unarmed youth left their school and walked to protest their educational limitations. The world not only stood together against the apartheid regime, but it also awarded four Nobel Peace Prizes to individuals who led its demise. "Never, never and never again shall it be that this beautiful land will experience the oppression of one by another," reads the inscription under a Mandela statue in Cape Town.

Military strength lent each of these villains temporary power that emerged from superior innovations and the prosperity they created. Although many of today's largest economies also derive their power from innovations, fewer are based on military might, as Japan, Norway, France, and South Korea exemplify. This is seen more clearly when GDPs are ranked on a per capita basis, as these include Luxembourg, Singapore, and Ireland.

Purchasing Power Parity is currently considered the most accurate metric of wealth; on its top 14 nations list, the USA has the only significant military.[193] Apart from those whose wealth is derived from the efficient management of their natural resources, the top PPP nations are best known for their fiscal and digital innovations. But the US military is also well-known in innovation circles for collaborating on pre-commercialization staged innovations, as experienced by Zimbabwe-born bioengineer, Shasha Jumbo. His Vibrome™ biosensing device is still

---

[193] Farraj, R.A., (2024, May 31). *Top 15 richest countries in the world by GDP per PPP*. Global Economy. https://economyglobal.com/news/top-15-richest-countries-in-the-world-by-gdp-per-capita-ppp/#:~:text=3.,a%20population%20of%205.32%20million.

in development, but it has already helped both South African miners and US military evacuees.[194]

According to recent data, the world's largest corporations by market capitalization include companies like Apple, Microsoft, Alphabet (Google), and NVIDIA. These digital superpowers gain or lose economic ground based on their innovations and their product-to-market-fit executions. Although their creations are often stolen, reverse-engineered, and mass-produced at lower prices by competitors in China and Russia, innovative corporations continue to grow in power and influence.

Why? Entrepreneurial global alliances: The speed and efficiency of free market supply chains and transactions outpace the speed of reverse engineering within closed and centrally controlled economies. In short, counterfeits miss their window of opportunity in rapidly developing markets.

Bill Gates says that his favorite book on AI is *The Coming Wave: Technology, Power, and the 21st Century's Greatest Dilemma*, in which DeepMind entrepreneur, Mustafa Suleyman, contrasts the fears of emerging technologies, which include synthetic biology, to the historic benefits they have brought. This same book was recommended by Siemens CEO, Barbara Humpton, at a Global Corporate Venture Capital conference in 2024. As a former VP at Booz Allen Hamilton, she was responsible for technology consulting at the US Departments of Justice and Homeland Security. While a VP at Lockheed, she was over biometrics and infrastructure programs for the FBI and TSA. Based on these roles, and as a grandmother, Barbara says the true purpose of technology is to expand what is humanly possible.

But investors and policymakers may find another book even more valuable, *Chip Wars: The Fight for the World's Most Critical Technology*. In it, Chris Miller, a young economic historian of Harvard, Yale, and Tufts Universities, offers quintessential case studies of the global competition for microprocessor superiority. These examples explain why free-market

---

[194] https://www.linkedin.com/in/drshasha/

corporations prevail. How? Because of their relative freedom to innovate, operate, and expand, they establish international collaborations that are reliable and efficient.

America's tech corporations secure partnerships from practically anywhere, which is not possible in more restrictive nations. Leading US companies leverage this freedom to build, retain, and reward supply chain alliances that are unique, reliable, and efficient. They can winnow out sub-optimal vendors. This level of flexibility leaves tightly controlled institutional competition in the dust.

What sets *Chip Wars* apart from others is Miller's insight that entrepreneurial freedom, personal initiative, and aligned incentives are what drive and reward winners. Does this theme sound familiar?

In prior chapters, we have seen the value of personal initiative, innovative ownership, and entrepreneurial sovereignty in people who are "Moving Out of Poverty." We've seen African argonauts, who innovate solutions and create ecosystems through collaboration. The spirit of Ubuntu is behind Africa's startup ecosystem successes. This cultural bias holds sacred the importance of building one's community.

Could it be that vicious **ego**-systems have now given way to virtuous innovation **eco**systems? If so, how should forward-looking investors and policymakers reposition their portfolios to realize maximal profits and impactful purposes?

Wrap-up: What's Not Working?

Fear, egos, and institutional strategies...enough said.

PART FOUR
What's Next?

Ours is a fragile planetary system that risks cosmic destruction daily. Consequently, humanity shares an imperative to become an interplanetary species. This goal mandates collaboration. The concepts discussed here are meant to enhance our future as one species inhabiting one planet.

"In today's wired world, the most important economic competition is no longer between countries or companies. It is actually between you and your own imagination. Today, just about everything is becoming a commodity, except imagination, except the ability to spark new ideas."[195] Thomas Friedman, 2010

---

[195] Friedman, T. (2010, March 21). Opinion: America's real dream team. *New York Times*. https://www.nytimes.com/2010/03/21/opinion/21friedman.html?src=me&ref=general

14. Leading Indicators

Predicting the future is our job as investors, and
leading indicators are our tools.

Study Sci-Fi

To understand the soul of a region, study its folklore: To fathom a country's future, study its science fiction. The lens of fantasy breaks down conventional boundaries, revealing a society's deepest longings and highest aspirations. Jules Verne (1828) and Isaac Asimov (1920) authored fantastical imaginations, each of which inspired a century of innovations that became commonplace. This begs the question, whose imaginations will most influence the next century?

According to award-winning Sci Fi author, Tade Thompson, one of this century's most respected and prolific luminaries is Nnedi Okorafor.[196] Born in America to Nigerian parents, Nnedi earned her PhD in literature and creative writing and coined the term Africanfuturism[197] for the Africa-centric and technology-driven themes that she and her peers focus on. In her book, Noor, the high-tech adventures of a partially bionic young woman in Northern Nigeria, explores a world beyond conventional boundaries. The region is superpowered by a mysterious energy source that is wirelessly transmitted from the heart of the Saharan desert.

---

[196] Thompson, T. (2018, September 19). *Please stop talking about the "rise" in African science fiction*. Lit Hub. African Science Fiction

[197] Okorafor, M. (2019, October 19). *Africanturism defined*. Nnedi's Wahala Zone Blog. Africanfuturism

Nnedi's inspirations for this tale came to her in three bursts. The essence of Noor's unique lead character flashed into Nnedi's mind as she walked out of the Lagos airport in 2017 and inhaled the energy of that vast city, stirring her to write the book's first paragraphs while waiting on a bench for her ride. Two years later, she toured the innovative Noor Solar Complex in Ouarzazate, Morocco, where she grasped the veracity of harvesting the energy of Africa's deserts. Finally, when she experienced a massive "haboob" dust storm that enveloped Phoenix, Arizona, she recognized a naturally intense power that might be harnessed to transport energy.

Among the top sci-fi picks of a team of journalism instructors at South African and European universities is Mothersound: The Sauútiverse Anthology.[198] This collection was edited by Wole Talabi, who hosted two years of author workshops. During these sessions, writers were challenged to imagine a freely shared and open universe from diverse perspectives. Since the Sauútiverse only exists as an amalgamation of viewpoints, readers are compelled to make sense of a myriad of realities. This anthology illustrates how radically new perspectives emerge when we look at the same event from different angles. Its collaborative origins echo a recurring theme explored in this book: that success requires us to respect multi-perspective partnerships. This mindset opens the future to attaining new horizons.

Star Trek was a SciFi TV show that shaped my teenage perspectives on global responsibility. Because of its interplanetary perspective, which acknowledged the role of ever-evolving cultures, the prime directive of non-interference was usually respected. By seeing cultural biases and integrations that were embedded in other worlds, totally alien to ours, it was easier for me to see how biases on Earth destroyed mutual opportunities, while collaborations were vital to progress and harmony.

---

[198] Ncugbe, G., Burger, B., et al. (2024, December 19). "*6 best African sci-fi and fantasy books to read.*" The Conservation. https://theconversation.com/6-best-african-sci-fi-and-fantasy-books-to-read-243493

Study Successes

Fintech

As Africa's entrepreneurs transform the continent's pain points into successful sectors, some investors are netting serious gains. If most citizens are poor, then where do these profits come from? Take fintech, for example, a newish investor focus area that has been supercharged by African innovators.

Fintech is not an investment sector; it's a platform that enables financial transactions across all sectors. It transforms digital devices into banks. Fintech similarly empowers economic progress across all sectors. In 2024, African fintechs attracted $1.4 billion in equity investment, a +59% year-over-year growth rate, and 60% of the continent's total startup equity funding.[199] McKinsey projects that Africa's fintech revenues will reach $47 billion annually by 2028, nearly fivefold 2023's revenues.[200]

Why?

Remember the challenges of informal African workers, who leave home and need to send earnings back to loved ones? They have already driven the mobile phone and mobile money industries. Since most Africans lack bank accounts, they previously had three options to move money, none of which are appealing, and all are potentially expensive.

African fintech startups compete with non-consumption, but non-consumption is both costly and risky. It is less expensive to pay for an SMS fintech app to deliver financial services safely than to carry cash or pay drivers to deliver it. Fintech innovations increase productivity and prosperity, and they create value within every market sector.

---

[199] Partech Africa. 2025, January 2). *2024 Partech Africa tech VC report: With US $3.2B raised, African startups show resilience despite 7% drop in funding.* Partech Africa VC report

[200] Kuyoro, M., Flototto, M., with Gathinki, C. (2024, December 10). *Redefining success: A new playbook for African fintech leaders.* McKinsey & Company. Playbook for African Fintech

The magnitude of their value-add, which is embedded in cell phones to relieve pain, is why Africans are leading fintech innovations and driving their adoption. Now, such innovations are valued not only inside Africa but around the world. Remember why Stripe bought Paystack when it was only four years old for $200M? Their innovations create profits in both African and global markets. And that acquisition freed ingenious African founders to keep innovating.

Why did African innovators lead this transition? They knew the pain point. Having an African bank account was deemed a privilege, exclusively for large corporates and wealthy families, not for aspiring entrepreneurs. Until mobile banking emerged, Africa's traditional banks were known to be highly profitable investments: They attracted buy-outs by global banking groups. These included Industrial and Commercial Bank of China (ICBC), BNP Paribas, Barclays, Credit Suisse, and Standard Chartered.

Because conventional banks did not service Africa's emerging commerce needs, digital innovators created workarounds. Their innovations initially negatively impacted big bank valuations. Some of those global investors are feeling the pain of owning elitist legacies that are losing significance. High growth fintech startups offer superior services.

Now these legacy banks are investing heavily in hiring digital designers and programmers and buying software platforms that fintech entrepreneurs innovate. In Nigeria, for example, this surge is thanks in part to a Central Bank of Nigeria (CBN) directive requiring all banks to onboard a new platform. By May 2025, 22 Nigerian commercial banks—including four tier-1 banks—had joined the Pan-African Payment and Settlement System (PAPSS), a financial rail making cross-border payments in Africa faster, cheaper, and local-currency friendly.

"African countries settle payments instantly in local currencies—no need for dollars or third-party intermediaries. This cuts costs, reduces friction, and, frankly, makes intra-African trade less of a paperwork nightmare," per TechCabal, May 28, 2025.[201]

Infrastructure

In the "What's Working?" section, we met Bayo Ogunlesi, the Nigerian founding CEO of Global Infrastructure Partners ("GIP"). His private equity teams successfully invest in airports, shipping ports, energy companies, and data centers around the world. At a time when people are expressing despair over infrastructure needs that exceed government resources, Bayo's private enterprise deals have secured a leadership role in the sector.

BlackRock, Inc. acquired Global Infrastructure Partners for over $12.5 billion in 2024, only 18 years after Bayo Ogunlesi launched it. Now that GIP is under BlackRock's well-financed private equity brand, it has even more opportunities to expand its reach, with responsible energy development at its core. Bayo has remained in leadership, having accepted board director positions at both BlackRock and OpenAI, creating a strategic bridge for the artificial general intelligence ("AGI") sector to access the financing, energy and data storage it needs.

The future of Africa's technology-driven ecosystem could be driven by leaders like Bayo, who efficiently link capital, infrastructure, and innovation. Africa does not lack indigenous sources of energy and innovation. We usually think it lacks capital and infrastructure, but what if over $4 trillion of suitable domestic capital were hiding in plain sight?

The 2025 State of Africa's Infrastructure (SAI) Report released by the Africa Finance Corporation (AFC) noted that this amount sits idle in the continent's commercial banks, long-term institutional funds, and central bank reserves. Africa already holds the financial capacity to transform its economic future; it is just locked up in low-risk, short-term investments,

---

[201] Nwosu, E. (2025, May 28). *22 Nigerian banks joined PAPPS; do they want to have the cake in cross-border payments too?* TechCabal. https://techcabal.com/2025/05/28/techcabal-daily-old-glo-ry/#Story3

which fail to empower the continent's urgent infrastructure and industrial development needs.

According to an Africa Global Funds article,[202]AFC's Infrastructure Report "presents a compelling argument for rethinking the continent's development finance paradigm. It calls for targeted policy reforms, innovative financial structures, and the deployment of risk-mitigation tools to mobilise African capital for African priorities. Rather than depending predominantly on external finance, AFC makes the case for repositioning African institutions—pension funds, insurance companies, sovereign wealth funds, and development banks—as lead investors in infrastructure." Perhaps Bayo's successes are shaking loose ripe fruit?

"AFC argues that Africa must shift from an energy access narrative focused on small-scale interventions to a large-scale strategy anchored in regional, interconnected power systems. The report calls for stronger regional grid integration, the introduction of private sector participation in electricity transmission, and a pipeline of cross-border power projects. It highlights Angola, the Democratic Republic of Congo (DRC), Tanzania, and Mauritania as strategic interconnection markets that could rebalance electricity supply and demand across national borders.

"In contrast to the stagnation in energy, the report identifies a resurgence in rail infrastructure as a signal of growing momentum. With more than 7,000 km of under-construction and planned railway lines, the continent could double its pace of rail development in the next decade. To support coordination and improve investor visibility, AFC has launched the Digital Map of African Railways, the first dynamic and interactive platform tracking rail development across the continent in real time.

The 2025 State of Africa's Infrastructure Report is a call to action. It underscores AFC's conviction that African capital, deployed strategically

---

[202] Africa Global Funds. (June 12, 2025). "AFC's 2025 Report urges Africa to channel $4 Trillion in domestic capital toward infrastructure-led industrial transformation." https://www.africaglobalfunds.com/news/funds/markets-and-industry-news/afcs-2025-report-urges-africa-to-channel-4-trillion-in-domestic-capital-toward-infrastructure-led-industrial-transformation/

through African institutions, holds the key to building a more industrial, connected, and resilient continent."[203]

SE Asia is already overwhelmed with commercial demand for potential data center locations and energy supply sources to support rapid sector development. This opens opportunities for Africa to engage with partners to fill the remaining global void. This data center expansion phase is increasing electricity demand across the continent, with some projections indicating a need for 1,000 megawatts of new power by 2025.

How might this increased demand for AI energy be met on a continent where over one billion entrepreneurial people are already constrained by a lack of access to energy? The continent has plenty of untapped energy resources. For example, African ingenuity could transform well-head gas flaring into energy to fuel data centers that drive AI capacity.[204]

With smart agreements in place, private sector developers of energy infrastructure for data centers will also enjoy robust demand from local consumers. Local energy demand offers developers compliant host countries, whose leadership recognizes the value of a well-powered populace. Developers will realize multiple revenue streams as they ramp up the continent's energy capacity. As Africa-based data centers grow, so will local economies, thanks to private investor-based funding of new energy supplies.

Which nation has the largest number of underserved energy consumers? Nigeria, of course! Interestingly, at the January 2025 World Economic Forum (WEF) meeting in Switzerland, Bayo Ogunlesi publicly committed to leading a global strategic investment group on biannual visits to his homeland. (A much-needed upgrade to the Lagos airport may actually

---

[203] Africa Global Funds. (June 12, 2025). "AFC's 2025 Report urges Africa to channel $4 Trillion in domestic capital toward infrastructure-led industrial transformation." https://www.africaglobalfunds.com/news/funds/markets-and-industry-news/afcs-2025-report-urges-africa-to-channel-4-trillion-in-domestic-capital-toward-infrastructure-led-industrial-transformation/

[204] https://green-flare.org/our-team/

become more front-of-mind for Bayo than energy access after a few trips, but this chapter is meant to inspire investors to reimagine the future.)

Bayo said his team will not just meet with political leaders but also collaborate with local industry leaders on using technology to tackle economic challenges. However, his commitment was conditional: These meetings must be coordinated by Nigeria's Industry, Trade, and Investment Minister, Dr. Jumoke Oduwole, herself. What should American investors know about Dr. Oduwole?

Jumoke was born and educated in Lagos before earning advanced degrees in law and international trade from Cambridge and Stanford, along with a Harvard Kennedy School fellowship. As brilliant as she is fashionable, Jumoke first built a career in investment banking, filling the match-making role between investors and enterprises. Then she served under former President Buhari, whose administration won its democratic election on an anti-corruption platform. According to official reports, Jumoke and her teams are credited with implementing over 200 reforms that improved Nigeria's standings for the ease of doing business, trade, and investment.[205] She also helped establish the Nigerian Office for Trade Negotiations.

Ogunlesi's meetings in Nigeria have already begun to position Nigeria as a preferred hub for international investors. His investment strategy group prioritized four sectors: infrastructure, technology, agriculture, and energy. Ogunlesi explained, "The swift progress in AI presents a unique chance to shape a better future. Strategic planning and investment in infrastructure will be crucial in fully realizing AI's potential and ensuring its benefits are delivered responsibly."[206]

As one publication phrased it, "For Nigeria, Ogunlesi's appointment to OpenAI's Board is both an inspiration and a testament to the vast

---

[205] Jumoke Oduwole. *Early life and education*. Wikipedia.
https://en.wikipedia.org/wiki/Jumoke_Oduwole#Early_life_and_education
[206]OpenAI Appoints Adebayo. https://www.techinafrica.com/openai-appoints-adebayo-ogunlesi-to-board-strengthening-global-strategy-and-ai-governance/

potential of its professional diaspora. As AI continues to drive global innovation, his role could encourage greater participation from African stakeholders in the evolving AI economy...Ogunlesi's appointment is not only a triumph for OpenAI but also a testament to the transformative impact of inclusive leadership."[207]

This shared leadership of AI's promising global impact opens doors for Africa's private sector development. Not the least of which may be fairer and more inclusive reporting of African entrepreneurial contributions to its economic successes by AI tools, a need cited above in *What's Not Working*.

Since this book highlights investing in tech startups, why focus on infrastructure here? Africa's startup ecosystem has done remarkably well, despite having minimal access to basics like clean water, electricity, or roads. Now, imagine what that startup ecosystem could do if it had abundant energy!

AI's demand for data centers is creating profit motives for the private sector to invest in Africa's energy supply. This could be another African tech workaround. Just as mobile phone tech leapfrogged landlines, and mobile money leapfrogged bricks-and-mortar banking, so too the tech-driven need for energy could resolve the continent's access issues. This access to energy will boost the continent's technology innovations, investments, and infrastructure. Bayo's focus on African enterprise development is among the strongest leading indicators that now is the time for investors to step up and engage.

Investors can learn more from The Africa Data Center Construction Report 2024,[208] that Africa's data center investments are expected to more than double, growing at a CAGR of 13.08% from 2023 to 2029. It also explains how the South African and Kenyan Governments have

---

[207] Ashiru, G. *OpenAI appoints Adebayo Ogunlesi to board, strengthening global strategy and AI governance.* Tech in Africa. <u>Tech in Africa</u>

[208] Research and Markets. (2024, April 25). *Africa data center construction report 2024.* Global Newswire. <u>Research and Markets</u>

partnered with private entities to develop digital infrastructure and have structured private investor incentives.

The lesson that Ogunlesi most wished to convey in a recent mentoring session was not about infrastructure or the financial capacity to build it; his mentee said Bayo emphasized intentional leadership and job creation.[209] "Africa's story is still being written. Ogunlesi's message sends both a warning and a path forward: we do not have to be original to be impactful, but we must be intentional. Especially when the costs of inaction, on youth, innovation, and infrastructure, are no longer theoretical...

"Ogunlesi also offered a refreshing counter-narrative to the U.S. job-loss rhetoric. "America is not primarily a manufacturing economy," he explained. "It is a services economy."[210] While around 500,000 manufacturing jobs have disappeared over the decades, more than triple that number have been created in the services sector, including in logistics, tech, finance, and insurance. Rather than romanticising the industrial past, Ogunlesi's analysis points us toward the need for economies, African or American, to build resilience by skilling for the future, not the past."

But most of us are not managing multibillion-dollar portfolios, so how do we personally translate leading indicators like these into viable investments?

---

[209] The Cable. (2025, April 20). *What Adebayo Ogunlesi taught me about Africa's future and its greatest threat*. The Cable. Ogunlesi on Leadership

[210] https://www.statista.com/topics/7997/service-sector-of-the-us/#topicOverview

15. Financing the Future

Get Started: Find your Herd...

Regardless of where you live or how much you have to invest, if you are curious about understanding Africa's opportunities, you can probably find African argonauts living near you and working at a local university, hospital, bank, or pharmacy. Invite them to go for a walk or have a coffee.

Silicon Valley is fortunate to have an Eritrea-born resident who is a master networker, named Almaz Negash. Her husband's tech engineering employer brought their family to Silicon Valley, where she established the African Diaspora Network. Now, hundreds of Afropreneurs and friends gather annually from around the country for ecosystem updates and to discuss emerging initiatives at investment symposiums.[211]

You may find a diaspora organization like this close to you. There, you'll meet African diaspora who love sharing what they know with truly curious investors, so non-Africans should not feel shy about asking for insights. But they are also juggling multiple balls, with limited time to mentor novices, so be considerate of their time.

Your first job is to rationally assess your personal assets and goals. If you have smallish amounts of money to invest periodically, in the $5000-to $200,000 range, and want to personally select your own African startups, then acquaint yourself with the continent's vibrant business angel sector. It is estimated to invest over $100 million a year in African Startups,[212] so you will find a lot of wisdom among seasoned angel

---

[211] https://africandiasporanetwork.org/programs/adis25/

[212] Africa: The Big Deal

investors. For instance, you may remember reading about Eric Osiakwan, one of Africa's first tech hub champions and tech investors in "What's Working." He cofounded Angel Fair Africa, which remains a vibrant startup investor resource that's aligned with many ecosystem participants.[213]

Photo: Teddy Ruge reunited with Eric Osiakwan at Hive Colab in Kampala, 2025
Source: Teddy Ruge

The African Business Angel Network,[214] boasts 75 membership groups that represent 5,000 business angels actively investing in 40 countries. They have banded together "towards an investment target of at least 500 startups to create over 10,000 jobs annually." You can also read up on current sector initiatives, sign up for a newsletter, and find the best investment practices for startups. ABAN membership benefits include matching investment capital from major donors, gaining eligibility to participate in Catalytic Africa's matching grant funds, designed to amplify your investment impact and foster growth in high-potential startups.[215] These will augment any positive returns. One of my dreams

---

[213] Angel Fair

[214] African Business Angel Network

[215] ABAN Membership Benefits

is for African angel networks like ABAN to link with US-based angel networks that have equally aspirational goals to collaborate on attaining shared investment objectives. This would truly add diversification to portfolios on both sides of "the pond."

On the VC4A[216] website, you can customize your profile of ventures you would like to learn about and find investor gatherings that you pair with your next holiday, where you will surely meet others who share your interests[217]. You can also attend training programs, curated pitch sessions, panel discussions, and networking opportunities.

Some of Africa's private investment clubs have rosters of several hundred who meld their professional skills into teams that collaborate on deal flow, due diligence, and co-investing, either individually or as a group. Tomi Balogun is another brilliant and beautiful woman whose passion for professionalizing startup investing clubs built, The Green Investment Club (TGIC) which became the lead Limited Partner in one of LoftyInc's Afropreneurs Funds. She is now a proponent of investment syndications and is bringing efficiencies to this high-potential tool.

Venture Capital and Private Equity Funds

If you have larger amounts to invest and want to learn as a Limited Partner (LP), looking over the shoulder of seed-stage teams with track records like LoftyInc's, then you have several to choose from. Our peer group of Africa-facing tech startup funds is astute, collaborative, and growing. Many are Delaware-registered funds and are still accepting new LPs with lowish minimum investments. Most of us attend the annual AVCA gathering, which qualified LPs can attend for free. These include employees of development finance institutions (DFIs), endowments, single-family offices, insurance companies, public and private pension funds, and sovereign wealth funds. Larger VC Funds that invest at later stages and Private Equity Funds also attend AVCA gatherings.

---

[216] VC4A Events. https://vc4a.com/events/

[217] Blog and Events. ABAN. ABAN Events

Funds of Funds:

Aggregating small funds under larger umbrellas managed by experienced managers makes sense. Theoretically, this could keep the best fund managers mentoring aspiring entrepreneurs instead of pulling them away to manage capital raising campaigns. An oft-cited objection is the double fee structure of two Funds, which may be a non-starter for investors.

But private fund investors already pay for both financial administration and fund management, so why not separate them with a Fund of Fund structure to reach economies of scale? The larger the funds, the lower the per-dollar fees. Or philanthropists could pay some of these fees to get more impact bang per buck by leveraging portfolios of funds that manage portfolios of impactful startups backed by private investors.

Also, on the fund level, it seems strange that non-profits with economic development mandates have not yet embraced local emerging fund managers by offering to help raise capital for their funds or to provide administrative oversight that would quell investor fears. These services would leverage non-profit strengths and networks, freeing local fund managers to focus on selecting and mentoring strong startup teams. Seasoned local managers could help portfolio companies reach sustainable revenues more rapidly. Instead, nonprofits try to set up their own teams of less experienced investors that are better funded than those with greater entrepreneurial skills and local insights. Such non-profit programs rarely build self-sustaining corporations and are often abandoned.

Investment Banking: As emerging market startup funds like ours increase in number, size, and expertise, hundreds of our successful ventures grow into sizable companies that deserve expert guidance on mergers, acquisitions, and IPOs on various exchanges globally. This is a fascinating, evolving area of finance that firms like LoftyInc Capital are starting to focus on. As Africans who have developed these deal-making skills abroad recognize the growth momentum of opportunities, they will return to the continent and fill the void.

Energy Funds:

The 2025 State of Africa's Infrastructure (SAI) Report[218] released by Africa Finance Corporation (AFC), estimates that the savings of Africans themselves hold at least $1.1T in long-term institutional capital, $2.5trn in commercial banking assets, and more than $470B in reserves held by central banks. Because most of this capital sits locked in low-risk, short-term investments, it fails to power the continent's urgent infrastructure and industrial needs.

AFC argues that Africans should deploy some of this capital to build large-scale energy generation via:

- stronger regional grid integration,
- private sector investment in electricity transmission,
- and a pipeline of cross-border power projects.

It highlights Angola, the Democratic Republic of Congo (DRC), Tanzania, and Mauritania as strategic sources of electricity supply that could meet demand across national borders.

This grid-focused energy recommendation from 40 African member countries[219] stands in stark contrast to the USAID's Power Africa Off-Grid Project (PAOP) initiative, which inexplicably rejected all grid development yet was funded from 2013 until the Trump administration terminated it in 2025.

In his comments on this report, AFC President & CEO Samaila Zubairu emphasised the urgency and opportunity ahead: "This report provides a practical roadmap for how Africa can channel its significant financial strength into the infrastructure needed to drive industrial transformation... The tools exist. The capital is available. What's needed now is coordinated action to unlock it."

---

[218] https://www.africaglobalfunds.com/news/funds/markets-and-industry-news/afcs-2025-report-urges-africa-to-channel-4-trillion-in-domestic-capital-toward-infrastructure-led-industrial-transformation/

[219] https://en.wikipedia.org/wiki/Africa_Finance_Corporation

16. Creating the Future:
African Pains Generate Investor Gains

"The best way to predict the future is to create it."
Abraham Lincoln

Internet Access

In addition to the continent's desperate need for energy, a similarly painful sector for Africans is internet access, which telecoms were best positioned to scale up, but they chose to neglect. Why? They felt unmotivated, as their industry was protected, making it a sacred cash cow. Accordingly, for over twenty years, innovative apps in sectors like telemedicine have sought to partner with telecoms to gain market share rapidly, with mixed results.

Telecoms' own rapid initial growth was similarly augmented by tech innovations that doomed landline companies, which clung to the same exclusivity as commercial banks. Based on Mo Ibrahim's Celtel launch, we know that popular demand for his cellular services skyrocketed precisely because of the pain point caused by landline phone providers that restricted services to a handful of elite customers. Given this history, telecoms should have been more alert to the danger created by their reticence in bringing high-speed internet services to rural areas.

We also learned from Funke Opeke's dream to bring connectivity to Nigerians. Although she was a respected executive leader at Verizon's headquarters, she was not able to enlist the Nigerian telecom's backing. She had to build a totally new corporation, but in doing so, she built tremendous value for her investors, while the legacy telco went bankrupt.

Funke has become a legend for her role in empowering Nigeria to become a digital innovation center. The reason she was able to raise the capital to bring an internet cable to West Africa is that the people who worked with her knew they could trust her to do what she said she would do. This fact-based confidence in Funke unlocked the funding she needed to fulfill her dream, delivering customer services and investor returns.

Because telecoms did not care enough to service their market's internet access, they now face a new threat from the sky: Starlink. Instead of partnering with Starlink, as T-Mobile did in the US, adding customer services, Kenya's dominant player, Safaricom, dug in, thinking that Kenya's local politicians and regulators would protect them from competition. But that did not happen. Broad-based economic development offers nations more benefits than bribes do.

The good news for Africa is that, thanks to Starlink competition, telcos have switched tactics, competing by increasing their internet speed and lowering prices. Again, we see that staid strategies have trouble competing with an innovative African argonaut, especially one whose costs to launch satellites are minimized via SpaceX-funded launches. Either way, this competition gives tech-driven Afropreneurs and their target markets an internet access edge.

From these examples, investors can see how African startups can be lower-risk investments than more established sector leaders and revenue generators.

Supply Chains

As we learned earlier from the demise of the USAID's health supply chain program, emerging markets are infamous for the pain of last-mile delivery of goods, while government solutions are sub-optimal. Solving this problem in Africa will transform the lives of hundreds of millions of small shop owners and subsistence farmers. It will also add productivity to consumers who now waste time and money trying to find everything they need, from toothpaste to cornflakes to fresh orange juice. At least one African startup seems to be on the right track...

While growing up in Nigeria, Deepankar Rustagi loathed the wealth gap he saw, so he decided to become an entrepreneur who helps small businesses grow. And that is precisely what he has done, but simply buying from distributors and delivering to retailers is not profitable in Africa, so he digitized their supply chain, consolidating key components on a single platform. This was neither easy to do nor sustainable– at first.

So, Deepanker built OmniRetail's online platform in 2019 to provide transparency between distributors and retailers. Its key product, OmniBiz, allows small shop owners to place digital orders online— directly with manufacturers—while keeping their retail shops open. The key to OmniRetail's last-mile success is its franchise partners who specialize in small-scale warehousing. Orders are delivered within 24 hours by third-party providers who are experts at hyper-local logistics.

In a recent interview, Deepankar revealed Omni's supply chain profitability edge. "Just buying from distributors and selling to retailers did not have enough margin and benefits, but engaging with distributors on the platform and embedding working capital tools like OmniPay increased the value chain margin for us to hit profitability."[220]

This referred to two embedded finance products: one empowers distributors with real-time visibility into inventory, orders, and analytics; the other offers payment and credit services for retailers as well as distributors. These platform offerings are credited with boosting Omni's margins into profits.

As of 2024, this OmniRetail system connects over 300 manufacturers that provide more than 1000 SKUs to 3,000 warehousing partners. These supply 140,000 retailers, who serve 14 million households in three countries. As complex as this all seems, OmniRetail is loved by its partners for making life easier, as seen in video clips posted on LinkedIn.

---

[220] Kene-Okafor, T. (2024, March 14). *What African B2B e-commerce startups can learn from OmniRetail's profitable run.* TechCrunch. TechCrunch Article by Tage Kene-Okafor, March 2024

Just as Walmart founder Sam Walton built value via low-cost operations and efficient warehousing and distribution, Deepanker has followed suit and gone further. OmniRetail runs asset-light operations by owning neither real estate nor delivery fleets. Instead of hiring, motivating, and managing a vast employee base, OmniRetail attracts entrepreneurs who are already engaged, motivated, and managing their own small shops. By offering supply chain tools that make these franchised shop owners more efficient, OmniRetail helps them add warehouse space, new products, and additional shops.

This low burn-rate model enabled the company to survive Nigeria's recent economic issues, and it is now profiting from the rapid growth of their partners. OmniRetail not only endured but topped the Financial Times' list of Africa's Fastest Growing Companies in 2024,[221]—a good omen for Omni!

Now they are innovating solutions to cold chain issues, which would open doors for African farmers to supply farm-fresh produce, as refrigerated train cars did for American farmers back in the day.

AI Factories in Africa

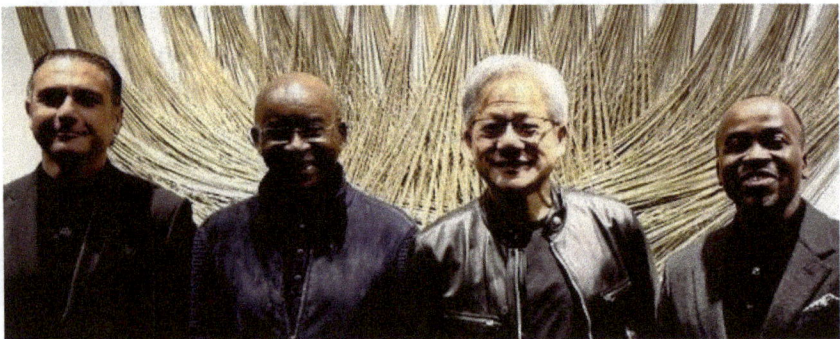

Photo: "Nvidia/Cassava AI Factory partnership.jpeg"
Source: https://www.linkedin.com/pulse/our-leap-faith-ai-compute-africa-most-powerful-ones-empower-masiyiwa-obime/

---

[221] Adeyoe, A. (2024, June 5). *OmniRetail holistic approach takes prize for Nigeria.* Financial Times. FT OmniBiz

Africa's first AI Factories are being built via a partnership of Cassava Technologies and Nvidia. In March 2025, a Zimbabwean-born, UK-educated Electrical Engineer named Strive Masiyiwa announced that his company is coupling NVIDIA's supercomputer Graphic Processing Units [GPUs] with Cassava Technology's existing hyperscale data centres in five African countries. These will empower local entrepreneurs to create high-compute processing projects, including Large Language AI model development.

"AI Factory" is a term coined by Nvidia CEO, Jensen Huang, for facilities that house and streamline the tech infrastructure for raw data aggregation, algorithm development and pilot testing. This level of "compute" capacity is required to tailor AI systems for specific uses. It is essential for Africa's researchers and industry-specific innovators to compete in global AI sandboxes.

Who is Strive Masiyiwa? Yet another successful African entrepreneur whose circular migrations for education and expertise included pioneering the continent's tech infrastructure. In 1992, Strive Masiyiwa took the Zimbabwe government to court over its monopoly of telecommunications. The five-year legal battle brought him to the brink of personal bankruptcy, but the favorable Supreme Court ruling helped open the sector to private investment. This victory paved the way for Strive to launch Econet Wireless, contributing to the growth of mobile communication across Africa.[222] [223]

> *"The most powerful force against corruption is one person saying 'no'."*—Strive Masiyiwa

In his LinkedIn post announcing the AI Factories, Strive shared that this technology leap forward was seeded while having coffee with two friends, billionaire businessman Aliko Dangote and Nigeria's former President Olusegun Obasanjo. After congratulating both Strive and Aliko on their successes, Olusegun challenged them to leverage their

---

[222] https://techcrunch.com/2016/02/17/not-another-african-tech-article/

[223] https://perbiexecutive.com/strife-success-significance-strive-masiyiwa/

expertise to "do more. Do big, audacious things for Africa!" Then Aliko explained his plans to build a liquefied natural gas refinery in Nigeria to transform its well-head gas flaring into low-carbon natural gas and urea for fertilizer. He has since completed that, at a cost of $19bn.

Sometime later, Strive was listening to tech conference speakers lamenting that Africans would "just be consumers of AI because of the costs," which made him reflect on what Aliko had done. He told himself that he, too, could raise a few billion dollars to get AI Compute started in Africa. He could even piggyback on existing data centers his team had already built!

When he told Aliko his thoughts, Strive got the final reassurances to push him over the starting line. "My brother, you got this," Aliko exclaimed. "It's your field now. If you can't do it, then who?" Of course, there is still the problem of capital raising, but their mutual friend offered to help. "We are always there for you as Afreximbank, even though you will also have to go global for such funding."[224]

One month after news of the AI Factory partnership, Cassava Technologies announced its intent to invest $720m in African AI factories.[225] Their financing includes both debt and equity from South African banks Standard, Rand Merchant, and Nedbank, as well as the US International Development Finance Corporation (DFC), the Finnish Fund for Industrial Cooperation (FinnFund), and Google. "If we don't take the first step to deploy our own capital, however limited it may be, we can't expect others to go first," said Cassava president and group chief executive Hardy Pemhiwa, a seasoned finance executive. "This is about ensuring that Africa doesn't get left behind." Pemhiwa added that one of the benefits of the partnership is the potential to sell surplus computing capacity to other Nvidia cloud clients globally.

---

[224] https://www.linkedin.com/pulse/our-leap-faith-ai-compute-africa-most-powerful-ones-empower-masiyiwa-obime/?trackingId=se%2FFMTyQRmm%2FNas1i0xihw%3D%3D
[225] https://www.verdict.co.uk/cassava-african-ai-factory/?cf-view

"This AI Factory creates opportunities for Africans to build and test their ideas locally." And they are hiring!

> *"The most powerful technologies are the ones that empower others."*
> —Jensen Huang

Final Thoughts

As you move forward from this book to potentially make courageous investments in the future, questions will emerge. You understand the value diverse teams, sectors, and countries bring to your portfolio, but you may wonder how to start. Partners, timing, scale, and pace are personal choices you have yet to muddle through. Also, you must find, vet, and choose which sectors, currencies, and countries best suit you personally.

Such challenges may overwhelm you at times. Yet you can find comfort in these pages, where you have seen Africa's diaspora return home to establish infrastructure and profit by doing so. You've learned how African-born entrepreneurs leveraged their day jobs while building startup ecosystems and enlisted visionary funders who helped them succeed.

You understand how their motives and expertise created economic opportunities. You've recognized their determination and admired their resilience as their companies and their support ecosystems built and sustained economic growth. They tested and proved strategies that worked.

Afropreneurs have de-risked their tech sector. By doing so, they are building a more secure future for us all. Investors can draw inspiration and confidence from their successes. These are the best leading indicators upon which non-Africans can make insightful investment decisions for their own portfolios.

When I see well-prepared Afropreneurs doing all they can, I reason that the least I can do is co-invest in their ventures. Our LoftyInc-led funds have done this about 200 times, which is a speck of dust on a continent the size of Africa. The total invested in African startups is 1% of the venture capital deployed by Americans annually. Yet, African youth comprise 23% of the world's youth, and by 2100, it will be close to 50%.[226] We are just getting started.

Early in this book, I mentioned the joys of reading inspirational posts from Afropreneurs I admire, and I promised to share one special post with you at the end of this book. It reflects the ambition, vision, and evolving strategies of "E" Aboyeji, a young Nigerian who was still a student when Idris began mentoring and investing in his ventures. E co-founded two Delaware-registered ventures that each attained over one-billion-dollar valuations before he turned 30. He immediately reinvested profits into the next crop of startups, empowering them to unicorn status as well.

In January 2024, A key African tech publication, the TechCabal headline read: "Exclusive: Backed by $750k grant, Aboyeji and Koschitzky-Kimani are launching the YC of Africa,[227] Also that week, in a LinkedIn post, this champion of Africa's tech startup ecosystem unknowingly wrote a suitable ending for this book.

"This week my Future Africa partner Mia von Koschitzky-Kimani [a German immigrant to Kenya] and I announced that we are re-launching Accelerate Africa as a full-fledged accelerator program that we hope will become the 'YC for Africa'. Prior to now, we have mostly run successful pre-accelerator programs to help get founders into actual accelerator programs like YC and Techstars. Now we are getting into the accelerator arena ourselves. I thought that, for posterity, I should pen a few thoughts about why I believe this has become necessary.

"As two of Africa's most prominent operator VCs with a track record for building some of Africa's most successful startups like Andela,

---

[226] https://mo.ibrahim.foundation/sites/default/files/2020-08/international-youth-day-research-brief.pdf

[227] https://techcabal.com/2024/01/17/iyin-aboyeji-and-koschitzky-kimani-the-yc-of-africa/

Flutterwave, Moove BV, Daystar Power, and DukaConnect, ...many of the companies we founded, funded, and advised are now billion dollar companies with hundreds of millions in revenue and some have been acquired by global businesses like Mastercard and Shell.

"However, ...with rising interest rates, the music's over and another dance has begun. From the days of Socketworks and Interswitch to the more recent past of IROKO and Konga, technology funding booms and busts have defined our ecosystem. Some ...[say] unicorns are alien to Africa, and we should lower our sights... I can understand the sentiment. Icarus is real.

"However, we can also choose a different path this time. The bull run of the last 10 years demonstrated what is possible, should we choose to scale innovative technology solutions to solve our development challenges as a continent. We have built billion-dollar companies, impacted hundreds of thousands of lives, delivered hundreds of millions of dollars in annual revenue, and raised tens of billions of dollars.

"I believe we have demonstrated that, in the words of the late General Murtala Mohammed, 'Africa has come of age'. However, this requires us to divorce ourselves from Silicon Valley's templates and forge our own unique path. It means building different technology companies that are not **worth** billions of dollars but are **earning** billions of dollars; not imported founders building solutions for the tiny minority who look like them and live on Victoria Island, but gritty founders who solve real world problems for the vast majority of Africans who require technology solutions that can make them more productive.

"This is why we are building African accelerators for bold and visionary founders of global businesses. Despite the long faces and downcast emotions cast on our industry, I believe that there is no better time to invest in African innovation. Our confidence comes from the fact that we've seen this movie before.

"All our billion-dollar businesses were built amidst deep downturns: Andela was founded in the throes of Ebola in 2014, Flutterwave was born in the midst of the banking and currency crisis of 2016..., Moove launched in the middle of COVID-19 in 2020. Rising inflation, a global capital crunch, and slow economic growth only suggest to us that this is the time for true entrepreneurs to come out and build.

"Second, there is no better time to take on this task. This decade has a new wave of talent, ready to take on new challenges. We have amassed an army of angels and venture capitalists who will fund African innovation. Nigeria's $50 billion stock exchange minted 13 unicorns in the last year. Governments in Africa are passing startup acts that protect and enhance homegrown tech startups. There is more dry powder seeking real returns in global VC than ever before. I couldn't think of a better time to build the future in Africa.

"Most importantly, our continent demands this of us. As African leadership wakes up to the realization that even though startups cannot innovate our way around the government, perhaps we can innovate hand in hand with them. True entrepreneurs are rising to the occasion and matching the scale of our continental challenges. A flurry of talented leadership is flowing from our technology ecosystems into government and charting a sustainable path to technology-driven progress and productivity.

"We thank the global accelerators and global venture capital community for all their support through the years. We have learned so much from them and we owe them for much of our success. Their sacrifice, belief, and generosity to our ecosystem will never be forgotten.

"Nevertheless, Africa has come of age, and in the words of General Murtala Mohammed –'the fortunes of Africa are in our hands to make or mar.'

"If you would like to partner with us on Accelerate Africa, please feel free to reach out...[228]"

---

[228] www.acceler8.africa

After reading his post, I thought, *"Thank you, E, for working so hard on your ventures that scores of early investors realized profitable returns, setting an example for hundreds of millions of Africa's tech-savvy youth. Thank you for returning home to Lagos from the US with your bride to help lead Africa's ecosystem development, for investing your own wealth into the ventures of Africa's youth, and for organizing investment vehicles that support thousands of worthy young founders seeking to make the world a better place for us all.*

"I am grateful for your father who invested all he had into your education, for your mother who held you accountable to be the best you could be, and for my LoftyInc partners who taught me to believe in you. Thank you for not letting us down."

I cannot think of a more fitting finale to this book than E's vision of a prosperous future for Africa.

Photo: Author and E at his wedding, 2018
Source: Author Archives

Photo: LoftyInc Capital Management Team, 2025, Lagos, Nigeria
Source: LCM Archives

The End

www.ingramcontent.com/pod-product-compliance
Lightning Source LLC
Chambersburg PA
CBHW071546210326
41597CB00019B/3136